Just The facts101
Textbook Key Facts

Doing Business and Investing in Senegal Guide

by Cram101
Textbook NOT Included

Table of Contents

Title Page

Copyright

Foundations of Business

Management

Business law

Finance

Human resource management

Information systems

Marketing

Manufacturing

Commerce

Business ethics

Accounting

Index: Answers

Just The Facts101

Exam Prep for

Doing Business and Investing in Senegal Guide

Just The Facts101 Exam Prep is your link from
the textbook and lecture to your exams.

**Just The Facts101 Exam Preps are unauthorized and comprehensive reviews
of your textbooks.**

All material provided by CTI Publications (c) 2019

Textbook publishers and textbook authors do not participate in or contribute to these reviews.

Just The Facts101 Exam Prep

Copyright © 2019 by CTI Publications. All rights reserved.

eAIN 444635

Foundations of Business

A business, also known as an enterprise, agency or a firm, is an entity involved in the provision of goods and/or services to consumers. Businesses are prevalent in capitalist economies, where most of them are privately owned and provide goods and services to customers in exchange for other goods, services, or money.

:: Insolvency ::

_____ is a legal process through which people or other entities who cannot repay debts to creditors may seek relief from some or all of their debts. In most jurisdictions, _____ is imposed by a court order, often initiated by the debtor.

Exam Probability: **Medium**

1. *Answer choices:*
(see index for correct answer)

- a. Official Committee of Equity Security Holders
- b. Conservatorship
- c. Personal Insolvency Arrangement
- d. Debt consolidation

Guidance: level 1

:: Production economics ::

_____ is the joint use of a resource or space. It is also the process of dividing and distributing. In its narrow sense, it refers to joint or alternating use of inherently finite goods, such as a common pasture or a shared residence. Still more loosely, "_____" can actually mean giving something as an outright gift: for example, to "share" one's food really means to give some of it as a gift. _____ is a basic component of human interaction, and is responsible for strengthening social ties and ensuring a person's well-being.

Exam Probability: **High**

2. *Answer choices:*

(see index for correct answer)

- a. Diseconomies of scale
- b. Split-off point
- c. Sharing
- d. Economic batch quantity

Guidance: level 1

:: Telecommunication theory ::

In reliability theory and reliability engineering, the term _____ has the following meanings.

Exam Probability: **Low**

3. *Answer choices:*

(see index for correct answer)

- a. Bipolar signal
- b. Availability
- c. Isochronous
- d. Information-bearer channel

Guidance: level 1

:: Health promotion ::

_____ , as defined by the World _____ Organization , is "a state of complete physical, mental and social well-being and not merely the absence of disease or infirmity." This definition has been subject to controversy, as it may have limited value for implementation. _____ may be defined as the ability to adapt and manage physical, mental and social challenges throughout life.

Exam Probability: **Low**

4. *Answer choices:*

(see index for correct answer)

- a. 10 Essential Public Health Services
- b. Alliance for Healthy Cities
- c. Breastfeeding promotion
- d. Lebensreform

Guidance: level 1

:: Income ::

_____ is a ratio between the net profit and cost of investment resulting from an investment of some resources. A high ROI means the investment's gains favorably to its cost. As a performance measure, ROI is used to evaluate the efficiency of an investment or to compare the efficiencies of several different investments. In purely economic terms, it is one way of relating profits to capital invested. _____ is a performance measure used by businesses to identify the efficiency of an investment or number of different investments.

Exam Probability: **High**

5. *Answer choices:*

(see index for correct answer)

- a. Passive income
- b. Implied level of government service
- c. Return on investment
- d. Per capita income

Guidance: level 1

:: Stock market ::

The _____ of a corporation is all of the shares into which ownership of the corporation is divided. In American English, the shares are commonly known as "_____ s". A single share of the _____ represents fractional ownership of the corporation in proportion to the total number of shares. This typically entitles the _____ holder to that fraction of the company's earnings, proceeds from liquidation of assets , or voting power, often dividing these up in proportion to the amount of money each _____ holder has invested. Not all _____ is necessarily equal, as certain classes of _____ may be issued for example without voting rights, with enhanced voting rights, or with a certain priority to receive profits or liquidation proceeds before or after other classes of shareholders.

Exam Probability: **Low**

6. *Answer choices:*

(see index for correct answer)

- a. Chip
- b. Instinet
- c. Stock
- d. Super-majority amendment

Guidance: level 1

:: Credit cards ::

A _____ is a payment card issued to users to enable the cardholder to pay a merchant for goods and services based on the cardholder's promise to the card issuer to pay them for the amounts plus the other agreed charges. The card issuer creates a revolving account and grants a line of credit to the cardholder, from which the cardholder can borrow money for payment to a merchant or as a cash advance.

Exam Probability: **Medium**

7. *Answer choices:*

(see index for correct answer)

- a. SBI Cards
- b. Credit card
- c. Credit Saison
- d. NexG PrePaid

Guidance: level 1

:: Energy and fuel journals ::

In physics, energy is the quantitative property that must be transferred to an object in order to perform work on, or to heat, the object. Energy is a conserved quantity; the law of conservation of energy states that energy can be converted in form, but not created or destroyed. The SI unit of energy is the joule, which is the energy transferred to an object by the work of moving it a distance of 1 metre against a force of 1 newton.

Exam Probability: **Low**

8. *Answer choices:*

(see index for correct answer)

- a. Fuel Cells
- b. Proceedings of the Institution of Mechanical Engineers, Part A: Journal of Power and Energy
- c. Energy-Safety and Energy-Economy
- d. Energy Procedia

Guidance: level 1

:: ::

_____ is the collection of techniques, skills, methods, and processes used in the production of goods or services or in the accomplishment of objectives, such as scientific investigation. _____ can be the knowledge of techniques, processes, and the like, or it can be embedded in machines to allow for operation without detailed knowledge of their workings. Systems applying _____ by taking an input, changing it according to the system's use, and then producing an outcome are referred to as _____ systems or technological systems.

Exam Probability: **High**

9. *Answer choices:*

(see index for correct answer)

- a. hierarchical perspective
- b. levels of analysis
- c. functional perspective
- d. Technology

Guidance: level 1

:: Generally Accepted Accounting Principles ::

An _____ or profit and loss account is one of the financial statements of a company and shows the company's revenues and expenses during a particular period.

Exam Probability: **Low**

10. *Answer choices:*
(see index for correct answer)

- a. Income statement
- b. Reserve
- c. Cost pool
- d. Long-term liabilities

Guidance: level 1

:: Occupations ::

An _____ is a person who has a position of authority in a hierarchical organization. The term derives from the late Latin from officiarius, meaning "official".

Exam Probability: **Low**

11. *Answer choices:*
(see index for correct answer)

- a. Key worker
- b. Receiver General
- c. Environmentalist
- d. Officer

Guidance: level 1

:: Derivatives (finance) ::

_____ is any bodily activity that enhances or maintains physical fitness and overall health and wellness. It is performed for various reasons, to aid growth and improve strength, preventing aging, developing muscles and the cardiovascular system, honing athletic skills, weight loss or maintenance, improving health and also for enjoyment. Many individuals choose to _____ outdoors where they can congregate in groups, socialize, and enhance well-being.

Exam Probability: **High**

12. *Answer choices:*
(see index for correct answer)

- a. Stock market index future
- b. Exercise
- c. Equity derivative
- d. Credit derivative

Guidance: level 1

:: Competition regulators ::

The _____ is an independent agency of the United States government, established in 1914 by the _____ Act. Its principal mission is the promotion of consumer protection and the elimination and prevention of anticompetitive business practices, such as coercive monopoly. It is headquartered in the _____ Building in Washington, D.C.

Exam Probability: **Low**

13. *Answer choices:*
(see index for correct answer)

- a. Superintendency of Industry and Commerce
- b. Federal Cartel Office
- c. Competition Appeal Tribunal
- d. Federal Trade Commission

Guidance: level 1

:: Business ::

The seller, or the provider of the goods or services, completes a sale in response to an acquisition, appropriation, requisition or a direct interaction with the buyer at the point of sale. There is a passing of title of the item, and the settlement of a price, in which agreement is reached on a price for which transfer of ownership of the item will occur. The seller, not the purchaser typically executes the sale and it may be completed prior to the obligation of payment. In the case of indirect interaction, a person who sells goods or service on behalf of the owner is known as a _____ man or _____ woman or _____ person, but this often refers to someone selling goods in a store/shop, in which case other terms are also common, including _____ clerk, shop assistant, and retail clerk.

Exam Probability: **Low**

14. *Answer choices:*
(see index for correct answer)

- a. EPG Model
- b. Kingdomality
- c. Sales
- d. Sustainopreneurship

Guidance: level 1

:: Production and manufacturing ::

_____ consists of organization-wide efforts to "install and make permanent climate where employees continuously improve their ability to provide on demand products and services that customers will find of particular value." "Total" emphasizes that departments in addition to production are obligated to improve their operations; "management" emphasizes that executives are obligated to actively manage quality through funding, training, staffing, and goal setting. While there is no widely agreed-upon approach, TQM efforts typically draw heavily on the previously developed tools and techniques of quality control. TQM enjoyed widespread attention during the late 1980s and early 1990s before being overshadowed by ISO 9000, Lean manufacturing, and Six Sigma.

Exam Probability: **Low**

15. *Answer choices:*
(see index for correct answer)

- a. Continuous production
- b. Manufacturing process management
- c. Transfer cars
- d. Plant layout study

Guidance: level 1

:: Strategic alliances ::

A _____ is an agreement between two or more parties to pursue a set of agreed upon objectives needed while remaining independent organizations. A _____ will usually fall short of a legal partnership entity, agency, or corporate affiliate relationship. Typically, two companies form a _____ when each possesses one or more business assets or have expertise that will help the other by enhancing their businesses. _____ s can develop in outsourcing relationships where the parties desire to achieve long-term win-win benefits and innovation based on mutually desired outcomes.

Exam Probability: **Low**

16. *Answer choices:*

(see index for correct answer)

- a. Defensive termination
- b. Strategic alliance
- c. International joint venture
- d. Management contract

Guidance: level 1

:: Globalization-related theories ::

_____ is the process in which a nation is being improved in the sector of the economic, political, and social well-being of its people. The term has been used frequently by economists, politicians, and others in the 20th and 21st centuries. The concept, however, has been in existence in the West for centuries. "Modernization, "westernization", and especially "industrialization" are other terms often used while discussing _____ . _____ has a direct relationship with the environment and environmental issues. _____ is very often confused with industrial development, even in some academic sources.

Exam Probability: **Low**

17. *Answer choices:*

(see index for correct answer)

- a. Economic Development
- b. post-industrial
- c. Capitalism

Guidance: level 1

:: Workplace ::

_____ is asystematic determination of a subject's merit, worth and significance, using criteria governed by a set of standards. It can assist an organization, program, design, project or any other intervention or initiative to assess any aim, realisable concept/proposal, or any alternative, to help in decision-making; or to ascertain the degree of achievement or value in regard to the aim and objectives and results of any such action that has been completed. The primary purpose of _____ , in addition to gaining insight into prior or existing initiatives, is to enable reflection and assist in the identification of future change.

Exam Probability: **Medium**

18. *Answer choices:*

(see index for correct answer)

- a. Workplace revenge
- b. Toxic workplace
- c. Workplace democracy
- d. Workplace relationships

Guidance: level 1

:: Stock market ::

_____ is a form of stock which may have any combination of features not possessed by common stock including properties of both an equity and a debt instrument, and is generally considered a hybrid instrument. _____ s are senior to common stock, but subordinate to bonds in terms of claim and may have priority over common stock in the payment of dividends and upon liquidation. Terms of the _____ are described in the issuing company's articles of association or articles of incorporation.

Exam Probability: **Medium**

19. *Answer choices:*

(see index for correct answer)

- a. Matchbook FX
- b. Reverse split
- c. Red chip
- d. Preferred stock

Guidance: level 1

:: Packaging ::

In work place, _____ or job _____ means good ranking with the hypothesized conception of requirements of a role. There are two types of job _____ s: contextual and task. Task _____ is related to cognitive ability while contextual _____ is dependent upon personality. Task _____ are behavioral roles that are recognized in job descriptions and by remuneration systems, they are directly related to organizational _____ , whereas, contextual _____ are value based and additional behavioral roles that are not recognized in job descriptions and covered by compensation; they are extra roles that are indirectly related to organizational _____ . Citizenship _____ like contextual _____ means a set of individual activity/contribution that supports the organizational culture.

Exam Probability: **High**

20. *Answer choices:*

(see index for correct answer)

- a. Squround
- b. Flavor scalping
- c. Phillumeny
- d. Performance

Guidance: level 1

:: Labour relations ::

_____ is a field of study that can have different meanings depending on the context in which it is used. In an international context, it is a subfield of labor history that studies the human relations with regard to work – in its broadest sense – and how this connects to questions of social inequality. It explicitly encompasses unregulated, historical, and non-Western forms of labor. Here, _____ define "for or with whom one works and under what rules. These rules determine the type of work, type and amount of remuneration, working hours, degrees of physical and psychological strain, as well as the degree of freedom and autonomy associated with the work."

Exam Probability: **Medium**

21. *Answer choices:*

(see index for correct answer)

- a. Labor relations
- b. Lockout
- c. Global union federation
- d. Open shop

Guidance: level 1

:: Semiconductor companies ::

_____ Corporation is a Japanese multinational conglomerate corporation headquartered in Konan, Minato, Tokyo. Its diversified business includes consumer and professional electronics, gaming, entertainment and financial services. The company owns the largest music entertainment business in the world, the largest video game console business and one of the largest video game publishing businesses, and is one of the leading manufacturers of electronic products for the consumer and professional markets, and a leading player in the film and television entertainment industry. _____ was ranked 97th on the 2018 Fortune Global 500 list.

Exam Probability: **Medium**

22. *Answer choices:*

(see index for correct answer)

- a. Fairchild Semiconductor
- b. Ingenic Semiconductor
- c. IXYS Corporation
- d. Sharp Corporation

Guidance: level 1

:: Infographics ::

A _____ is a graphical representation of data, in which "the data is represented by symbols, such as bars in a bar _____, lines in a line _____, or slices in a pie _____". A _____ can represent tabular numeric data, functions or some kinds of qualitative structure and provides different info.

Exam Probability: **Medium**

23. *Answer choices:*

(see index for correct answer)

- a. Diagram
- b. Chart
- c. Cutaway drawing
- d. Motion chart

Guidance: level 1

:: Business models ::

A _____ is "an autonomous association of persons united voluntarily to meet their common economic, social, and cultural needs and aspirations through a jointly-owned and democratically-controlled enterprise". _____ s may include.

Exam Probability: **Low**

24. *Answer choices:*

(see index for correct answer)

- a. Cooperative
- b. The India Way
- c. Low-cost carrier
- d. Freemium

Guidance: level 1

:: Organizational structure ::

An _____ defines how activities such as task allocation, coordination, and supervision are directed toward the achievement of organizational aims.

Exam Probability: **Medium**

25. *Answer choices:*

(see index for correct answer)

- a. Organizational structure
- b. Blessed Unrest
- c. Unorganisation
- d. The Starfish and the Spider

Guidance: level 1

:: ::

An _____ is a contingent motivator. Traditional _____ s are extrinsic motivators which reward actions to yield a desired outcome. The effectiveness of traditional _____ s has changed as the needs of Western society have evolved. While the traditional _____ model is effective when there is a defined procedure and goal for a task, Western society started to require a higher volume of critical thinkers, so the traditional model became less effective. Institutions are now following a trend in implementing strategies that rely on intrinsic motivations rather than the extrinsic motivations that the traditional _____ s foster.

Exam Probability: **High**

26. *Answer choices:*

(see index for correct answer)

- a. open system
- b. process perspective
- c. deep-level diversity
- d. Incentive

Guidance: level 1

:: Marketing ::

_____ comes from the Latin neg and otsia referring to businessmen who, unlike the patricians, had no leisure time in their industriousness; it held the meaning of business until the 17th century when it took on the diplomatic connotation as a dialogue between two or more people or parties intended to reach a beneficial outcome over one or more issues where a conflict exists with respect to at least one of these issues. Thus, _____ is a process of combining divergent positions into a joint agreement under a decision rule of unanimity.

Exam Probability: **Medium**

27. *Answer choices:*
(see index for correct answer)

- a. Existing visitor optimisation
- b. Negotiation
- c. Customer lifetime value
- d. Buyer decision process

Guidance: level 1

:: Management ::

_____ is the identification, evaluation, and prioritization of risks followed by coordinated and economical application of resources to minimize, monitor, and control the probability or impact of unfortunate events or to maximize the realization of opportunities.

Exam Probability: **Medium**

28. *Answer choices:*
(see index for correct answer)

- a. Relational view
- b. Risk management
- c. Crisis management
- d. Semiconductor consolidation

Guidance: level 1

:: Business law ::

_____ is where a person's financial liability is limited to a fixed sum, most commonly the value of a person's investment in a company or partnership. If a company with _____ is sued, then the claimants are suing the company, not its owners or investors. A shareholder in a limited company is not personally liable for any of the debts of the company, other than for the amount already invested in the company and for any unpaid amount on the shares in the company, if any. The same is true for the members of a _____ partnership and the limited partners in a limited partnership. By contrast, sole proprietors and partners in general partnerships are each liable for all the debts of the business.

Exam Probability: **High**

29. *Answer choices:*

(see index for correct answer)

- a. Uniform Partnership Act
- b. TRIPS Agreement
- c. Lessor
- d. Limited liability

Guidance: level 1

:: Management ::

_____ is a process by which entities review the quality of all factors involved in production. ISO 9000 defines _____ as "A part of quality management focused on fulfilling quality requirements".

Exam Probability: **Low**

30. *Answer choices:*

(see index for correct answer)

- a. Continuous monitoring
- b. Iterative and incremental development
- c. Dominant design
- d. Personal offshoring

Guidance: level 1

:: E-commerce ::

_____ is the activity of buying or selling of products on online services or over the Internet. Electronic commerce draws on technologies such as mobile commerce, electronic funds transfer, supply chain management, Internet marketing, online transaction processing, electronic data interchange , inventory management systems, and automated data collection systems.

Exam Probability: **High**

31. *Answer choices:*

(see index for correct answer)

- a. E-commerce
- b. Customer Access and Retrieval System
- c. Soldsie
- d. SAF-T

Guidance: level 1

:: Goods ::

In most contexts, the concept of _____ denotes the conduct that should be preferred when posed with a choice between possible actions. _____ is generally considered to be the opposite of evil, and is of interest in the study of morality, ethics, religion and philosophy. The specific meaning and etymology of the term and its associated translations among ancient and contemporary languages show substantial variation in its inflection and meaning depending on circumstances of place, history, religious, or philosophical context.

Exam Probability: **High**

32. *Answer choices:*

(see index for correct answer)

- a. Good
- b. Information good
- c. Neutral good
- d. Case

Guidance: level 1

:: Regression analysis ::

A _____ often refers to a set of documented requirements to be satisfied by a material, design, product, or service. A _____ is often a type of technical standard.

Exam Probability: **Medium**

33. *Answer choices:*

(see index for correct answer)

- a. Local regression
- b. Tobit model
- c. Generalized least squares
- d. Specification

Guidance: level 1

:: Organizational behavior ::

_____ is the state or fact of exclusive rights and control over property, which may be an object, land/real estate or intellectual property. _____ involves multiple rights, collectively referred to as title, which may be separated and held by different parties.

Exam Probability: **Low**

34. *Answer choices:*

(see index for correct answer)

- a. Organizational citizenship behavior
- b. Satisficing
- c. Ownership
- d. Achievement Motivation Inventory

Guidance: level 1

:: ::

_____ or accountancy is the measurement, processing, and communication of financial information about economic entities such as businesses and corporations. The modern field was established by the Italian mathematician Luca Pacioli in 1494. _____ , which has been called the "language of business", measures the results of an organization's economic activities and conveys this information to a variety of users, including investors, creditors, management, and regulators. Practitioners of _____ are known as accountants. The terms "_____" and "financial reporting" are often used as synonyms.

Exam Probability: **Low**

35. *Answer choices:*
(see index for correct answer)

- a. empathy
- b. corporate values
- c. surface-level diversity
- d. Accounting

Guidance: level 1

:: Currency ::

A _____ , in the most specific sense is money in any form when in use or circulation as a medium of exchange, especially circulating banknotes and coins. A more general definition is that a _____ is a system of money in common use, especially for people in a nation. Under this definition, US dollars , pounds sterling , Australian dollars , European euros , Russian rubles and Indian Rupees are examples of currencies. These various currencies are recognized as stores of value and are traded between nations in foreign exchange markets, which determine the relative values of the different currencies. Currencies in this sense are defined by governments, and each type has limited boundaries of acceptance.

Exam Probability: **High**

36. *Answer choices:*
(see index for correct answer)

- a. Currency
- b. Remonetisation
- c. Currency intervention

- d. Circulation

Guidance: level 1

:: Industrial Revolution ::

The _____, now also known as the First _____, was the transition to new manufacturing processes in Europe and the US, in the period from about 1760 to sometime between 1820 and 1840. This transition included going from hand production methods to machines, new chemical manufacturing and iron production processes, the increasing use of steam power and water power, the development of machine tools and the rise of the mechanized factory system. The _____ also led to an unprecedented rise in the rate of population growth.

Exam Probability: **High**

37. *Answer choices:*

(see index for correct answer)

- a. Leawood Pump House
- b. Bowling Iron Works
- c. Hulett
- d. Blast furnace

Guidance: level 1

:: Human resource management ::

_____ are the people who make up the workforce of an organization, business sector, or economy. "Human capital" is sometimes used synonymously with "_____", although human capital typically refers to a narrower effect. Likewise, other terms sometimes used include manpower, talent, labor, personnel, or simply people.

Exam Probability: **Low**

38. *Answer choices:*

(see index for correct answer)

- a. Cross-functional team
- b. Job performance
- c. Job description management
- d. Human resources

Guidance: level 1

:: ::

_____ is the administration of an organization, whether it is a business, a not-for-profit organization, or government body. _____ includes the activities of setting the strategy of an organization and coordinating the efforts of its employees to accomplish its objectives through the application of available resources, such as financial, natural, technological, and human resources. The term "_____" may also refer to those people who manage an organization.

Exam Probability: **High**

39. *Answer choices:*
(see index for correct answer)

- a. Management
- b. process perspective
- c. hierarchical
- d. cultural

Guidance: level 1

:: Export and import control ::

"_____" means the Government Service which is responsible for the administration of _____ law and the collection of duties and taxes and which also has the responsibility for the application of other laws and regulations relating to the importation, exportation, movement or storage of goods.

Exam Probability: **High**

40. *Answer choices:*
(see index for correct answer)

- a. Canadian Export and Import Controls Bureau
- b. Customs Modernization Act
- c. Customs
- d. Customs valuation

Guidance: level 1

:: Decision theory ::

A _____ is a deliberate system of principles to guide decisions and achieve rational outcomes. A _____ is a statement of intent, and is implemented as a procedure or protocol. Policies are generally adopted by a governance body within an organization. Policies can assist in both subjective and objective decision making. Policies to assist in subjective decision making usually assist senior management with decisions that must be based on the relative merits of a number of factors, and as a result are often hard to test objectively, e.g. work-life balance _____. In contrast policies to assist in objective decision making are usually operational in nature and can be objectively tested, e.g. password _____.

Exam Probability: **Medium**

41. *Answer choices:*

(see index for correct answer)

- a. Binary decision
- b. Decision rule
- c. Statistical murder
- d. Policy

Guidance: level 1

:: Land value taxation ::

_____, sometimes referred to as dry _____, is the solid surface of Earth that is not permanently covered by water. The vast majority of human activity throughout history has occurred in _____ areas that support agriculture, habitat, and various natural resources. Some life forms have developed from predecessor species that lived in bodies of water.

Exam Probability: **Medium**

42. *Answer choices:*

(see index for correct answer)

- a. Henry George
- b. Harry Gunnison Brown
- c. Land
- d. Physiocracy

Guidance: level 1

:: International trade ::

In finance, an _____ is the rate at which one currency will be exchanged for another. It is also regarded as the value of one country's currency in relation to another currency. For example, an interbank _____ of 114 Japanese yen to the United States dollar means that ¥114 will be exchanged for each US$1 or that US$1 will be exchanged for each ¥114. In this case it is said that the price of a dollar in relation to yen is ¥114, or equivalently that the price of a yen in relation to dollars is $1/114.

Exam Probability: **High**

43. *Answer choices:*

(see index for correct answer)

- a. Export-oriented
- b. Trans-Atlantic trade
- c. Reciprocity
- d. International Association for Technology Trade

Guidance: level 1

:: Casting (manufacturing) ::

A _____ is a regularity in the world, man-made design, or abstract ideas. As such, the elements of a _____ repeat in a predictable manner. A geometric _____ is a kind of _____ formed of geometric shapes and typically repeated like a wallpaper design.

Exam Probability: **High**

44. *Answer choices:*

(see index for correct answer)

- a. Vacuum casting
- b. Lost-foam casting
- c. Plaster mold casting
- d. Sand casting

Guidance: level 1

:: Alchemical processes ::

In chemistry, a _____ is a special type of homogeneous mixture composed of two or more substances. In such a mixture, a solute is a substance dissolved in another substance, known as a solvent. The mixing process of a _____ happens at a scale where the effects of chemical polarity are involved, resulting in interactions that are specific to solvation. The _____ assumes the phase of the solvent when the solvent is the larger fraction of the mixture, as is commonly the case. The concentration of a solute in a _____ is the mass of that solute expressed as a percentage of the mass of the whole _____ . The term aqueous _____ is when one of the solvents is water.

Exam Probability: **Low**

45. *Answer choices:*

(see index for correct answer)

- a. Fermentation
- b. Fixation
- c. Corporification
- d. Solution

Guidance: level 1

:: ::

_____ is a marketing communication that employs an openly sponsored, non-personal message to promote or sell a product, service or idea. Sponsors of _____ are typically businesses wishing to promote their products or services. _____ is differentiated from public relations in that an advertiser pays for and has control over the message. It differs from personal selling in that the message is non-personal, i.e., not directed to a particular individual. _____ is communicated through various mass media, including traditional media such as newspapers, magazines, television, radio, outdoor _____ or direct mail; and new media such as search results, blogs, social media, websites or text messages. The actual presentation of the message in a medium is referred to as an advertisement, or "ad" or advert for short.

Exam Probability: **Low**

46. *Answer choices:*

(see index for correct answer)

- a. process perspective
- b. information systems assessment

- c. similarity-attraction theory
- d. Advertising

Guidance: level 1

:: ::

_____ is a means of protection from financial loss. It is a form of risk management, primarily used to hedge against the risk of a contingent or uncertain loss

Exam Probability: **High**

47. *Answer choices:*
(see index for correct answer)

- a. levels of analysis
- b. Insurance
- c. co-culture
- d. personal values

Guidance: level 1

:: Marketing ::

A _____ is an overall experience of a customer that distinguishes an organization or product from its rivals in the eyes of the customer. _____ s are used in business, marketing, and advertising. Name _____ s are sometimes distinguished from generic or store _____ s.

Exam Probability: **Low**

48. *Answer choices:*
(see index for correct answer)

- a. Brand
- b. Marketing operations
- c. Disruptive innovation
- d. Multicultural marketing

Guidance: level 1

:: Commerce ::

_____ relates to "the exchange of goods and services, especially on a large scale". It includes legal, economic, political, social, cultural and technological systems that operate in a country or in international trade.

Exam Probability: **Medium**

49. *Answer choices:*

(see index for correct answer)

- a. Weight
- b. Commerce
- c. Hauls
- d. Organ trade

Guidance: level 1

:: Management ::

In business, a _____ is the attribute that allows an organization to outperform its competitors. A _____ may include access to natural resources, such as high-grade ores or a low-cost power source, highly skilled labor, geographic location, high entry barriers, and access to new technology.

Exam Probability: **Low**

50. *Answer choices:*

(see index for correct answer)

- a. Competitive advantage
- b. Participative decision-making
- c. Balanced scorecard
- d. Environmental stewardship

Guidance: level 1

:: Evaluation ::

_____ solving consists of using generic or ad hoc methods in an orderly manner to find solutions to _____ s. Some of the _____ -solving techniques developed and used in philosophy, artificial intelligence, computer science, engineering, mathematics, or medicine are related to mental _____ -solving techniques studied in psychology.

Exam Probability: **Low**

51. *Answer choices:*

(see index for correct answer)

- a. Problem
- b. Evaluation Assurance Level
- c. Australian Drug Evaluation Committee
- d. SPECpower

Guidance: level 1

:: Contract law ::

A _____ is a legally-binding agreement which recognises and governs the rights and duties of the parties to the agreement. A _____ is legally enforceable because it meets the requirements and approval of the law. An agreement typically involves the exchange of goods, services, money, or promises of any of those. In the event of breach of _____ , the law awards the injured party access to legal remedies such as damages and cancellation.

Exam Probability: **Medium**

52. *Answer choices:*

(see index for correct answer)

- a. Contract
- b. Non-repudiation
- c. Personal contract purchase
- d. Force majeure

Guidance: level 1

:: Monopoly (economics) ::

A _____ is a form of intellectual property that gives its owner the legal right to exclude others from making, using, selling, and importing an invention for a limited period of years, in exchange for publishing an enabling public disclosure of the invention. In most countries _____ rights fall under civil law and the _____ holder needs to sue someone infringing the _____ in order to enforce his or her rights. In some industries _____ s are an essential form of competitive advantage; in others they are irrelevant.

Exam Probability: **High**

53. *Answer choices:*

(see index for correct answer)

- a. Network effect
- b. Ownership unbundling
- c. History of monopoly
- d. Patent

Guidance: level 1

:: Project management ::

Contemporary business and science treat as a _____ any undertaking, carried out individually or collaboratively and possibly involving research or design, that is carefully planned to achieve a particular aim.

Exam Probability: **High**

54. *Answer choices:*

(see index for correct answer)

- a. Project
- b. Mandated lead arranger
- c. Site survey
- d. Transfer of Burden

Guidance: level 1

:: Stochastic processes ::

_____ in its modern meaning is a "new idea, creative thoughts, new imaginations in form of device or method". _____ is often also viewed as the application of better solutions that meet new requirements, unarticulated needs, or existing market needs. Such _____ takes place through the provision of more-effective products, processes, services, technologies, or business models that are made available to markets, governments and society. An _____ is something original and more effective and, as a consequence, new, that "breaks into" the market or society. _____ is related to, but not the same as, invention, as _____ is more apt to involve the practical implementation of an invention to make a meaningful impact in the market or society, and not all _____ s require an invention. _____ often manifests itself via the engineering process, when the problem being solved is of a technical or scientific nature. The opposite of _____ is exnovation.

Exam Probability: **High**

55. *Answer choices:*

(see index for correct answer)

- a. Random dynamical system
- b. Stochastic quantization
- c. Innovation
- d. Moran process

Guidance: level 1

:: Information science ::

_____ is the resolution of uncertainty; it is that which answers the question of "what an entity is" and thus defines both its essence and nature of its characteristics. _____ relates to both data and knowledge, as data is meaningful _____ representing values attributed to parameters, and knowledge signifies understanding of a concept. _____ is uncoupled from an observer, which is an entity that can access _____ and thus discern what it specifies; _____ exists beyond an event horizon for example. In the case of knowledge, the _____ itself requires a cognitive observer to be obtained.

Exam Probability: **High**

56. *Answer choices:*

(see index for correct answer)

- a. Knowledge Organization Systems
- b. CENDI
- c. Cultural informatics
- d. Information

Guidance: level 1

:: Investment ::

In finance, the benefit from an _____ is called a return. The return may consist of a gain realised from the sale of property or an _____, unrealised capital appreciation, or _____ income such as dividends, interest, rental income etc., or a combination of capital gain and income. The return may also include currency gains or losses due to changes in foreign currency exchange rates.

Exam Probability: **Low**

57. *Answer choices:*
(see index for correct answer)

- a. Lehman Formula
- b. Investor awareness
- c. Investment
- d. Investment outsourcing

Guidance: level 1

:: Financial regulatory authorities of the United States ::

The _____ is the revenue service of the United States federal government. The government agency is a bureau of the Department of the Treasury, and is under the immediate direction of the Commissioner of Internal Revenue, who is appointed to a five-year term by the President of the United States. The IRS is responsible for collecting taxes and administering the Internal Revenue Code, the main body of federal statutory tax law of the United States. The duties of the IRS include providing tax assistance to taxpayers and pursuing and resolving instances of erroneous or fraudulent tax filings. The IRS has also overseen various benefits programs, and enforces portions of the Affordable Care Act.

Exam Probability: **High**

58. *Answer choices:*

(see index for correct answer)

- a. Office of Thrift Supervision
- b. Operation Choke Point
- c. Commodity Futures Trading Commission
- d. Internal Revenue Service

Guidance: level 1

:: ::

Competition arises whenever at least two parties strive for a goal which cannot be shared: where one's gain is the other's loss.

Exam Probability: **High**

59. *Answer choices:*

(see index for correct answer)

- a. Competitor
- b. Sarbanes-Oxley act of 2002
- c. hierarchical perspective
- d. cultural

Guidance: level 1

Management

Management is the administration of an organization, whether it is a business, a not-for-profit organization, or government body. Management includes the activities of setting the strategy of an organization and coordinating the efforts of its employees (or of volunteers) to accomplish its objectives through the application of available resources, such as financial, natural, technological, and human resources.

:: Supply chain management ::

_____ is the process of finding and agreeing to terms, and acquiring goods, services, or works from an external source, often via a tendering or competitive bidding process. _____ is used to ensure the buyer receives goods, services, or works at the best possible price when aspects such as quality, quantity, time, and location are compared. Corporations and public bodies often define processes intended to promote fair and open competition for their business while minimizing risks such as exposure to fraud and collusion.

Exam Probability: **Low**

1. *Answer choices:*

(see index for correct answer)

- a. Pharmacode
- b. Journal of Supply Chain Management
- c. Pacific Access
- d. Procurement

Guidance: level 1

:: ::

_____ is the amount of time someone works beyond normal working hours. The term is also used for the pay received for this time. Normal hours may be determined in several ways.

Exam Probability: **Low**

2. *Answer choices:*

(see index for correct answer)

- a. Overtime
- b. empathy
- c. interpersonal communication
- d. personal values

Guidance: level 1

:: Management ::

_____ is a method of quality control which employs statistical methods to monitor and control a process. This helps to ensure that the process operates efficiently, producing more specification-conforming products with less waste . SPC can be applied to any process where the "conforming product" output can be measured. Key tools used in SPC include run charts, control charts, a focus on continuous improvement, and the design of experiments. An example of a process where SPC is applied is manufacturing lines.

Exam Probability: **High**

3. *Answer choices:*

(see index for correct answer)

- a. Statistical process control
- b. Outrage constraint
- c. Allegiance
- d. Force-field analysis

Guidance: level 1

:: ::

In sales, commerce and economics, a _____ is the recipient of a good, service, product or an idea - obtained from a seller, vendor, or supplier via a financial transaction or exchange for money or some other valuable consideration.

Exam Probability: **High**

4. *Answer choices:*
(see index for correct answer)

- a. hierarchical
- b. Customer
- c. co-culture
- d. Sarbanes-Oxley act of 2002

Guidance: level 1

:: ::

_____ is the administration of an organization, whether it is a business, a not-for-profit organization, or government body. _____ includes the activities of setting the strategy of an organization and coordinating the efforts of its employees to accomplish its objectives through the application of available resources, such as financial, natural, technological, and human resources. The term "_____" may also refer to those people who manage an organization.

Exam Probability: **Low**

5. *Answer choices:*
(see index for correct answer)

- a. open system
- b. hierarchical perspective
- c. information systems assessment
- d. Character

Guidance: level 1

:: Production economics ::

In microeconomics, _____ are the cost advantages that enterprises obtain due to their scale of operation, with cost per unit of output decreasing with increasing scale.

Exam Probability: **Medium**

6. *Answer choices:*

(see index for correct answer)

- a. Split-off point
- b. Marginal product
- c. Multifactor productivity
- d. Economies of scale

Guidance: level 1

:: Business law ::

A _____ is a business entity created by two or more parties, generally characterized by shared ownership, shared returns and risks, and shared governance. Companies typically pursue _____ s for one of four reasons: to access a new market, particularly emerging markets; to gain scale efficiencies by combining assets and operations; to share risk for major investments or projects; or to access skills and capabilities.

Exam Probability: **Low**

7. *Answer choices:*

(see index for correct answer)

- a. Single business enterprise
- b. Partnership
- c. Joint venture
- d. Interest of the company

Guidance: level 1

:: ::

_____ refers to the confirmation of certain characteristics of an object, person, or organization. This confirmation is often, but not always, provided by some form of external review, education, assessment, or audit. Accreditation is a specific organization's process of _____ . According to the National Council on Measurement in Education, a _____ test is a credentialing test used to determine whether individuals are knowledgeable enough in a given occupational area to be labeled "competent to practice" in that area.

Exam Probability: **High**

8. *Answer choices:*

(see index for correct answer)

- a. process perspective
- b. corporate values
- c. cultural
- d. functional perspective

Guidance: level 1

:: Power (social and political) ::

In a notable study of power conducted by social psychologists John R. P. French and Bertram Raven in 1959, power is divided into five separate and distinct forms. In 1965 Raven revised this model to include a sixth form by separating the informational power base as distinct from the _____ base.

Exam Probability: **High**

9. *Answer choices:*

(see index for correct answer)

- a. Expert power
- b. need for power
- c. Referent power

Guidance: level 1

:: ::

_____ is the process of making predictions of the future based on past and present data and most commonly by analysis of trends. A commonplace example might be estimation of some variable of interest at some specified future date. Prediction is a similar, but more general term. Both might refer to formal statistical methods employing time series, cross-sectional or longitudinal data, or alternatively to less formal judgmental methods. Usage can differ between areas of application: for example, in hydrology the terms "forecast" and "_____" are sometimes reserved for estimates of values at certain specific future times, while the term "prediction" is used for more general estimates, such as the number of times floods will occur over a long period.

Exam Probability: **High**

10. *Answer choices:*

(see index for correct answer)

- a. corporate values
- b. Sarbanes-Oxley act of 2002
- c. Forecasting
- d. hierarchical

Guidance: level 1

:: Outsourcing ::

_____ is the relocation of a business process from one country to another—typically an operational process, such as manufacturing, or supporting processes, such as accounting. Typically this refers to a company business, although state governments may also employ _____ . More recently, technical and administrative services have been offshored.

Exam Probability: **Low**

11. *Answer choices:*

(see index for correct answer)

- a. Offshoring
- b. Counsel On Call
- c. Pillsbury Winthrop Shaw Pittman
- d. Website Management Outsourcing

Guidance: level 1

:: ::

_____ is the assignment of any responsibility or authority to another person to carry out specific activities. It is one of the core concepts of management leadership. However, the person who delegated the work remains accountable for the outcome of the delegated work. _____ empowers a subordinate to make decisions, i.e. it is a shifting of decision-making authority from one organizational level to a lower one. _____, if properly done, is not fabrication. The opposite of effective _____ is micromanagement, where a manager provides too much input, direction, and review of delegated work. In general, _____ is good and can save money and time, help in building skills, and motivate people. On the other hand, poor _____ might cause frustration and confusion to all the involved parties. Some agents, however, do not favour a _____ and consider the power of making a decision rather burdensome.

Exam Probability: **High**

12. *Answer choices:*

(see index for correct answer)

- a. Delegation
- b. Character
- c. imperative
- d. open system

Guidance: level 1

:: Customs duties ::

A _____ is a tax on imports or exports between sovereign states. It is a form of regulation of foreign trade and a policy that taxes foreign products to encourage or safeguard domestic industry. _____ s are the simplest and oldest instrument of trade policy. Traditionally, states have used them as a source of income. Now, they are among the most widely used instruments of protection, along with import and export quotas.

Exam Probability: **High**

13. *Answer choices:*

(see index for correct answer)

- a. Tariff
- b. Tariffication

- c. Court of Exchequer
- d. Wines in bond

Guidance: level 1

:: Management ::

In the field of management, _____ involves the formulation and implementation of the major goals and initiatives taken by an organization's top management on behalf of owners, based on consideration of resources and an assessment of the internal and external environments in which the organization operates.

Exam Probability: **Medium**

14. *Answer choices:*
(see index for correct answer)

- a. Performance indicator
- b. Industrial forensics
- c. Certified Energy Manager
- d. Critical path method

Guidance: level 1

:: ::

An _____ is a process where candidates are examined to determine their suitability for specific types of employment, especially management or military command. The candidates' personality and aptitudes are determined by techniques including interviews, group exercises, presentations, examinations and psychometric testing.

Exam Probability: **High**

15. *Answer choices:*
(see index for correct answer)

- a. Assessment center
- b. empathy
- c. cultural
- d. process perspective

Guidance: level 1

:: Systems theory ::

A _____ is a set of policies, processes and procedures used by an organization to ensure that it can fulfill the tasks required to achieve its objectives. These objectives cover many aspects of the organization's operations. For instance, an environmental _____ enables organizations to improve their environmental performance and an occupational health and safety _____ enables an organization to control its occupational health and safety risks, etc.

Exam Probability: **Medium**

16. *Answer choices:*

(see index for correct answer)

- a. subsystem
- b. Management system
- c. transient state
- d. process system

Guidance: level 1

:: Organizational behavior ::

_____ is the state or fact of exclusive rights and control over property, which may be an object, land/real estate or intellectual property. _____ involves multiple rights, collectively referred to as title, which may be separated and held by different parties.

Exam Probability: **Medium**

17. *Answer choices:*

(see index for correct answer)

- a. Ownership
- b. Nut Island effect
- c. Organizational justice
- d. Span of control

Guidance: level 1

:: Training ::

_____ is action or inaction that is regulated to be in accordance with a particular system of governance. _____ is commonly applied to regulating human and animal behavior, and furthermore, it is applied to each activity-branch in all branches of organized activity, knowledge, and other fields of study and observation. _____ can be a set of expectations that are required by any governing entity including the self, groups, classes, fields, industries, or societies.

Exam Probability: **Low**

18. *Answer choices:*

(see index for correct answer)

- a. Youth Training Scheme
- b. Adobe Captivate
- c. Practicum
- d. ISpring Suite

Guidance: level 1

:: Business ethics ::

_____ is a type of harassment technique that relates to a sexual nature and the unwelcome or inappropriate promise of rewards in exchange for sexual favors. _____ includes a range of actions from mild transgressions to sexual abuse or assault. Harassment can occur in many different social settings such as the workplace, the home, school, churches, etc. Harassers or victims may be of any gender.

Exam Probability: **Low**

19. *Answer choices:*

(see index for correct answer)

- a. Whistleblower
- b. Sexual harassment
- c. Resource Conservation and Recovery Act
- d. Walmarting

Guidance: level 1

:: Management ::

A _____ is a method or technique that has been generally accepted as superior to any alternatives because it produces results that are superior to those achieved by other means or because it has become a standard way of doing things, e.g., a standard way of complying with legal or ethical requirements.

Exam Probability: **Medium**

20. *Answer choices:*
(see index for correct answer)

- a. Business rule
- b. Community management
- c. Best practice
- d. Earned value management

Guidance: level 1

:: Business terms ::

Centralisation or _____ is the process by which the activities of an organization, particularly those regarding planning and decision-making, framing strategy and policies become concentrated within a particular geographical location group. This moves the important decision-making and planning powers within the center of the organisation.

Exam Probability: **Medium**

21. *Answer choices:*
(see index for correct answer)

- a. organizational capital
- b. strategic plan
- c. granular
- d. front office

Guidance: level 1

:: ::

The _____ is an intergovernmental organization that is concerned with the regulation of international trade between nations. The WTO officially commenced on 1 January 1995 under the Marrakesh Agreement, signed by 124 nations on 15 April 1994, replacing the General Agreement on Tariffs and Trade , which commenced in 1948. It is the largest international economic organization in the world.

Exam Probability: **Medium**

22. *Answer choices:*

(see index for correct answer)

- a. World Trade Organization
- b. Sarbanes-Oxley act of 2002
- c. Character
- d. deep-level diversity

Guidance: level 1

:: ::

An _____ is a contingent motivator. Traditional _____ s are extrinsic motivators which reward actions to yield a desired outcome. The effectiveness of traditional _____ s has changed as the needs of Western society have evolved. While the traditional _____ model is effective when there is a defined procedure and goal for a task, Western society started to require a higher volume of critical thinkers, so the traditional model became less effective. Institutions are now following a trend in implementing strategies that rely on intrinsic motivations rather than the extrinsic motivations that the traditional _____ s foster.

Exam Probability: **High**

23. *Answer choices:*

(see index for correct answer)

- a. Incentive
- b. surface-level diversity
- c. open system
- d. co-culture

Guidance: level 1

:: Management ::

_____ is the identification, evaluation, and prioritization of risks followed by coordinated and economical application of resources to minimize, monitor, and control the probability or impact of unfortunate events or to maximize the realization of opportunities.

Exam Probability: **Medium**

24. *Answer choices:*

(see index for correct answer)

- a. Double linking
- b. Design leadership
- c. Pareto analysis
- d. Risk management

Guidance: level 1

:: Leadership ::

_____ /Management is a part of a style of leadership that focuses on supervision, organization, and performance; it is an integral part of the Full Range Leadership Model. _____ is a style of leadership in which leaders promote compliance by followers through both rewards and punishments. Through a rewards and punishments system, transactional leaders are able to keep followers motivated for the short-term. Unlike transformational leaders, those using the transactional approach are not looking to change the future, they look to keep things the same. Leaders using _____ as a model pay attention to followers' work in order to find faults and deviations.

Exam Probability: **Medium**

25. *Answer choices:*

(see index for correct answer)

- a. Moral example
- b. The Leadership Council
- c. BTS Group
- d. Inspired Leadership Award

Guidance: level 1

:: Industrial relations ::

_____ or employee satisfaction is a measure of workers' contentedness with their job, whether or not they like the job or individual aspects or facets of jobs, such as nature of work or supervision. _____ can be measured in cognitive, affective, and behavioral components. Researchers have also noted that _____ measures vary in the extent to which they measure feelings about the job, or cognitions about the job.

Exam Probability: **High**

26. *Answer choices:*

(see index for correct answer)

- a. Job satisfaction
- b. Workforce Investment Board
- c. Injury prevention
- d. European Journal of Industrial Relations

Guidance: level 1

:: Organizational theory ::

_____ refers to both a body of non-elective government officials and an administrative policy-making group. Historically, a _____ was a government administration managed by departments staffed with non-elected officials. Today, _____ is the administrative system governing any large institution, whether publicly owned or privately owned. The public administration in many countries is an example of a _____, but so is the centralized hierarchical structure of a business firm.

Exam Probability: **Low**

27. *Answer choices:*

(see index for correct answer)

- a. Organisational semiotics
- b. Constructive Developmental Framework
- c. Organizational ecology
- d. Bureaucracy

Guidance: level 1

:: Project management ::

A _____ is a professional in the field of project management. _____ s have the responsibility of the planning, procurement and execution of a project, in any undertaking that has a defined scope, defined start and a defined finish; regardless of industry. _____ s are first point of contact for any issues or discrepancies arising from within the heads of various departments in an organization before the problem escalates to higher authorities. Project management is the responsibility of a _____ . This individual seldom participates directly in the activities that produce the end result, but rather strives to maintain the progress, mutual interaction and tasks of various parties in such a way that reduces the risk of overall failure, maximizes benefits, and minimizes costs.

Exam Probability: **Low**

28. *Answer choices:*
(see index for correct answer)

- a. Gold plating
- b. Time horizon
- c. Phased implementation
- d. Outcome mapping

Guidance: level 1

:: Production and manufacturing ::

Automatic _____ in continuous production processes is a combination of control engineering and chemical engineering disciplines that uses industrial control systems to achieve a production level of consistency, economy and safety which could not be achieved purely by human manual control. It is implemented widely in industries such as oil refining, pulp and paper manufacturing, chemical processing and power generating plants.

Exam Probability: **Medium**

29. *Answer choices:*
(see index for correct answer)

- a. production control
- b. Product data record
- c. Alarm management
- d. Accelerated aging

Guidance: level 1

:: Evaluation ::

_____ is a way of preventing mistakes and defects in manufactured products and avoiding problems when delivering products or services to customers; which ISO 9000 defines as "part of quality management focused on providing confidence that quality requirements will be fulfilled". This defect prevention in _____ differs subtly from defect detection and rejection in quality control and has been referred to as a shift left since it focuses on quality earlier in the process .

Exam Probability: **Low**

30. *Answer choices:*
(see index for correct answer)

- a. Narrative evaluation
- b. Academic equivalency evaluation
- c. Technology assessment
- d. Quality assurance

Guidance: level 1

:: Life skills ::

_____ , emotional leadership , emotional quotient and _____ quotient , is the capability of individuals to recognize their own emotions and those of others, discern between different feelings and label them appropriately, use emotional information to guide thinking and behavior, and manage and/or adjust emotions to adapt to environments or achieve one's goal.

Exam Probability: **Medium**

31. *Answer choices:*
(see index for correct answer)

- a. emotion work
- b. Social intelligence
- c. multiple intelligence
- d. coping mechanism

Guidance: level 1

:: ::

_____ is the process of two or more people or organizations working together to complete a task or achieve a goal. _____ is similar to cooperation. Most _____ requires leadership, although the form of leadership can be social within a decentralized and egalitarian group. Teams that work collaboratively often access greater resources, recognition and rewards when facing competition for finite resources.

Exam Probability: **High**

32. *Answer choices:*
(see index for correct answer)

- a. Collaboration
- b. Character
- c. hierarchical perspective
- d. empathy

Guidance: level 1

:: Workplace ::

A _____, also referred to as a performance review, performance evaluation, development discussion, or employee appraisal is a method by which the job performance of an employee is documented and evaluated. _____ s are a part of career development and consist of regular reviews of employee performance within organizations.

Exam Probability: **Low**

33. *Answer choices:*
(see index for correct answer)

- a. Performance appraisal
- b. Queen bee syndrome
- c. Open allocation
- d. Workplace romance

Guidance: level 1

:: Critical thinking ::

An _____ is a set of statements usually constructed to describe a set of facts which clarifies the causes, context, and consequences of those facts. This description of the facts et cetera may establish rules or laws, and may clarify the existing rules or laws in relation to any objects, or phenomena examined. The components of an _____ can be implicit, and interwoven with one another.

Exam Probability: **Low**

34. *Answer choices:*

(see index for correct answer)

- a. Explanation
- b. Adviser
- c. Proof
- d. Seven Types of Ambiguity

Guidance: level 1

:: ::

_____ is the consumption and saving opportunity gained by an entity within a specified timeframe, which is generally expressed in monetary terms. For households and individuals, " _____ is the sum of all the wages, salaries, profits, interest payments, rents, and other forms of earnings received in a given period of time."

Exam Probability: **Low**

35. *Answer choices:*

(see index for correct answer)

- a. corporate values
- b. interpersonal communication
- c. imperative
- d. Sarbanes-Oxley act of 2002

Guidance: level 1

:: Legal terms ::

_____ is a type of meaning in which a phrase, statement or resolution is not explicitly defined, making several interpretations plausible. A common aspect of _____ is uncertainty. It is thus an attribute of any idea or statement whose intended meaning cannot be definitively resolved according to a rule or process with a finite number of steps.

Exam Probability: **High**

36. *Answer choices:*

(see index for correct answer)

- a. Legal benefit
- b. Third party complaint
- c. Judicial estoppel
- d. Ambiguity

Guidance: level 1

:: International trade ::

_____ involves the transfer of goods or services from one person or entity to another, often in exchange for money. A system or network that allows _____ is called a market.

Exam Probability: **Low**

37. *Answer choices:*

(see index for correct answer)

- a. Trading nation
- b. Trade
- c. Pauper labor argument
- d. Parallel import

Guidance: level 1

:: Social psychology ::

In social psychology, _____ is the phenomenon of a person exerting less effort to achieve a goal when he or she works in a group than when working alone. This is seen as one of the main reasons groups are sometimes less productive than the combined performance of their members working as individuals, but should be distinguished from the accidental coordination problems that groups sometimes experience.

Exam Probability: **High**

38. *Answer choices:*
(see index for correct answer)

- a. Social loafing
- b. self-disclosure
- c. thought control
- d. externalization

Guidance: level 1

:: Project management ::

_____ is the right to exercise power, which can be formalized by a state and exercised by way of judges, appointed executives of government, or the ecclesiastical or priestly appointed representatives of a God or other deities.

Exam Probability: **Medium**

39. *Answer choices:*
(see index for correct answer)

- a. Structured data analysis
- b. Defense Acquisition Guide
- c. Project appraisal
- d. Authority

Guidance: level 1

:: ::

In production, research, retail, and accounting, a _____ is the value of money that has been used up to produce something or deliver a service, and hence is not available for use anymore. In business, the _____ may be one of acquisition, in which case the amount of money expended to acquire it is counted as _____. In this case, money is the input that is gone in order to acquire the thing. This acquisition _____ may be the sum of the _____ of production as incurred by the original producer, and further _____ s of transaction as incurred by the acquirer over and above the price paid to the producer. Usually, the price also includes a mark-up for profit over the _____ of production.

Exam Probability: **Low**

40. *Answer choices:*

(see index for correct answer)

- a. hierarchical perspective
- b. personal values
- c. information systems assessment
- d. surface-level diversity

Guidance: level 1

:: Business law ::

A _____ is an arrangement where parties, known as partners, agree to cooperate to advance their mutual interests. The partners in a _____ may be individuals, businesses, interest-based organizations, schools, governments or combinations. Organizations may partner to increase the likelihood of each achieving their mission and to amplify their reach. A _____ may result in issuing and holding equity or may be only governed by a contract.

Exam Probability: **Low**

41. *Answer choices:*

(see index for correct answer)

- a. Consumer privacy
- b. Partnership
- c. Ladenschlussgesetz
- d. Leave of absence

Guidance: level 1

:: Cognitive biases ::

The _____ is a type of immediate judgement discrepancy, or cognitive bias, where a person making an initial assessment of another person, place, or thing will assume ambiguous information based upon concrete information. A simplified example of the _____ is when an individual noticing that the person in the photograph is attractive, well groomed, and properly attired, assumes, using a mental heuristic, that the person in the photograph is a good person based upon the rules of that individual's social concept. This constant error in judgment is reflective of the individual's preferences, prejudices, ideology, aspirations, and social perception. The _____ is an evaluation by an individual and can affect the perception of a decision, action, idea, business, person, group, entity, or other whenever concrete data is generalized or influences ambiguous information.

Exam Probability: **Medium**

42. *Answer choices:*

(see index for correct answer)

- a. Halo effect
- b. Hindsight bias
- c. Familiarity heuristic
- d. Time-saving bias

Guidance: level 1

:: Employment discrimination ::

A _____ is a metaphor used to represent an invisible barrier that keeps a given demographic from rising beyond a certain level in a hierarchy.

Exam Probability: **Medium**

43. *Answer choices:*

(see index for correct answer)

- a. Glass cliff
- b. LGBT employment discrimination in the United States
- c. United Kingdom employment equality law
- d. MacBride Principles

Guidance: level 1

:: Management ::

_____ is the practice of initiating, planning, executing, controlling, and closing the work of a team to achieve specific goals and meet specific success criteria at the specified time.

Exam Probability: **Low**

44. *Answer choices:*

(see index for correct answer)

- a. Product Development and Systems Engineering Consortium
- b. Project management
- c. Management fad
- d. Linear scheduling method

Guidance: level 1

:: Regression analysis ::

A _____ often refers to a set of documented requirements to be satisfied by a material, design, product, or service. A _____ is often a type of technical standard.

Exam Probability: **High**

45. *Answer choices:*

(see index for correct answer)

- a. Multinomial logistic regression
- b. Omitted-variable bias
- c. Specification
- d. Proper linear model

Guidance: level 1

:: Psychometrics ::

_____ is a dynamic, structured, interactive process where a neutral third party assists disputing parties in resolving conflict through the use of specialized communication and negotiation techniques. All participants in _____ are encouraged to actively participate in the process. _____ is a "party-centered" process in that it is focused primarily upon the needs, rights, and interests of the parties. The mediator uses a wide variety of techniques to guide the process in a constructive direction and to help the parties find their optimal solution. A mediator is facilitative in that she/he manages the interaction between parties and facilitates open communication. _____ is also evaluative in that the mediator analyzes issues and relevant norms , while refraining from providing prescriptive advice to the parties .

Exam Probability: **Low**

46. *Answer choices:*

(see index for correct answer)

- a. Mediation
- b. William H. Tucker
- c. Assessment Systems Corporation
- d. Thurstonian model

Guidance: level 1

:: Logistics ::

_____ is generally the detailed organization and implementation of a complex operation. In a general business sense, _____ is the management of the flow of things between the point of origin and the point of consumption in order to meet requirements of customers or corporations. The resources managed in _____ may include tangible goods such as materials, equipment, and supplies, as well as food and other consumable items. The _____ of physical items usually involves the integration of information flow, materials handling, production, packaging, inventory, transportation, warehousing, and often security.

Exam Probability: **Low**

47. *Answer choices:*

(see index for correct answer)

- a. Phase jitter modulation
- b. Space logistics

- c. Logistics
- d. Freightos

Guidance: level 1

:: Internet privacy ::

An _____ is a private network accessible only to an organization's staff. Often, a wide range of information and services are available on an organization's internal _____ that are unavailable to the public, unlike the Internet. A company-wide _____ can constitute an important focal point of internal communication and collaboration, and provide a single starting point to access internal and external resources. In its simplest form, an _____ is established with the technologies for local area networks and wide area networks . Many modern _____ s have search engines, user profiles, blogs, mobile apps with notifications, and events planning within their infrastructure.

Exam Probability: **Medium**

48. *Answer choices:*

(see index for correct answer)

- a. Internet privacy
- b. Intranet
- c. Right to be forgotten
- d. Shiva Smart Tunneling

Guidance: level 1

:: Product design ::

_____ as a verb is to create a new product to be sold by a business to its customers. A very broad coefficient and effective generation and development of ideas through a process that leads to new products. Thus, it is a major aspect of new product development.

Exam Probability: **Low**

49. *Answer choices:*

(see index for correct answer)

- a. Sara Little Turnbull
- b. Rodney Fitch

- c. Product design
- d. Happily Unmarried

Guidance: level 1

:: Management ::

The term _____ refers to measures designed to increase the degree of autonomy and self-determination in people and in communities in order to enable them to represent their interests in a responsible and self-determined way, acting on their own authority. It is the process of becoming stronger and more confident, especially in controlling one's life and claiming one's rights. _____ as action refers both to the process of self- _____ and to professional support of people, which enables them to overcome their sense of powerlessness and lack of influence, and to recognize and use their resources. To do work with power.

Exam Probability: **High**

50. *Answer choices:*
(see index for correct answer)

- a. Resource management
- b. Empowerment
- c. Pareto analysis
- d. Fredmund Malik

Guidance: level 1

:: Management ::

The _____ is a strategy performance management tool – a semi-standard structured report, that can be used by managers to keep track of the execution of activities by the staff within their control and to monitor the consequences arising from these actions.

Exam Probability: **High**

51. *Answer choices:*
(see index for correct answer)

- a. Quality
- b. Strategic management
- c. SimulTrain

- d. Balanced scorecard

Guidance: level 1

:: Information technology management ::

_____ is a collective term for all approaches to prepare, support and help individuals, teams, and organizations in making organizational change. The most common change drivers include: technological evolution, process reviews, crisis, and consumer habit changes; pressure from new business entrants, acquisitions, mergers, and organizational restructuring. It includes methods that redirect or redefine the use of resources, business process, budget allocations, or other modes of operation that significantly change a company or organization. Organizational _____ considers the full organization and what needs to change, while _____ may be used solely to refer to how people and teams are affected by such organizational transition. It deals with many different disciplines, from behavioral and social sciences to information technology and business solutions.

Exam Probability: **High**

52. *Answer choices:*

(see index for correct answer)

- a. Change management
- b. Contract management
- c. Lean IT
- d. Knowledge balance sheet

Guidance: level 1

:: Project management ::

Some scenarios associate "this kind of planning" with learning "life skills". _____ s are necessary, or at least useful, in situations where individuals need to know what time they must be at a specific location to receive a specific service, and where people need to accomplish a set of goals within a set time period.

Exam Probability: **High**

53. *Answer choices:*

(see index for correct answer)

- a. Small-scale project management
- b. Deliverable
- c. Mandated lead arranger
- d. Code name

Guidance: level 1

:: Management occupations ::

_____ is the process of designing, launching and running a new business, which is often initially a small business. The people who create these businesses are called entrepreneurs.

Exam Probability: **Low**

54. *Answer choices:*
(see index for correct answer)

- a. Pit manager
- b. Vorstandsassistent
- c. Ceco
- d. Entrepreneurship

Guidance: level 1

:: ::

In business strategy, _____ is establishing a competitive advantage by having the lowest cost of operation in the industry. _____ is often driven by company efficiency, size, scale, scope and cumulative experience .A _____ strategy aims to exploit scale of production, well-defined scope and other economies , producing highly standardized products, using advanced technology.In recent years, more and more companies have chosen a strategic mix to achieve market leadership. These patterns consist of simultaneous _____ , superior customer service and product leadership. Walmart has succeeded across the world due to its _____ strategy. The company has cut down on exesses at every point of production and thus are able to provide the consumers with quality products at low prices.

Exam Probability: **Medium**

55. *Answer choices:*
(see index for correct answer)

- a. Cost leadership
- b. similarity-attraction theory
- c. information systems assessment
- d. personal values

Guidance: level 1

:: ::

The _____ is a political and economic union of 28 member states that are located primarily in Europe. It has an area of 4,475,757 km2 and an estimated population of about 513 million. The EU has developed an internal single market through a standardised system of laws that apply in all member states in those matters, and only those matters, where members have agreed to act as one. EU policies aim to ensure the free movement of people, goods, services and capital within the internal market, enact legislation in justice and home affairs and maintain common policies on trade, agriculture, fisheries and regional development. For travel within the Schengen Area, passport controls have been abolished. A monetary union was established in 1999 and came into full force in 2002 and is composed of 19 EU member states which use the euro currency.

Exam Probability: **Low**

56. *Answer choices:*
(see index for correct answer)

- a. Character
- b. deep-level diversity
- c. personal values
- d. European Union

Guidance: level 1

:: Marketing ::

_____ is based on a marketing concept which can be adopted by an organization as a strategy for business expansion. Where implemented, a franchisor licenses its know-how, procedures, intellectual property, use of its business model, brand, and rights to sell its branded products and services to a franchisee. In return the franchisee pays certain fees and agrees to comply with certain obligations, typically set out in a Franchise Agreement.

Exam Probability: **Low**

57. *Answer choices:*

(see index for correct answer)

- a. Mass-market theory
- b. Behance
- c. Narrowcasting
- d. Preference-rank translation

Guidance: level 1

:: Statistical terminology ::

_____ is the ability to avoid wasting materials, energy, efforts, money, and time in doing something or in producing a desired result. In a more general sense, it is the ability to do things well, successfully, and without waste. In more mathematical or scientific terms, it is a measure of the extent to which input is well used for an intended task or function. It often specifically comprises the capability of a specific application of effort to produce a specific outcome with a minimum amount or quantity of waste, expense, or unnecessary effort. _____ refers to very different inputs and outputs in different fields and industries.

Exam Probability: **Medium**

58. *Answer choices:*

(see index for correct answer)

- a. Concentration parameter
- b. Statistical error
- c. Efficiency
- d. Central limit theorem

Guidance: level 1

:: Marketing ::

_____ is the percentage of a market accounted for by a specific entity. In a survey of nearly 200 senior marketing managers, 67% responded that they found the revenue- "dollar _____" metric very useful, while 61% found "unit _____" very useful.

Exam Probability: **Medium**

59. *Answer choices:*

(see index for correct answer)

- a. Kano model
- b. Marketing communications
- c. Market share
- d. Digital strategy

Guidance: level 1

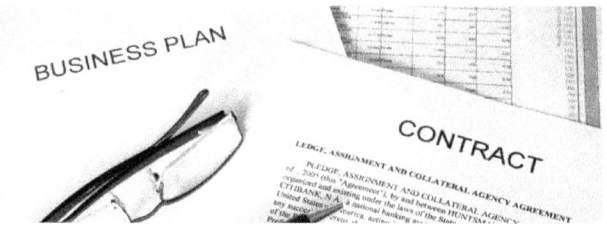

Business law

Corporate law (also known as business law) is the body of law governing the rights, relations, and conduct of persons, companies, organizations and businesses. It refers to the legal practice relating to, or the theory of corporations. Corporate law often describes the law relating to matters which derive directly from the life-cycle of a corporation. It thus encompasses the formation, funding, governance, and death of a corporation.

:: Ethically disputed business practices ::

_____ is the trading of a public company's stock or other securities by individuals with access to nonpublic information about the company. In various countries, some kinds of trading based on insider information is illegal. This is because it is seen as unfair to other investors who do not have access to the information, as the investor with insider information could potentially make larger profits than a typical investor could make. The rules governing _____ are complex and vary significantly from country to country. The extent of enforcement also varies from one country to another. The definition of insider in one jurisdiction can be broad, and may cover not only insiders themselves but also any persons related to them, such as brokers, associates and even family members. A person who becomes aware of non-public information and trades on that basis may be guilty of a crime.

Exam Probability: **High**

1. *Answer choices:*
(see index for correct answer)

- a. Cream skimming
- b. Boiler room
- c. Constructive dismissal
- d. Insider trading

Guidance: level 1

:: ::

A _____, in common law jurisdictions, is a civil wrong that causes a claimant to suffer loss or harm resulting in legal liability for the person who commits the _____ ious act. It can include the intentional infliction of emotional distress, negligence, financial losses, injuries, invasion of privacy, and many other things.

Exam Probability: **High**

2. *Answer choices:*

(see index for correct answer)

- a. Tort
- b. co-culture
- c. deep-level diversity
- d. personal values

Guidance: level 1

:: Asset ::

In financial accounting, an _____ is any resource owned by the business. Anything tangible or intangible that can be owned or controlled to produce value and that is held by a company to produce positive economic value is an _____. Simply stated, _____ s represent value of ownership that can be converted into cash. The balance sheet of a firm records the monetary value of the _____ s owned by that firm. It covers money and other valuables belonging to an individual or to a business.

Exam Probability: **Medium**

3. *Answer choices:*

(see index for correct answer)

- a. Fixed asset
- b. Asset

Guidance: level 1

:: Majority–minority relations ::

_____ , also known as reservation in India and Nepal, positive discrimination / action in the United Kingdom, and employment equity in Canada and South Africa, is the policy of promoting the education and employment of members of groups that are known to have previously suffered from discrimination. Historically and internationally, support for _____ has sought to achieve goals such as bridging inequalities in employment and pay, increasing access to education, promoting diversity, and redressing apparent past wrongs, harms, or hindrances.

Exam Probability: **Medium**

4. *Answer choices:*

(see index for correct answer)

- a. cultural Relativism
- b. cultural dissonance
- c. Affirmative action

Guidance: level 1

:: Real property law ::

A _____ is any legal instrument in writing which passes, affirms or confirms an interest, right, or property and that is signed, attested, delivered, and in some jurisdictions, sealed. It is commonly associated with transferring title to property. The _____ has a greater presumption of validity and is less rebuttable than an instrument signed by the party to the _____ . A _____ can be unilateral or bilateral. _____ s include conveyances, commissions, licenses, patents, diplomas, and conditionally powers of attorney if executed as _____ s. The _____ is the modern descendant of the medieval charter, and delivery is thought to symbolically replace the ancient ceremony of livery of seisin.

Exam Probability: **Medium**

5. *Answer choices:*

(see index for correct answer)

- a. Common area
- b. Deed
- c. Claim club
- d. Paper road

Guidance: level 1

:: Legal terms ::

_____ s may be governments, corporations or investment trusts. _____ s are legally responsible for the obligations of the issue and for reporting financial conditions, material developments and any other operational activities as required by the regulations of their jurisdictions.

Exam Probability: **Medium**

6. *Answer choices:*
(see index for correct answer)

- a. Comparative negligence
- b. Market capitalization
- c. Issuer
- d. Adverse

Guidance: level 1

:: Monopoly (economics) ::

_____ is a category of property that includes intangible creations of the human intellect. _____ encompasses two types of rights: industrial property rights and copyright. It was not until the 19th century that the term " _____ " began to be used, and not until the late 20th century that it became commonplace in the majority of the world.

Exam Probability: **Low**

7. *Answer choices:*
(see index for correct answer)

- a. Economies of scope
- b. National Competition Policy
- c. Special 301 Report
- d. Intellectual property

Guidance: level 1

:: Contract law ::

Generally, a _____ is a loan or a credit transaction in which the lender acquires a security interest in collateral owned by the borrower and is entitled to foreclose on or repossess the collateral in the event of the borrower's default. The terms of the relationship are governed by a contract, or security agreement. A common example would be a consumer who purchases a car on credit. If the consumer fails to make the payments on time, the lender will take the car and resell it, applying the proceeds of the sale toward the loan. Mortgages and deeds of trust are another example. In the United States, _____ s in personal property are governed by Article 9 of the Uniform Commercial Code .

Exam Probability: **High**

8. *Answer choices:*
(see index for correct answer)

- a. Secured transaction
- b. Culpa in contrahendo
- c. Implied authority
- d. Extended warranty

Guidance: level 1

:: Commercial item transport and distribution ::

_____ s may be negotiable or non-negotiable. Negotiable _____ s allow transfer of ownership of that commodity without having to deliver the physical commodity. See Delivery order.

Exam Probability: **High**

9. *Answer choices:*
(see index for correct answer)

- a. Export Yellow Pages
- b. Warehouse receipt
- c. Supply chain management
- d. Intermodal freight transport

Guidance: level 1

:: Progressive Era in the United States ::

The Clayton Antitrust Act of 1914 , was a part of United States antitrust law with the goal of adding further substance to the U.S. antitrust law regime; the _____ sought to prevent anticompetitive practices in their incipiency. That regime started with the Sherman Antitrust Act of 1890, the first Federal law outlawing practices considered harmful to consumers . The _____ specified particular prohibited conduct, the three-level enforcement scheme, the exemptions, and the remedial measures.

Exam Probability: **Low**

10. *Answer choices:*

(see index for correct answer)

- a. Clayton Antitrust Act
- b. Clayton Act
- c. pragmatism

Guidance: level 1

:: Chemical industry ::

The _____ for the Protection of Literary and Artistic Works, usually known as the _____, is an international agreement governing copyright, which was first accepted in Berne, Switzerland, in 1886.

Exam Probability: **Medium**

11. *Answer choices:*

(see index for correct answer)

- a. Blue colour works
- b. Berne Convention
- c. Middle German Chemical Triangle
- d. Chemical leasing

Guidance: level 1

:: United States corporate law ::

In tort law, a _____ is a legal obligation which is imposed on an individual requiring adherence to a standard of reasonable care while performing any acts that could foreseeably harm others. It is the first element that must be established to proceed with an action in negligence. The claimant must be able to show a _____ imposed by law which the defendant has breached. In turn, breaching a duty may subject an individual to liability. The _____ may be imposed by operation of law between individuals who have no current direct relationship but eventually become related in some manner, as defined by common law.

Exam Probability: **Low**

12. *Answer choices:*
(see index for correct answer)

- a. Corporate law in the United States
- b. Model Nonprofit Corporation Act
- c. NYSE Listed Company Manual
- d. New York Business Corporation Law

Guidance: level 1

:: Fraud ::

_____ is the deliberate use of someone else's identity, usually as a method to gain a financial advantage or obtain credit and other benefits in the other person's name, and perhaps to the other person's disadvantage or loss. The person whose identity has been assumed may suffer adverse consequences, especially if they are held responsible for the perpetrator's actions. _____ occurs when someone uses another's personally identifying information, like their name, identifying number, or credit card number, without their permission, to commit fraud or other crimes. The term _____ was coined in 1964. Since that time, the definition of _____ has been statutorily prescribed throughout both the U.K. and the United States as the theft of personally identifying information, generally including a person's name, date of birth, social security number, driver's license number, bank account or credit card numbers, PIN numbers, electronic signatures, fingerprints, passwords, or any other information that can be used to access a person's financial resources.

Exam Probability: **Medium**

13. *Answer choices:*

(see index for correct answer)

- a. Identity theft
- b. Control fraud
- c. Lottery scam
- d. Lip sync

Guidance: level 1

:: ::

An _____, for United States federal income tax, is a closely held corporation that makes a valid election to be taxed under Subchapter S of Chapter 1 of the Internal Revenue Code. In general, _____ s do not pay any income taxes. Instead, the corporation's income or losses are divided among and passed through to its shareholders. The shareholders must then report the income or loss on their own individual income tax returns.

Exam Probability: **Medium**

14. *Answer choices:*

(see index for correct answer)

- a. deep-level diversity
- b. S corporation
- c. functional perspective
- d. personal values

Guidance: level 1

:: Intention ::

_____ is the mental element of a person's intention to commit a crime; or knowledge that one's action or lack of action would cause a crime to be committed. It is a necessary element of many crimes.

Exam Probability: **High**

15. *Answer choices:*

(see index for correct answer)

- a. Mens rea
- b. Letter of Intent

Guidance: level 1

:: Labour relations ::

_____ is a field of study that can have different meanings depending on the context in which it is used. In an international context, it is a subfield of labor history that studies the human relations with regard to work – in its broadest sense – and how this connects to questions of social inequality. It explicitly encompasses unregulated, historical, and non-Western forms of labor. Here, _____ define "for or with whom one works and under what rules. These rules determine the type of work, type and amount of remuneration, working hours, degrees of physical and psychological strain, as well as the degree of freedom and autonomy associated with the work."

Exam Probability: **Medium**

16. *Answer choices:*

(see index for correct answer)

- a. Labor relations
- b. Labour council
- c. Minnesota Nurses Association
- d. Big labor

Guidance: level 1

:: Legal doctrines and principles ::

_____ is a failure to exercise appropriate and or ethical ruled care expected to be exercised amongst specified circumstances. The area of tort law known as _____ involves harm caused by failing to act as a form of carelessness possibly with extenuating circumstances. The core concept of _____ is that people should exercise reasonable care in their actions, by taking account of the potential harm that they might foreseeably cause to other people or property.

Exam Probability: **High**

17. *Answer choices:*

(see index for correct answer)

- a. Negligence
- b. Contributory negligence
- c. Attractive nuisance doctrine
- d. compulsory purchase

Guidance: level 1

:: ::

A concept of English law, a _____ is an untrue or misleading statement of fact made during negotiations by one party to another, the statement then inducing that other party into the contract. The misled party may normally rescind the contract, and sometimes may be awarded damages as well

Exam Probability: **Low**

18. *Answer choices:*

(see index for correct answer)

- a. Misrepresentation
- b. interpersonal communication
- c. information systems assessment
- d. empathy

Guidance: level 1

:: ::

_____ refers to a business or organization attempting to acquire goods or services to accomplish its goals. Although there are several organizations that attempt to set standards in the _____ process, processes can vary greatly between organizations. Typically the word " _____ " is not used interchangeably with the word "procurement", since procurement typically includes expediting, supplier quality, and transportation and logistics in addition to _____ .

Exam Probability: **Low**

19. *Answer choices:*

(see index for correct answer)

- a. personal values
- b. interpersonal communication
- c. Character
- d. Purchasing

Guidance: level 1

:: Monopoly (economics) ::

A _____ is a form of intellectual property that gives its owner the legal right to exclude others from making, using, selling, and importing an invention for a limited period of years, in exchange for publishing an enabling public disclosure of the invention. In most countries _____ rights fall under civil law and the _____ holder needs to sue someone infringing the _____ in order to enforce his or her rights. In some industries _____ s are an essential form of competitive advantage; in others they are irrelevant.

Exam Probability: **High**

20. *Answer choices:*

(see index for correct answer)

- a. Practice of law
- b. Privatization
- c. Patent
- d. Contestable market

Guidance: level 1

:: ::

In common law legal systems, _____ is a principle or rule established in a previous legal case that is either binding on or persuasive for a court or other tribunal when deciding subsequent cases with similar issues or facts. Common-law legal systems place great value on deciding cases according to consistent principled rules, so that similar facts will yield similar and predictable outcomes, and observance of _____ is the mechanism by which that goal is attained. The principle by which judges are bound to _____ s is known as stare decisis. Common-law _____ is a third kind of law, on equal footing with statutory law and delegated legislation or regulatory law.

Exam Probability: **High**

21. *Answer choices:*

(see index for correct answer)

- a. surface-level diversity
- b. functional perspective

- c. levels of analysis
- d. Sarbanes-Oxley act of 2002

Guidance: level 1

:: International relations ::

_____ is double mindedness or double heartedness in duplicity, fraud, or deception. It may involve intentional deceit of others, or self-deception.

Exam Probability: **Low**

22. *Answer choices:*

(see index for correct answer)

- a. Asia Society
- b. European balance of power
- c. E9
- d. Fragile state

Guidance: level 1

:: Contract law ::

Offer and acceptance analysis is a traditional approach in contract law. The offer and acceptance formula, developed in the 19th century, identifies a moment of formation when the parties are of one mind. This classical approach to contract formation has been modified by developments in the law of estoppel, misleading conduct, misrepresentation and unjust enrichment.

Exam Probability: **Low**

23. *Answer choices:*

(see index for correct answer)

- a. Pirate code
- b. Condition precedent
- c. Substantial performance
- d. Offeror

Guidance: level 1

:: Generally Accepted Accounting Principles ::

In accounting, _____ is the income that a business have from its normal business activities, usually from the sale of goods and services to customers. _____ is also referred to as sales or turnover. Some companies receive _____ from interest, royalties, or other fees. _____ may refer to business income in general, or it may refer to the amount, in a monetary unit, earned during a period of time, as in "Last year, Company X had _____ of $42 million". Profits or net income generally imply total _____ minus total expenses in a given period. In accounting, in the balance statement it is a subsection of the Equity section and _____ increases equity, it is often referred to as the "top line" due to its position on the income statement at the very top. This is to be contrasted with the "bottom line" which denotes net income.

Exam Probability: **High**

24. *Answer choices:*
(see index for correct answer)

- a. Liability
- b. Matching principle
- c. Normal balance
- d. Closing entries

Guidance: level 1

:: ::

A _____ is a person or firm who arranges transactions between a buyer and a seller for a commission when the deal is executed. A _____ who also acts as a seller or as a buyer becomes a principal party to the deal. Neither role should be confused with that of an agent—one who acts on behalf of a principal party in a deal.

Exam Probability: **High**

25. *Answer choices:*
(see index for correct answer)

- a. Character
- b. Broker
- c. open system
- d. hierarchical

Guidance: level 1

:: Clauses of the United States Constitution ::

The _____ describes an enumerated power listed in the United States Constitution. The clause states that the United States Congress shall have power "To regulate Commerce with foreign Nations, and among the several States, and with the Indian Tribes." Courts and commentators have tended to discuss each of these three areas of commerce as a separate power granted to Congress. It is common to see the individual components of the _____ referred to under specific terms: the Foreign _____, the Interstate _____, and the Indian _____.

Exam Probability: **Medium**

26. *Answer choices:*

(see index for correct answer)

- a. Full Faith and Credit Clause
- b. Full faith and credit
- c. Commerce Clause

Guidance: level 1

:: Employment discrimination ::

_____ is a form of discrimination based on race, gender, religion, national origin, physical or mental disability, age, sexual orientation, and gender identity by employers. Earnings differentials or occupational differentiation—where differences in pay come from differences in qualifications or responsibilities—should not be confused with _____. Discrimination can be intended and involve disparate treatment of a group or be unintended, yet create disparate impact for a group.

Exam Probability: **High**

27. *Answer choices:*

(see index for correct answer)

- a. United Kingdom employment equality law
- b. Employment discrimination
- c. Glass ceiling
- d. New South Wales selection bias

Guidance: level 1

:: ::

A _____ is a law passed by a legislative body in a common law system to set the maximum time after an event within which legal proceedings may be initiated.

Exam Probability: **High**

28. *Answer choices:*

(see index for correct answer)

- a. co-culture
- b. hierarchical
- c. imperative
- d. corporate values

Guidance: level 1

:: Business law ::

A _____ is a group of people who jointly supervise the activities of an organization, which can be either a for-profit business, nonprofit organization, or a government agency. Such a board's powers, duties, and responsibilities are determined by government regulations and the organization's own constitution and bylaws. These authorities may specify the number of members of the board, how they are to be chosen, and how often they are to meet.

Exam Probability: **Medium**

29. *Answer choices:*

(see index for correct answer)

- a. Refusal to deal
- b. Bulk sale
- c. Trading while insolvent
- d. Undervalue transaction

Guidance: level 1

:: Business models ::

A _____, _____ company or daughter company is a company that is owned or controlled by another company, which is called the parent company, parent, or holding company. The _____ can be a company, corporation, or limited liability company. In some cases it is a government or state-owned enterprise. In some cases, particularly in the music and book publishing industries, subsidiaries are referred to as imprints.

Exam Probability: **High**

30. *Answer choices:*

(see index for correct answer)

- a. One stop shop
- b. Consumer cooperative
- c. Legacy carrier
- d. Subsidiary

Guidance: level 1

:: Contract law ::

In contract law, a _____ is a promise which is not a condition of the contract or an innominate term: it is a term "not going to the root of the contract", and which only entitles the innocent party to damages if it is breached: i.e. the _____ is not true or the defaulting party does not perform the contract in accordance with the terms of the _____ . A _____ is not guarantee. It is a mere promise. It may be enforced if it is breached by an award for the legal remedy of damages.

Exam Probability: **Medium**

31. *Answer choices:*

(see index for correct answer)

- a. Warranty
- b. Mistake
- c. Offeree
- d. Quasi-contract

Guidance: level 1

:: Decision theory ::

A _____ is a deliberate system of principles to guide decisions and achieve rational outcomes. A _____ is a statement of intent, and is implemented as a procedure or protocol. Policies are generally adopted by a governance body within an organization. Policies can assist in both subjective and objective decision making. Policies to assist in subjective decision making usually assist senior management with decisions that must be based on the relative merits of a number of factors, and as a result are often hard to test objectively, e.g. work-life balance _____ . In contrast policies to assist in objective decision making are usually operational in nature and can be objectively tested, e.g. password _____ .

Exam Probability: **Medium**

32. *Answer choices:*

(see index for correct answer)

- a. Policy
- b. Quantum cognition
- c. Kepner-Tregoe
- d. Decision-theoretic rough sets

Guidance: level 1

:: ::

_____ is a legal term which, in its broadest sense, is a synonym for anyone in a position of trust and so can refer to any person who holds property, authority, or a position of trust or responsibility for the benefit of another. A _____ can also refer to a person who is allowed to do certain tasks but not able to gain income. Although in the strictest sense of the term a _____ is the holder of property on behalf of a beneficiary, the more expansive sense encompasses persons who serve, for example, on the board of _____ s of an institution that operates for a charity, for the benefit of the general public, or a person in the local government.

Exam Probability: **Medium**

33. *Answer choices:*

(see index for correct answer)

- a. levels of analysis
- b. co-culture
- c. Trustee

- d. corporate values

Guidance: level 1

:: ::

_____ is that part of a civil law legal system which is part of the jus commune that involves relationships between individuals, such as the law of contracts or torts , and the law of obligations . It is to be distinguished from public law, which deals with relationships between both natural and artificial persons and the state, including regulatory statutes, penal law and other law that affects the public order. In general terms, _____ involves interactions between private citizens, whereas public law involves interrelations between the state and the general population.

Exam Probability: **High**

34. *Answer choices:*
(see index for correct answer)

- a. deep-level diversity
- b. imperative
- c. levels of analysis
- d. personal values

Guidance: level 1

:: Utilitarianism ::

_____ is a family of consequentialist ethical theories that promotes actions that maximize happiness and well-being for the majority of a population. Although different varieties of _____ admit different characterizations, the basic idea behind all of them is to in some sense maximize utility, which is often defined in terms of well-being or related concepts. For instance, Jeremy Bentham, the founder of _____ , described utility as

Exam Probability: **Medium**

35. *Answer choices:*
(see index for correct answer)

- a. Felicific calculus
- b. Utilitarianism

- c. Utilitarian bioethics
- d. The Methods of Ethics

Guidance: level 1

:: Product liability ::

_____ is the area of law in which manufacturers, distributors, suppliers, retailers, and others who make products available to the public are held responsible for the injuries those products cause. Although the word "product" has broad connotations, _____ as an area of law is traditionally limited to products in the form of tangible personal property.

Exam Probability: **Low**

36. *Answer choices:*
(see index for correct answer)

- a. Product liability
- b. Product Liability Directive
- c. Consumer Protection Act 1987
- d. Market share liability

Guidance: level 1

:: ::

_____ is a concept of English common law and is a necessity for simple contracts but not for special contracts . The concept has been adopted by other common law jurisdictions, including the US.

Exam Probability: **Medium**

37. *Answer choices:*
(see index for correct answer)

- a. hierarchical perspective
- b. Consideration
- c. empathy
- d. personal values

Guidance: level 1

:: Business ethics ::

_____ is a type of harassment technique that relates to a sexual nature and the unwelcome or inappropriate promise of rewards in exchange for sexual favors. _____ includes a range of actions from mild transgressions to sexual abuse or assault. Harassment can occur in many different social settings such as the workplace, the home, school, churches, etc. Harassers or victims may be of any gender.

Exam Probability: **High**

38. *Answer choices:*
(see index for correct answer)

- a. The Crooked E: The Unshredded Truth About Enron
- b. Perfect Relations
- c. Black Company
- d. Sexual harassment

Guidance: level 1

:: Investment ::

In finance, the benefit from an _____ is called a return. The return may consist of a gain realised from the sale of property or an _____, unrealised capital appreciation, or _____ income such as dividends, interest, rental income etc., or a combination of capital gain and income. The return may also include currency gains or losses due to changes in foreign currency exchange rates.

Exam Probability: **High**

39. *Answer choices:*
(see index for correct answer)

- a. Insurance bond
- b. Shock absorber fee
- c. Investment
- d. Inventory investment

Guidance: level 1

:: ::

The _____ is an independent agency of the Federal government of the United States with responsibilities for enforcing U.S. labor law in relation to collective bargaining and unfair labor practices. Under the National Labor Relations Act of 1935 it supervises elections for labor union representation and can investigate and remedy unfair labor practices. Unfair labor practices may involve union-related situations or instances of protected concerted activity. The NLRB is governed by a five-person board and a General Counsel, all of whom are appointed by the President with the consent of the Senate. Board members are appointed to five-year terms and the General Counsel is appointed to a four-year term. The General Counsel acts as a prosecutor and the Board acts as an appellate quasi-judicial body from decisions of administrative law judges.

Exam Probability: **High**

40. *Answer choices:*

(see index for correct answer)

- a. National Labor Relations Board
- b. information systems assessment
- c. imperative
- d. hierarchical

Guidance: level 1

:: ::

_____ is the consumption and saving opportunity gained by an entity within a specified timeframe, which is generally expressed in monetary terms. For households and individuals, "_____ is the sum of all the wages, salaries, profits, interest payments, rents, and other forms of earnings received in a given period of time."

Exam Probability: **High**

41. *Answer choices:*

(see index for correct answer)

- a. Sarbanes-Oxley act of 2002
- b. open system
- c. levels of analysis
- d. Income

Guidance: level 1

:: ::

_____ is the practical authority granted to a legal body to administer justice within a defined field of responsibility, e.g., Michigan tax law. In federations like the United States, areas of _____ apply to local, state, and federal levels; e.g. the court has _____ to apply federal law.

Exam Probability: **Medium**

42. *Answer choices:*

(see index for correct answer)

- a. Sarbanes-Oxley act of 2002
- b. levels of analysis
- c. Character
- d. surface-level diversity

Guidance: level 1

:: ::

A _____ is a formal written enactment of a legislative authority that governs the legal entities of a city, state, or country by way of consent. Typically, _____ s command or prohibit something, or declare policy. _____ s are rules made by legislative bodies; they are distinguished from case law or precedent, which is decided by courts, and regulations issued by government agencies.

Exam Probability: **Medium**

43. *Answer choices:*

(see index for correct answer)

- a. hierarchical perspective
- b. Statute
- c. corporate values
- d. levels of analysis

Guidance: level 1

:: Auctioneering ::

An _____ is a process of buying and selling goods or services by offering them up for bid, taking bids, and then selling the item to the highest bidder. The open ascending price _____ is arguably the most common form of _____ in use today. Participants bid openly against one another, with each subsequent bid required to be higher than the previous bid. An _____ eer may announce prices, bidders may call out their bids themselves, or bids may be submitted electronically with the highest current bid publicly displayed. In a Dutch _____, the _____ eer begins with a high asking price for some quantity of like items; the price is lowered until a participant is willing to accept the _____ eer's price for some quantity of the goods in the lot or until the seller's reserve price is met. While _____ s are most associated in the public imagination with the sale of antiques, paintings, rare collectibles and expensive wines, _____ s are also used for commodities, livestock, radio spectrum and used cars. In economic theory, an _____ may refer to any mechanism or set of trading rules for exchange.

Exam Probability: **Low**

44. *Answer choices:*
(see index for correct answer)

- a. Auction
- b. Proxy bid
- c. Call for bids
- d. Calor licitantis

Guidance: level 1

:: ::

_____ is the body of law that governs the activities of administrative agencies of government. Government agency action can include rule making, adjudication, or the enforcement of a specific regulatory agenda. _____ is considered a branch of public law. As a body of law, _____ deals with the decision-making of the administrative units of government that are part of a national regulatory scheme in such areas as police law, international trade, manufacturing, the environment, taxation, broadcasting, immigration and transport. _____ expanded greatly during the twentieth century, as legislative bodies worldwide created more government agencies to regulate the social, economic and political spheres of human interaction.

Exam Probability: **Medium**

45. *Answer choices:*

(see index for correct answer)

- a. Administrative law
- b. levels of analysis
- c. hierarchical
- d. empathy

Guidance: level 1

:: Finance ::

_____ is the investigation or exercise of care that a reasonable business or person is expected to take before entering into an agreement or contract with another party, or an act with a certain standard of care.

Exam Probability: **Low**

46. *Answer choices:*

(see index for correct answer)

- a. Equity
- b. Pet banks
- c. Due diligence
- d. Swap rate

Guidance: level 1

:: Forgery ::

_____ is a white-collar crime that generally refers to the false making or material alteration of a legal instrument with the specific intent to defraud anyone . Tampering with a certain legal instrument may be forbidden by law in some jurisdictions but such an offense is not related to _____ unless the tampered legal instrument was actually used in the course of the crime to defraud another person or entity. Copies, studio replicas, and reproductions are not considered forgeries, though they may later become forgeries through knowing and willful misrepresentations.

Exam Probability: **Medium**

47. *Answer choices:*

(see index for correct answer)

- a. Signature forgery
- b. Forgery Act 1913
- c. Counterfeit electronic components
- d. Void pantograph

Guidance: level 1

:: ::

_____ is the practice of protecting the natural environment by individuals, organizations and governments. Its objectives are to conserve natural resources and the existing natural environment and, where possible, to repair damage and reverse trends.

Exam Probability: **Medium**

48. *Answer choices:*

(see index for correct answer)

- a. Character
- b. Environmental Protection
- c. interpersonal communication
- d. information systems assessment

Guidance: level 1

:: ::

A _____ is a sworn body of people convened to render an impartial verdict officially submitted to them by a court, or to set a penalty or judgment. Modern juries tend to be found in courts to ascertain the guilt or lack thereof in a crime. In Anglophone jurisdictions, the verdict may be guilty or not guilty. The old institution of grand juries still exists in some places, particularly the United States, to investigate whether enough evidence of a crime exists to bring someone to trial.

Exam Probability: **High**

49. *Answer choices:*

(see index for correct answer)

- a. Jury
- b. open system
- c. cultural
- d. imperative

Guidance: level 1

:: Contract law ::

In the law of contracts, the _____ , also referred to as an unequivocal and absolute acceptance requirement, states that an offer must be accepted exactly with no modifications. The offeror is the master of one's own offer. An attempt to accept the offer on different terms instead creates a counter-offer, and this constitutes a rejection of the original offer.

Exam Probability: **Low**

50. *Answer choices:*

(see index for correct answer)

- a. Recording contract
- b. first refusal
- c. Contract B
- d. Mirror image rule

Guidance: level 1

:: Criminal procedure ::

In law, a verdict is the formal finding of fact made by a jury on matters or questions submitted to the jury by a judge. In a bench trial, the judge's decision near the end of the trial is simply referred to as a finding. In England and Wales, a coroner's findings are called verdicts .

Exam Probability: **High**

51. *Answer choices:*

(see index for correct answer)

- a. criminal procedure
- b. Exoneration

Guidance: level 1

:: Insurance terms ::

A _____ in the broadest sense is a natural person or other legal entity who receives money or other benefits from a benefactor. For example, the _____ of a life insurance policy is the person who receives the payment of the amount of insurance after the death of the insured.

Exam Probability: **Medium**

52. *Answer choices:*

(see index for correct answer)

- a. Split billing
- b. Beneficiary
- c. Omnibus clause
- d. Segregated fund

Guidance: level 1

:: ::

_____ , in law, is a transaction or action that is valid but may be annulled by one of the parties to the transaction. _____ is usually used in distinction to void ab initio and unenforceable.

Exam Probability: **Low**

53. *Answer choices:*

(see index for correct answer)

- a. functional perspective
- b. surface-level diversity
- c. Voidable
- d. interpersonal communication

Guidance: level 1

:: ::

Punishment is the imposition of an undesirable or unpleasant outcome upon a group or individual, meted out by an authority—in contexts ranging from child discipline to criminal law—as a response and deterrent to a particular action or behaviour that is deemed undesirable or unacceptable. The reasoning may be to condition a child to avoid self-endangerment, to impose social conformity, to defend norms, to protect against future harms, and to maintain the law—and respect for rule of law—under which the social group is governed. Punishment may be self-inflicted as with self-flagellation and mortification of the flesh in the religious setting, but is most often a form of social coercion.

Exam Probability: **Medium**

54. *Answer choices:*
(see index for correct answer)

- a. hierarchical perspective
- b. Punitive
- c. similarity-attraction theory
- d. information systems assessment

Guidance: level 1

:: ::

In logic and philosophy, an _____ is a series of statements, called the premises or premisses, intended to determine the degree of truth of another statement, the conclusion. The logical form of an _____ in a natural language can be represented in a symbolic formal language, and independently of natural language formally defined " _____ s" can be made in math and computer science.

Exam Probability: **High**

55. *Answer choices:*
(see index for correct answer)

- a. process perspective
- b. open system
- c. Argument
- d. deep-level diversity

Guidance: level 1

:: Contract law ::

_____ are damages whose amount the parties designate during the formation of a contract for the injured party to collect as compensation upon a specific breach.

Exam Probability: **High**

56. *Answer choices:*

(see index for correct answer)

- a. Liquidated damages
- b. Pirate code
- c. Beneficial interest
- d. Morals clause

Guidance: level 1

:: ::

_____ is widespread, interconnected digital technology. The term entered the popular culture from science fiction and the arts but is now used by technology strategists, security professionals, government, military and industry leaders and entrepreneurs to describe the domain of the global technology environment. Others consider _____ to be just a notional environment in which communication over computer networks occurs. The word became popular in the 1990s when the uses of the Internet, networking, and digital communication were all growing dramatically and the term "_____" was able to represent the many new ideas and phenomena that were emerging. It has been called the largest unregulated and uncontrolled domain in the history of mankind, and is also unique because it is a domain created by people vice the traditional physical domains.

Exam Probability: **Medium**

57. *Answer choices:*

(see index for correct answer)

- a. Cyberspace
- b. similarity-attraction theory
- c. open system
- d. cultural

Guidance: level 1

:: Contract law ::

_____ , also called an anticipatory breach, is a term in the law of contracts that describes a declaration by the promising party to a contract that he or she does not intend to live up to his or her obligations under the contract.

Exam Probability: **Medium**

58. *Answer choices:*

(see index for correct answer)

- a. Community Benefits Agreement
- b. Contra proferentem
- c. Anticipatory repudiation
- d. Quasi-contract

Guidance: level 1

:: ::

The _____ is one of the several United States Uniform Acts proposed by the National Conference of Commissioners on Uniform State Laws . Forty-seven states, the District of Columbia, and the U.S. Virgin Islands have adopted the UETA . Its purpose is to harmonize state laws concerning retention of paper records and the validity of electronic signatures.

Exam Probability: **Medium**

59. *Answer choices:*

(see index for correct answer)

- a. hierarchical
- b. Uniform Electronic Transactions Act
- c. hierarchical perspective
- d. corporate values

Guidance: level 1

Finance

Finance is a field that is concerned with the allocation (investment) of assets and liabilities over space and time, often under conditions of risk or uncertainty. Finance can also be defined as the science of money management. Participants in the market aim to price assets based on their risk level, fundamental value, and their expected rate of return. Finance can be split into three sub-categories: public finance, corporate finance and personal finance.

:: Fraud ::

In law, _____ is intentional deception to secure unfair or unlawful gain, or to deprive a victim of a legal right. _____ can violate civil law, a criminal law, or it may cause no loss of money, property or legal right but still be an element of another civil or criminal wrong. The purpose of _____ may be monetary gain or other benefits, for example by obtaining a passport, travel document, or driver's license, or mortgage _____, where the perpetrator may attempt to qualify for a mortgage by way of false statements.

Exam Probability: **Low**

1. *Answer choices:*
(see index for correct answer)

- a. Fraud
- b. Lottery scam
- c. Missing trader fraud
- d. Check kiting

Guidance: level 1

:: Markets (customer bases) ::

In economics, _____ is the economic price for which a good or service is offered in the marketplace. It is of interest mainly in the study of microeconomics. Market value and _____ are equal only under conditions of market efficiency, equilibrium, and rational expectations.

Exam Probability: **Medium**

2. *Answer choices:*

(see index for correct answer)

- a. Vertical market
- b. Competitive equilibrium
- c. Horizontal market
- d. Williamson trade-off

Guidance: level 1

:: Corporate finance ::

_____ in corporate finance is the way a corporation finances its assets through some combination of equity, debt, or hybrid securities.

Exam Probability: **Medium**

3. *Answer choices:*

(see index for correct answer)

- a. Golden share
- b. Management buy-in
- c. Rights issue
- d. Capital structure

Guidance: level 1

:: ::

An _____ is an area of the production, distribution, or trade, and consumption of goods and services by different agents. Understood in its broadest sense, `The _____ is defined as a social domain that emphasize the practices, discourses, and material expressions associated with the production, use, and management of resources`. Economic agents can be individuals, businesses, organizations, or governments. Economic transactions occur when two parties agree to the value or price of the transacted good or service, commonly expressed in a certain currency. However, monetary transactions only account for a small part of the economic domain.

Exam Probability: **Medium**

4. *Answer choices:*
(see index for correct answer)

- a. interpersonal communication
- b. Character
- c. similarity-attraction theory
- d. Economy

Guidance: level 1

:: ::

A _____, in the word's original meaning, is a sheet of paper on which one performs work. They come in many forms, most commonly associated with children's school work assignments, tax forms, and accounting or other business environments. Software is increasingly taking over the paper-based _____.

Exam Probability: **Medium**

5. *Answer choices:*
(see index for correct answer)

- a. surface-level diversity
- b. deep-level diversity
- c. Sarbanes-Oxley act of 2002
- d. process perspective

Guidance: level 1

:: Expense ::

An _____, operating expenditure, operational expense, operational expenditure or opex is an ongoing cost for running a product, business, or system. Its counterpart, a capital expenditure, is the cost of developing or providing non-consumable parts for the product or system. For example, the purchase of a photocopier involves capex, and the annual paper, toner, power and maintenance costs represents opex. For larger systems like businesses, opex may also include the cost of workers and facility expenses such as rent and utilities.

Exam Probability: **Medium**

6. *Answer choices:*

(see index for correct answer)

- a. Corporate travel
- b. Operating expense
- c. Expense account
- d. expenditure

Guidance: level 1

:: Financial markets ::

The _____ is the part of the capital market that deals with the issuance and sale of equity-backed securities to investors directly by the issuer. Investor buy securities that were never traded before. _____ s create long term instruments through which corporate entities raise funds from the capital market. It is also known as the New Issue Market.

Exam Probability: **Low**

7. *Answer choices:*

(see index for correct answer)

- a. Primary market
- b. Holy grail distribution
- c. Long
- d. Options Price Reporting Authority

Guidance: level 1

:: Costs ::

The _____ is computed by dividing the total cost of goods available for sale by the total units available for sale. This gives a weighted-average unit cost that is applied to the units in the ending inventory.

Exam Probability: **Medium**

8. *Answer choices:*

(see index for correct answer)

- a. Khozraschyot
- b. Quality costs
- c. Direct labor cost
- d. Direct materials cost

Guidance: level 1

:: Business law ::

The expression " _____ " is somewhat confusing as it has a different meaning based on the context that is under consideration. From a product characteristic stand point, this type of a lease, as distinguished from a finance lease, is one where the lessor takes residual risk. As such, the lease is non full payout. From an accounting stand point, this type of lease results in off balance sheet financing.

Exam Probability: **Low**

9. *Answer choices:*

(see index for correct answer)

- a. Family and Medical Leave Act of 1993
- b. OHADA
- c. Statutory authority
- d. Operating lease

Guidance: level 1

:: Expense ::

A company's _____, or As a result, the computation of the _____ is considerably more complex. Tax law may provide for different treatment of items of income and expenses as a result of tax policy. The differences may be of permanent or temporary nature. Permanent items are in the form of non taxable income and non taxable expenses. Things such as expenses considered not deductible by taxing authorities , the range of tax rates applicable to various levels of income, different tax rates in different jurisdictions, multiple layers of tax on income, and other issues.

Exam Probability: **Low**

10. *Answer choices:*

(see index for correct answer)

- a. Business overhead expense disability insurance
- b. Tax expense
- c. Expense account
- d. Stock option expensing

Guidance: level 1

:: Business law ::

A _____ is an arrangement where parties, known as partners, agree to cooperate to advance their mutual interests. The partners in a _____ may be individuals, businesses, interest-based organizations, schools, governments or combinations. Organizations may partner to increase the likelihood of each achieving their mission and to amplify their reach. A _____ may result in issuing and holding equity or may be only governed by a contract.

Exam Probability: **Medium**

11. *Answer choices:*

(see index for correct answer)

- a. Partnership
- b. Inslaw
- c. Unfair business practices
- d. Limited liability company

Guidance: level 1

:: Accounting systems ::

In bookkeeping, a _____ statement is a process that explains the difference on a specified date between the bank balance shown in an organization's bank statement, as supplied by the bank and the corresponding amount shown in the organization's own accounting records.

Exam Probability: **Low**

12. *Answer choices:*

(see index for correct answer)

- a. Purchase ledger
- b. Debits and credits
- c. Confidence accounting
- d. Bank reconciliation

Guidance: level 1

:: Insolvency ::

_____ is the process in accounting by which a company is brought to an end in the United Kingdom, Republic of Ireland and United States. The assets and property of the company are redistributed. _____ is also sometimes referred to as winding-up or dissolution, although dissolution technically refers to the last stage of _____ . The process of _____ also arises when customs, an authority or agency in a country responsible for collecting and safeguarding customs duties, determines the final computation or ascertainment of the duties or drawback accruing on an entry.

Exam Probability: **Medium**

13. *Answer choices:*

(see index for correct answer)

- a. Debt consolidation
- b. Conservatorship
- c. Insolvency law of Russia
- d. Liquidation

Guidance: level 1

:: Business ::

The seller, or the provider of the goods or services, completes a sale in response to an acquisition, appropriation, requisition or a direct interaction with the buyer at the point of sale. There is a passing of title of the item, and the settlement of a price, in which agreement is reached on a price for which transfer of ownership of the item will occur. The seller, not the purchaser typically executes the sale and it may be completed prior to the obligation of payment. In the case of indirect interaction, a person who sells goods or service on behalf of the owner is known as a salesman or saleswoman or salesperson, but this often refers to someone _____ goods in a store/shop, in which case other terms are also common, including salesclerk, shop assistant, and retail clerk.

Exam Probability: **Medium**

14. *Answer choices:*

(see index for correct answer)

- a. Selling
- b. Counter trade
- c. Price-based selling
- d. GoCardless

Guidance: level 1

:: ::

_____ is an eight-block-long street running roughly northwest to southeast from Broadway to South Street, at the East River, in the Financial District of Lower Manhattan in New York City. Over time, the term has become a metonym for the financial markets of the United States as a whole, the American financial services industry, or New York–based financial interests.

Exam Probability: **High**

15. *Answer choices:*

(see index for correct answer)

- a. Character
- b. corporate values
- c. co-culture
- d. Wall Street

Guidance: level 1

:: ::

_____ is the field of accounting concerned with the summary, analysis and reporting of financial transactions related to a business. This involves the preparation of financial statements available for public use. Stockholders, suppliers, banks, employees, government agencies, business owners, and other stakeholders are examples of people interested in receiving such information for decision making purposes.

Exam Probability: **Low**

16. *Answer choices:*
(see index for correct answer)

- a. similarity-attraction theory
- b. imperative
- c. Financial accounting
- d. hierarchical

Guidance: level 1

:: Hazard analysis ::

Broadly speaking, a _____ is the combined effort of 1. identifying and analyzing potential events that may negatively impact individuals, assets, and/or the environment ; and 2. making judgments "on the tolerability of the risk on the basis of a risk analysis" while considering influencing factors . Put in simpler terms, a _____ analyzes what can go wrong, how likely it is to happen, what the potential consequences are, and how tolerable the identified risk is. As part of this process, the resulting determination of risk may be expressed in a quantitative or qualitative fashion. The _____ is an inherent part of an overall risk management strategy, which attempts to, after a _____ , "introduce control measures to eliminate or reduce" any potential risk-related consequences.

Exam Probability: **Low**

17. *Answer choices:*
(see index for correct answer)

- a. Hazard
- b. Hazardous Materials Identification System
- c. Swiss cheese model
- d. Hazard identification

Guidance: level 1

:: International trade ::

In finance, an _____ is the rate at which one currency will be exchanged for another. It is also regarded as the value of one country's currency in relation to another currency. For example, an interbank _____ of 114 Japanese yen to the United States dollar means that ¥114 will be exchanged for each US$1 or that US$1 will be exchanged for each ¥114. In this case it is said that the price of a dollar in relation to yen is ¥114, or equivalently that the price of a yen in relation to dollars is $1/114.

Exam Probability: **Medium**

18. *Answer choices:*
(see index for correct answer)

- a. Concertina model
- b. National Trade Estimate Report
- c. The Product Space
- d. Agreement on Agriculture

Guidance: level 1

:: Inventory ::

_____ is the amount of inventory a company has in stock at the end of its fiscal year. It is closely related with _____ cost, which is the amount of money spent to get these goods in stock. It should be calculated at the lower of cost or market.

Exam Probability: **Medium**

19. *Answer choices:*
(see index for correct answer)

- a. Ending inventory
- b. Cost of goods sold
- c. Perpetual inventory
- d. Cost of goods available for sale

Guidance: level 1

:: ::

A _____ is an individual or institution that legally owns one or more shares of stock in a public or private corporation. _____ s may be referred to as members of a corporation. Legally, a person is not a _____ in a corporation until their name and other details are entered in the corporation's register of _____ s or members.

Exam Probability: **Low**

20. *Answer choices:*

(see index for correct answer)

- a. Character
- b. process perspective
- c. personal values
- d. Shareholder

Guidance: level 1

:: Derivatives (finance) ::

In finance, a _____ or simply a forward is a non-standardized contract between two parties to buy or to sell an asset at a specified future time at a price agreed upon today, making it a type of derivative instrument. The party agreeing to buy the underlying asset in the future assumes a long position, and the party agreeing to sell the asset in the future assumes a short position. The price agreed upon is called the delivery price, which is equal to the forward price at the time the contract is entered into.

Exam Probability: **High**

21. *Answer choices:*

(see index for correct answer)

- a. Repurchase agreement
- b. Forward contract
- c. Singapore Mercantile Exchange
- d. Net volatility

Guidance: level 1

:: Accounting journals and ledgers ::

_____ is a daybook or journal which is used to record transactions relating to adjustment entries, opening stock, accounting errors etc. The source documents of this prime entry book are journal voucher, copy of management reports and invoices.

Exam Probability: **Medium**

22. *Answer choices:*
(see index for correct answer)

- a. General journal
- b. Journal entry
- c. Cash receipts journal
- d. Sales journal

Guidance: level 1

:: Business law ::

_____ is where a person's financial liability is limited to a fixed sum, most commonly the value of a person's investment in a company or partnership. If a company with _____ is sued, then the claimants are suing the company, not its owners or investors. A shareholder in a limited company is not personally liable for any of the debts of the company, other than for the amount already invested in the company and for any unpaid amount on the shares in the company, if any. The same is true for the members of a _____ partnership and the limited partners in a limited partnership. By contrast, sole proprietors and partners in general partnerships are each liable for all the debts of the business .

Exam Probability: **Medium**

23. *Answer choices:*
(see index for correct answer)

- a. Turnkey
- b. Advertising regulation
- c. Limited liability
- d. Ladenschlussgesetz

Guidance: level 1

:: Business economics ::

In finance, _____ is the risk of losses caused by interest rate changes. The prices of most financial instruments, such as stocks and bonds move inversely with interest rates, so investors are subject to capital loss when rates rise.

Exam Probability: **High**

24. *Answer choices:*
(see index for correct answer)

- a. Willingness to accept
- b. Conglomerate merger
- c. EBITA
- d. Risk financing

Guidance: level 1

:: Fundamental analysis ::

_____ is the monetary value of earnings per outstanding share of common stock for a company.

Exam Probability: **Medium**

25. *Answer choices:*
(see index for correct answer)

- a. Economic Value Added
- b. Goldman Sachs asset management factor model
- c. Public float
- d. Earnings per share

Guidance: level 1

:: Inventory ::

In business and accounting/accountancy, _____ or continuous inventory describes systems of inventory where information on inventory quantity and availability is updated on a continuous basis as a function of doing business. Generally this is accomplished by connecting the inventory system with order entry and in retail the point of sale system. In this case, book inventory would be exactly the same as, or almost the same, as the real inventory.

Exam Probability: **High**

26. *Answer choices:*

(see index for correct answer)

- a. Perpetual inventory
- b. Cost of goods sold
- c. Stock mix
- d. New old stock

Guidance: level 1

:: Generally Accepted Accounting Principles ::

A _____ , in accrual accounting, is any account where the asset or liability is not realized until a future date , e.g. annuities, charges, taxes, income, etc. The deferred item may be carried, dependent on type of _____ , as either an asset or liability. See also accrual.

Exam Probability: **Low**

27. *Answer choices:*

(see index for correct answer)

- a. Deferral
- b. Deprival value
- c. Cost principle
- d. Operating profit

Guidance: level 1

:: Business law ::

A _____ is a group of people who jointly supervise the activities of an organization, which can be either a for-profit business, nonprofit organization, or a government agency. Such a board's powers, duties, and responsibilities are determined by government regulations and the organization's own constitution and bylaws. These authorities may specify the number of members of the board, how they are to be chosen, and how often they are to meet.

Exam Probability: **Low**

28. *Answer choices:*

(see index for correct answer)

- a. Undervalue transaction
- b. Bulk sale
- c. Commercial law
- d. Fraudulent trading

Guidance: level 1

:: Financial ratios ::

The _____ or dividend-price ratio of a share is the dividend per share, divided by the price per share. It is also a company's total annual dividend payments divided by its market capitalization, assuming the number of shares is constant. It is often expressed as a percentage.

Exam Probability: **Medium**

29. *Answer choices:*
(see index for correct answer)

- a. Dividend yield
- b. Capital employed
- c. Retention rate
- d. Times interest earned

Guidance: level 1

:: Financial risk ::

The _____ on a financial investment is the expected value of its return. It is a measure of the center of the distribution of the random variable that is the return.

Exam Probability: **Low**

30. *Answer choices:*
(see index for correct answer)

- a. Entropic risk measure
- b. Expected return
- c. Risk metric
- d. Fuel price risk management

Guidance: level 1

:: Occupations ::

An _____ is a practitioner of accounting or accountancy, which is the measurement, disclosure or provision of assurance about financial information that helps managers, investors, tax authorities and others make decisions about allocating resource.

Exam Probability: **High**

31. *Answer choices:*

(see index for correct answer)

- a. Accountant
- b. Avocation
- c. Biochemist
- d. Middleware analyst

Guidance: level 1

:: Manufacturing ::

_____ s are goods that have completed the manufacturing process but have not yet been sold or distributed to the end user.

Exam Probability: **High**

32. *Answer choices:*

(see index for correct answer)

- a. Useful art
- b. Finished good
- c. Taguchi methods
- d. International Organization of Legal Metrology

Guidance: level 1

:: ::

A _____ is a fund into which a sum of money is added during an employee's employment years, and from which payments are drawn to support the person's retirement from work in the form of periodic payments. A _____ may be a "defined benefit plan" where a fixed sum is paid regularly to a person, or a "defined contribution plan" under which a fixed sum is invested and then becomes available at retirement age. _____ s should not be confused with severance pay; the former is usually paid in regular installments for life after retirement, while the latter is typically paid as a fixed amount after involuntary termination of employment prior to retirement.

Exam Probability: **High**

33. *Answer choices:*

(see index for correct answer)

- a. Character
- b. co-culture
- c. imperative
- d. Pension

Guidance: level 1

:: Financial ratios ::

_____ is a financial ratio that indicates the percentage of a company's assets that are provided via debt. It is the ratio of total debt and total assets .

Exam Probability: **High**

34. *Answer choices:*

(see index for correct answer)

- a. Average propensity to save
- b. Debt ratio
- c. PB ratio
- d. Dividend payout ratio

Guidance: level 1

:: Consumer theory ::

_____ is the quantity of a good that consumers are willing and able to purchase at various prices during a given period of time.

Exam Probability: **Medium**

35. *Answer choices:*

(see index for correct answer)

- a. Autonomous consumption
- b. Income effect
- c. Demand vacuum
- d. Demand

Guidance: level 1

:: Financial markets ::

As money became a commodity, the _____ became a component of the financial market for assets involved in short-term borrowing, lending, buying and selling with original maturities of one year or less. Trading in _____ s is done over the counter and is wholesale.

Exam Probability: **Medium**

36. *Answer choices:*

(see index for correct answer)

- a. Broker-dealer
- b. Money market
- c. Index cohesive force
- d. Spread trade

Guidance: level 1

:: International taxation ::

_____ is the levying of tax by two or more jurisdictions on the same declared income, asset, or financial transaction. Double liability is mitigated in a number of ways, for example.

Exam Probability: **High**

37. *Answer choices:*

(see index for correct answer)

- a. Controlled foreign corporation
- b. Double taxation
- c. Euromod
- d. Foreign personal holding company

Guidance: level 1

:: ::

A _____ loan or, simply, _____ is used either by purchasers of real property to raise funds to buy real estate, or alternatively by existing property owners to raise funds for any purpose, while putting a lien on the property being _____ d. The loan is "secured" on the borrower`s property through a process known as _____ origination. This means that a legal mechanism is put into place which allows the lender to take possession and sell the secured property to pay off the loan in the event the borrower defaults on the loan or otherwise fails to abide by its terms. The word _____ is derived from a Law French term used in Britain in the Middle Ages meaning "death pledge" and refers to the pledge ending when either the obligation is fulfilled or the property is taken through foreclosure. A _____ can also be described as "a borrower giving consideration in the form of a collateral for a benefit ".

Exam Probability: **High**

38. *Answer choices:*
(see index for correct answer)

- a. interpersonal communication
- b. Mortgage
- c. similarity-attraction theory
- d. hierarchical

Guidance: level 1

:: ::

From an accounting perspective, _____ is crucial because _____ and _____ taxes considerably affect the net income of most companies and because they are subject to laws and regulations .

Exam Probability: **High**

39. *Answer choices:*

(see index for correct answer)

- a. cultural
- b. functional perspective
- c. information systems assessment
- d. co-culture

Guidance: level 1

:: Options (finance) ::

A _____ , often simply labeled a "call", is a financial contract between two parties, the buyer and the seller of this type of option. The buyer of the _____ has the right, but not the obligation, to buy an agreed quantity of a particular commodity or financial instrument from the seller of the option at a certain time for a certain price . The seller is obligated to sell the commodity or financial instrument to the buyer if the buyer so decides. The buyer pays a fee for this right. The term "call" comes from the fact that the owner has the right to "call the stock away" from the seller.

Exam Probability: **Low**

40. *Answer choices:*

(see index for correct answer)

- a. LEAPS
- b. Naked put
- c. Rainbow option
- d. Compound option

Guidance: level 1

:: Generally Accepted Accounting Principles ::

In accounting and finance, earnings before interest and taxes is a measure of a firm's profit that includes all incomes and expenses except interest expenses and income tax expenses.

Exam Probability: **High**

41. *Answer choices:*

(see index for correct answer)

- a. Net profit
- b. Operating Income
- c. Deprival value
- d. Closing entries

Guidance: level 1

:: Accounting in the United States ::

The _____ is a private-sector, nonprofit corporation created by the Sarbanes–Oxley Act of 2002 to oversee the audits of public companies and other issuers in order to protect the interests of investors and further the public interest in the preparation of informative, accurate and independent audit reports. The PCAOB also oversees the audits of broker-dealers, including compliance reports filed pursuant to federal securities laws, to promote investor protection. All PCAOB rules and standards must be approved by the U.S. Securities and Exchange Commission .

Exam Probability: **High**

42. *Answer choices:*
(see index for correct answer)

- a. Comprehensive Performance Assessment
- b. Public Company Accounting Oversight Board
- c. Accounting Today
- d. Joseph Eve, Certified Public Accountants

Guidance: level 1

:: Legal terms ::

_____ s may be governments, corporations or investment trusts. _____ s are legally responsible for the obligations of the issue and for reporting financial conditions, material developments and any other operational activities as required by the regulations of their jurisdictions.

Exam Probability: **Low**

43. *Answer choices:*
(see index for correct answer)

- a. Marital power
- b. Issuer
- c. Natural person

- d. Commanding precedent

Guidance: level 1

:: ::

A _____ is the process of presenting a topic to an audience. It is typically a demonstration, introduction, lecture, or speech meant to inform, persuade, inspire, motivate, or to build good will or to present a new idea or product. The term can also be used for a formal or ritualized introduction or offering, as with the _____ of a debutante. _____ s in certain formats are also known as keynote address.

Exam Probability: **Medium**

44. *Answer choices:*
(see index for correct answer)

- a. empathy
- b. Sarbanes-Oxley act of 2002
- c. Presentation
- d. process perspective

Guidance: level 1

:: ::

An _____ is the production of goods or related services within an economy. The major source of revenue of a group or company is the indicator of its relevant _____. When a large group has multiple sources of revenue generation, it is considered to be working in different industries. Manufacturing _____ became a key sector of production and labour in European and North American countries during the Industrial Revolution, upsetting previous mercantile and feudal economies. This came through many successive rapid advances in technology, such as the production of steel and coal.

Exam Probability: **High**

45. *Answer choices:*
(see index for correct answer)

- a. Industry

- b. personal values
- c. hierarchical perspective
- d. levels of analysis

Guidance: level 1

:: ::

_____ or accountancy is the measurement, processing, and communication of financial information about economic entities such as businesses and corporations. The modern field was established by the Italian mathematician Luca Pacioli in 1494. _____ , which has been called the "language of business", measures the results of an organization's economic activities and conveys this information to a variety of users, including investors, creditors, management, and regulators. Practitioners of _____ are known as accountants. The terms "_____" and "financial reporting" are often used as synonyms.

Exam Probability: **High**

46. *Answer choices:*
(see index for correct answer)

- a. functional perspective
- b. Accounting
- c. hierarchical
- d. cultural

Guidance: level 1

:: Loans ::

In corporate finance, a _____ is a medium- to long-term debt instrument used by large companies to borrow money, at a fixed rate of interest. The legal term "_____" originally referred to a document that either creates a debt or acknowledges it, but in some countries the term is now used interchangeably with bond, loan stock or note. A _____ is thus like a certificate of loan or a loan bond evidencing the fact that the company is liable to pay a specified amount with interest and although the money raised by the _____ s becomes a part of the company's capital structure, it does not become share capital. Senior _____ s get paid before subordinate _____ s, and there are varying rates of risk and payoff for these categories.

Exam Probability: **Medium**

47. *Answer choices:*

(see index for correct answer)

- a. Forgivable loan
- b. Marriage loan
- c. Mortgage assumption
- d. Debenture

Guidance: level 1

:: Fixed income market ::

The _____ is a financial market where participants can issue new debt, known as the primary market, or buy and sell debt securities, known as the secondary market. This is usually in the form of bonds, but it may include notes, bills, and so on.

Exam Probability: **High**

48. *Answer choices:*

(see index for correct answer)

- a. Bond market
- b. Fixed income
- c. Bond Exchange of South Africa
- d. Fixed-income attribution

Guidance: level 1

:: Financial ratios ::

In finance, the _____ , also known as the acid-test ratio is a type of liquidity ratio which measures the ability of a company to use its near cash or quick assets to extinguish or retire its current liabilities immediately. Quick assets include those current assets that presumably can be quickly converted to cash at close to their book values. It is the ratio between quickly available or liquid assets and current liabilities.

Exam Probability: **High**

49. *Answer choices:*

(see index for correct answer)

- a. Days payable outstanding
- b. Operating ratio
- c. Cost accrual ratio
- d. Quick ratio

Guidance: level 1

:: Management accounting ::

_____ is the process of recording, classifying, analyzing, summarizing, and allocating costs associated with a process, after that developing various courses of action to control the costs. Its goal is to advise the management on how to optimize business practices and processes based on cost efficiency and capability. _____ provides the detailed cost information that management needs to control current operations and plan for the future.

Exam Probability: **High**

50. *Answer choices:*

(see index for correct answer)

- a. Cost accounting
- b. Cash and cash equivalents
- c. Responsibility center
- d. Hedge accounting

Guidance: level 1

:: Investment ::

The _____ is a measure of an investment's rate of return. The term internal refers to the fact that the calculation excludes external factors, such as the risk-free rate, inflation, the cost of capital, or various financial risks.

Exam Probability: **High**

51. *Answer choices:*

(see index for correct answer)

- a. Internal rate of return
- b. Passive investor
- c. With-profits policy
- d. Enhanced indexing

Guidance: level 1

:: Financial markets ::

_____ s are monetary contracts between parties. They can be created, traded, modified and settled. They can be cash , evidence of an ownership interest in an entity , or a contractual right to receive or deliver cash .

Exam Probability: **High**

52. *Answer choices:*
(see index for correct answer)

- a. Earnings guidance
- b. Price-weighted
- c. Financial instrument
- d. Virtual bidding

Guidance: level 1

:: Loans ::

In finance, a _____ is the lending of money by one or more individuals, organizations, or other entities to other individuals, organizations etc. The recipient incurs a debt, and is usually liable to pay interest on that debt until it is repaid, and also to repay the principal amount borrowed.

Exam Probability: **Low**

53. *Answer choices:*
(see index for correct answer)

- a. SGE Loans
- b. Refund anticipation
- c. Loan
- d. Debenture

Guidance: level 1

:: Accounting terminology ::

_____ or capital expense is the money a company spends to buy, maintain, or improve its fixed assets, such as buildings, vehicles, equipment, or land. It is considered a _____ when the asset is newly purchased or when money is used towards extending the useful life of an existing asset, such as repairing the roof.

Exam Probability: **High**

54. *Answer choices:*

(see index for correct answer)

- a. Capital expenditure
- b. Fund accounting
- c. Adjusting entries
- d. Record to report

Guidance: level 1

:: Asset ::

In financial accounting, an _____ is any resource owned by the business. Anything tangible or intangible that can be owned or controlled to produce value and that is held by a company to produce positive economic value is an _____ . Simply stated, _____ s represent value of ownership that can be converted into cash . The balance sheet of a firm records the monetary value of the _____ s owned by that firm. It covers money and other valuables belonging to an individual or to a business.

Exam Probability: **Medium**

55. *Answer choices:*

(see index for correct answer)

- a. Current asset
- b. Fixed asset

Guidance: level 1

:: Accounting in the United States ::

_____ is the title of qualified accountants in numerous countries in the English-speaking world. In the United States, the CPA is a license to provide accounting services to the public. It is awarded by each of the 50 states for practice in that state. Additionally, almost every state has passed mobility laws to allow CPAs from other states to practice in their state. State licensing requirements vary, but the minimum standard requirements include passing the Uniform _____ Examination, 150 semester units of college education, and one year of accounting related experience.

Exam Probability: **High**

56. *Answer choices:*

(see index for correct answer)

- a. Institute of Internal Auditors
- b. American Institute of Certified Public Accountants
- c. Norwalk Agreement
- d. Revolving fund

Guidance: level 1

:: Financial markets ::

In economics and finance, _____ is the practice of taking advantage of a price difference between two or more markets: striking a combination of matching deals that capitalize upon the imbalance, the profit being the difference between the market prices. When used by academics, an _____ is a transaction that involves no negative cash flow at any probabilistic or temporal state and a positive cash flow in at least one state; in simple terms, it is the possibility of a risk-free profit after transaction costs. For example, an _____ opportunity is present when there is the opportunity to instantaneously buy something for a low price and sell it for a higher price.

Exam Probability: **Medium**

57. *Answer choices:*

(see index for correct answer)

- a. Alternative trading system
- b. Ultra-low latency direct market access
- c. Subscription
- d. Price limit

Guidance: level 1

:: ::

_____ is a costing method that identifies activities in an organization and assigns the cost of each activity to all products and services according to the actual consumption by each. This model assigns more indirect costs into direct costs compared to conventional costing.

Exam Probability: **High**

58. *Answer choices:*

(see index for correct answer)

- a. corporate values
- b. similarity-attraction theory
- c. Activity-based costing
- d. hierarchical

Guidance: level 1

:: Pension funds ::

_____ s typically have large amounts of money to invest and are the major investors in listed and private companies. They are especially important to the stock market where large institutional investors dominate. The largest 300 _____ s collectively hold about $6 trillion in assets. In January 2008, The Economist reported that Morgan Stanley estimates that _____ s worldwide hold over US$20 trillion in assets, the largest for any category of investor ahead of mutual funds, insurance companies, currency reserves, sovereign wealth funds, hedge funds, or private equity.

Exam Probability: **Medium**

59. *Answer choices:*

(see index for correct answer)

- a. Pension buyout
- b. Pension led funding
- c. Pension fund

Guidance: level 1

Human resource management

Human resource (HR) management is the strategic approach to the effective management of organization workers so that they help the business gain a competitive advantage. It is designed to maximize employee performance in service of an employer's strategic objectives. HR is primarily concerned with the management of people within organizations, focusing on policies and on systems. HR departments are responsible for overseeing employee-benefits design, employee recruitment, training and development, performance appraisal, and rewarding (e.g., managing pay and benefit systems). HR also concerns itself with organizational change and industrial relations, that is, the balancing of organizational practices with requirements arising from collective bargaining and from governmental laws.

:: ::

_____ , also known as drug abuse, is a patterned use of a drug in which the user consumes the substance in amounts or with methods which are harmful to themselves or others, and is a form of substance-related disorder. Widely differing definitions of drug abuse are used in public health, medical and criminal justice contexts. In some cases criminal or anti-social behaviour occurs when the person is under the influence of a drug, and long term personality changes in individuals may occur as well. In addition to possible physical, social, and psychological harm, use of some drugs may also lead to criminal penalties, although these vary widely depending on the local jurisdiction.

Exam Probability: **Low**

1. *Answer choices:*
(see index for correct answer)

- a. imperative
- b. empathy
- c. surface-level diversity
- d. Substance abuse

Guidance: level 1

:: Socialism ::

In sociology, _____ is the process of internalizing the norms and ideologies of society. _____ encompasses both learning and teaching and is thus "the means by which social and cultural continuity are attained".

Exam Probability: **Low**

2. *Answer choices:*

(see index for correct answer)

- a. Socialization
- b. Proletarian internationalism
- c. Economic calculation problem
- d. Authoritarian socialism

Guidance: level 1

:: ::

_____ is the process of gathering and measuring information on targeted variables in an established system, which then enables one to answer relevant questions and evaluate outcomes. _____ is a component of research in all fields of study including physical and social sciences, humanities, and business. While methods vary by discipline, the emphasis on ensuring accurate and honest collection remains the same. The goal for all _____ is to capture quality evidence that allows analysis to lead to the formulation of convincing and credible answers to the questions that have been posed.

Exam Probability: **Low**

3. *Answer choices:*

(see index for correct answer)

- a. interpersonal communication
- b. corporate values
- c. Sarbanes-Oxley act of 2002
- d. functional perspective

Guidance: level 1

:: Meetings ::

A _____ is a body of one or more persons that is subordinate to a deliberative assembly. Usually, the assembly sends matters into a _____ as a way to explore them more fully than would be possible if the assembly itself were considering them. _____ s may have different functions and their type of work differ depending on the type of the organization and its needs.

Exam Probability: **Low**

4. *Answer choices:*

(see index for correct answer)

- a. Committee
- b. Over the Air
- c. CodeCamp
- d. Altenberg Workshops in Theoretical Biology

Guidance: level 1

:: Business ethics ::

_____ is a type of harassment technique that relates to a sexual nature and the unwelcome or inappropriate promise of rewards in exchange for sexual favors. _____ includes a range of actions from mild transgressions to sexual abuse or assault. Harassment can occur in many different social settings such as the workplace, the home, school, churches, etc. Harassers or victims may be of any gender.

Exam Probability: **High**

5. *Answer choices:*

(see index for correct answer)

- a. Anti-consumerism
- b. Repugnant market
- c. Sexual harassment
- d. The FCPA Blog

Guidance: level 1

:: Training ::

A _____ is commonly known as an individual taking part in a _____ program or a graduate program within a company after having graduated from university or college.

Exam Probability: **High**

6. *Answer choices:*
(see index for correct answer)

- a. Makers Academy
- b. Training
- c. International Society for Performance Improvement
- d. Biography Work

Guidance: level 1

:: Employment compensation ::

_____ , merit increase or pay for performance, is performance-related pay, most frequently in the context of educational reform or government civil service reform. It provides bonuses for workers who perform their jobs effectively, according to easily measurable criteria. In the United States, policy makers are divided on whether _____ should be offered to public school teachers, and other public employees, as is commonly the case in the United Kingdom.

Exam Probability: **Low**

7. *Answer choices:*
(see index for correct answer)

- a. Lockstep compensation
- b. Duvet day
- c. Fringe benefits tax
- d. ADP, LLC

Guidance: level 1

:: ::

A _____ is a fund into which a sum of money is added during an employee's employment years, and from which payments are drawn to support the person's retirement from work in the form of periodic payments. A _____ may be a "defined benefit plan" where a fixed sum is paid regularly to a person, or a "defined contribution plan" under which a fixed sum is invested and then becomes available at retirement age. _____ s should not be confused with severance pay; the former is usually paid in regular installments for life after retirement, while the latter is typically paid as a fixed amount after involuntary termination of employment prior to retirement.

Exam Probability: **Medium**

8. *Answer choices:*

(see index for correct answer)

- a. Sarbanes-Oxley act of 2002
- b. open system
- c. Pension
- d. deep-level diversity

Guidance: level 1

:: Human resource management ::

_____ , Inc. is an American office staffing company that operates globally. The company places employees at all levels in various sectors including financial services, information technology, and law. Also, its professional services include human resource and management consulting, outsourcing, recruitment, career transition, and vendor management. _____ was founded by William Russell Kelly in 1946 and is headquartered in Troy, Michigan. In 2015, the company reported 8,100 employees, $5.5 billion in revenue, and placed 550,000 employees to work in positions in various sectors, making it one of the world's largest staffing firms.

Exam Probability: **Medium**

9. *Answer choices:*

(see index for correct answer)

- a. Employeeship
- b. Human relations movement
- c. Workforce planning
- d. Kelly Services

Guidance: level 1

:: Employment compensation ::

A _____ is pay and benefits employees receive when they leave employment at a company unwillfully. In addition to their remaining regular pay, it may include some of the following.

Exam Probability: **Medium**

10. *Answer choices:*
(see index for correct answer)

- a. Performance-related pay
- b. Severance package
- c. Labour code
- d. Golden handcuffs

Guidance: level 1

:: Workplace ::

A _____, also referred to as a performance review, performance evaluation, development discussion, or employee appraisal is a method by which the job performance of an employee is documented and evaluated. _____ s are a part of career development and consist of regular reviews of employee performance within organizations.

Exam Probability: **Low**

11. *Answer choices:*
(see index for correct answer)

- a. Workplace phobia
- b. Workplace aggression
- c. Workplace harassment
- d. Feminisation of the workplace

Guidance: level 1

:: Psychometrics ::

A _____ is a set of categories designed to elicit information about a quantitative or a qualitative attribute. In the social sciences, particularly psychology, common examples are the Likert response scale and 1-10 _____ s in which a person selects the number which is considered to reflect the perceived quality of a product.

Exam Probability: **Low**

12. *Answer choices:*

(see index for correct answer)

- a. Base rate
- b. Rating scale
- c. Fuzzy concept
- d. Common-method variance

Guidance: level 1

:: Industrial agreements ::

_____ is a process of negotiation between employers and a group of employees aimed at agreements to regulate working salaries, working conditions, benefits, and other aspects of workers' compensation and rights for workers. The interests of the employees are commonly presented by representatives of a trade union to which the employees belong. The collective agreements reached by these negotiations usually set out wage scales, working hours, training, health and safety, overtime, grievance mechanisms, and rights to participate in workplace or company affairs.

Exam Probability: **Low**

13. *Answer choices:*

(see index for correct answer)

- a. Union security agreement
- b. Bargaining unit
- c. Collective bargaining
- d. Compromise agreement

Guidance: level 1

:: Grounds for termination of employment ::

_____ is a habitual pattern of absence from a duty or obligation without good reason. Generally, _____ is unplanned absences. _____ has been viewed as an indicator of poor individual performance, as well as a breach of an implicit contract between employee and employer. It is seen as a management problem, and framed in economic or quasi-economic terms. More recent scholarship seeks to understand _____ as an indicator of psychological, medical, or social adjustment to work.

Exam Probability: **Low**

14. *Answer choices:*

(see index for correct answer)

- a. Absenteeism
- b. No call, no show
- c. Huffman v. Office of Personnel Management
- d. Presidential Policy Directive 19

Guidance: level 1

:: Social psychology ::

In social psychology, _____ is the phenomenon of a person exerting less effort to achieve a goal when he or she works in a group than when working alone. This is seen as one of the main reasons groups are sometimes less productive than the combined performance of their members working as individuals, but should be distinguished from the accidental coordination problems that groups sometimes experience.

Exam Probability: **Medium**

15. *Answer choices:*

(see index for correct answer)

- a. Social loafing
- b. Social character
- c. brainwriting
- d. Prosocial

Guidance: level 1

:: ::

_____ is a form of government characterized by strong central power and limited political freedoms. Individual freedoms are subordinate to the state and there is no constitutional accountability and rule of law under an authoritarian regime. Authoritarian regimes can be autocratic with power concentrated in one person or it can be more spread out between multiple officials and government institutions. Juan Linz's influential 1964 description of _____ characterized authoritarian political systems by four qualities.

Exam Probability: **Medium**

16. *Answer choices:*

(see index for correct answer)

- a. similarity-attraction theory
- b. cultural
- c. Authoritarianism
- d. hierarchical perspective

Guidance: level 1

:: Behavioral and social facets of systemic risk ::

_____ is the difficulty in understanding an issue and effectively making decisions when one has too much information about that issue. Generally, the term is associated with the excessive quantity of daily information. _____ most likely originated from information theory, which are studies in the storage, preservation, communication, compression, and extraction of information. The term, _____, was first used in Bertram Gross' 1964 book, The Managing of Organizations, and it was further popularized by Alvin Toffler in his bestselling 1970 book Future Shock. Speier et al. stated.

Exam Probability: **High**

17. *Answer choices:*

(see index for correct answer)

- a. Attention management
- b. Meme
- c. Behavioral Finance
- d. Latent human error

Guidance: level 1

:: Evaluation methods ::

In social psychology, _____ is the process of looking at oneself in order to assess aspects that are important to one's identity. It is one of the motives that drive self-evaluation, along with self-verification and self-enhancement. Sedikides suggests that the _____ motive will prompt people to seek information to confirm their uncertain self-concept rather than their certain self-concept and at the same time people use _____ to enhance their certainty of their own self-knowledge. However, the _____ motive could be seen as quite different from the other two self-evaluation motives. Unlike the other two motives through _____ people are interested in the accuracy of their current self view, rather than improving their self-view. This makes _____ the only self-evaluative motive that may cause a person's self-esteem to be damaged.

Exam Probability: **High**

18. *Answer choices:*

(see index for correct answer)

- a. Self-assessment
- b. Qualitative research
- c. Event correlation
- d. Moral statistics

Guidance: level 1

:: Labor relations in the United States ::

In the context of U.S. labor politics, "_____ s" refers to state laws that prohibit union security agreements between companies and labor unions. Under these laws, employees in unionized workplaces are banned from negotiating contracts which require all members who benefit from the union contract to contribute to the costs of union representation.

Exam Probability: **Medium**

19. *Answer choices:*

(see index for correct answer)

- a. Project Labor Agreement
- b. Public Safety Employer-Employee Cooperation Act of 2007
- c. Jewish Labor Committee
- d. Terror of the Tug

Guidance: level 1

:: Behavior ::

_____ refers to behavior-change procedures that were employed during the 1970s and early 1980s. Based on methodological behaviorism, overt behavior was modified with presumed consequences, including artificial positive and negative reinforcement contingencies to increase desirable behavior, or administering positive and negative punishment and/or extinction to reduce problematic behavior. For the treatment of phobias, habituation and punishment were the basic principles used in flooding, a subcategory of desensitization.

Exam Probability: **Medium**

20. *Answer choices:*
(see index for correct answer)

- a. theory of reasoned action
- b. theory of planned behavior

Guidance: level 1

:: Business ethics ::

In United States labor law, a _____ exists when one's behavior within a workplace creates an environment that is difficult or uncomfortable for another person to work in, due to discrimination. Common complaints in sexual harassment lawsuits include fondling, suggestive remarks, sexually-suggestive photos displayed in the workplace, use of sexual language, or off-color jokes. Small matters, annoyances, and isolated incidents are usually not considered to be statutory violations of the discrimination laws. For a violation to impose liability, the conduct must create a work environment that would be intimidating, hostile, or offensive to a reasonable person. An employer can be held liable for failing to prevent these workplace conditions, unless it can prove that it attempted to prevent the harassment and that the employee failed to take advantage of existing harassment counter-measures or tools provided by the employer.

Exam Probability: **Low**

21. *Answer choices:*
(see index for correct answer)

- a. Minecode
- b. United Nations Global Compact
- c. Impact investing
- d. Hostile work environment

Guidance: level 1

:: Employment discrimination ::

A _____ is a metaphor used to represent an invisible barrier that keeps a given demographic from rising beyond a certain level in a hierarchy.

Exam Probability: **Low**

22. *Answer choices:*

(see index for correct answer)

- a. Employment discrimination
- b. Marriage bars
- c. LGBT employment discrimination in the United States
- d. Glass ceiling

Guidance: level 1

:: Labor terms ::

_____, often called DI or disability income insurance, or income protection, is a form of insurance that insures the beneficiary's earned income against the risk that a disability creates a barrier for a worker to complete the core functions of their work. For example, the worker may suffer from an inability to maintain composure in the case of psychological disorders or an injury, illness or condition that causes physical impairment or incapacity to work. It encompasses paid sick leave, short-term disability benefits , and long-term disability benefits . Statistics show that in the US a disabling accident occurs, on average, once every second. In fact, nearly 18.5% of Americans are currently living with a disability, and 1 out of every 4 persons in the US workforce will suffer a disabling injury before retirement.

Exam Probability: **High**

23. *Answer choices:*

(see index for correct answer)

- a. Disability insurance

- b. Displaced workers
- c. Deflator
- d. Consumer unit

Guidance: level 1

:: Management ::

In business, a _____ is the attribute that allows an organization to outperform its competitors. A _____ may include access to natural resources, such as high-grade ores or a low-cost power source, highly skilled labor, geographic location, high entry barriers, and access to new technology.

Exam Probability: **High**

24. *Answer choices:*
(see index for correct answer)

- a. Smiling curve
- b. Process-based management
- c. Competitive advantage
- d. Best current practice

Guidance: level 1

:: Organizational theory ::

Decentralisation is the process by which the activities of an organization, particularly those regarding planning and decision making, are distributed or delegated away from a central, authoritative location or group. Concepts of _____ have been applied to group dynamics and management science in private businesses and organizations, political science, law and public administration, economics, money and technology.

Exam Probability: **Low**

25. *Answer choices:*
(see index for correct answer)

- a. Decentralization
- b. Constructive Developmental Framework
- c. Identity negotiation
- d. Organizational learning

Guidance: level 1

:: Business planning ::

_____ is an organization's process of defining its strategy, or direction, and making decisions on allocating its resources to pursue this strategy. It may also extend to control mechanisms for guiding the implementation of the strategy. _____ became prominent in corporations during the 1960s and remains an important aspect of strategic management. It is executed by strategic planners or strategists, who involve many parties and research sources in their analysis of the organization and its relationship to the environment in which it competes.

Exam Probability: **Low**

26. *Answer choices:*
(see index for correct answer)

- a. Joint decision trap
- b. Business war games
- c. Customer Demand Planning
- d. Strategic planning

Guidance: level 1

:: Survey methodology ::

_____ is often used to assess thoughts, opinions, and feelings. Surveys can be specific and limited, or they can have more global, widespread goals. Psychologists and sociologists often use surveys to analyze behavior, while it is also used to meet the more pragmatic needs of the media, such as, in evaluating political candidates, public health officials, professional organizations, and advertising and marketing directors. A survey consists of a predetermined set of questions that is given to a sample. With a representative sample, that is, one that is representative of the larger population of interest, one can describe the attitudes of the population from which the sample was drawn. Further, one can compare the attitudes of different populations as well as look for changes in attitudes over time. A good sample selection is key as it allows one to generalize the findings from the sample to the population, which is the whole purpose of _____ .

Exam Probability: **High**

27. *Answer choices:*

(see index for correct answer)

- a. Coverage error
- b. Group concept mapping
- c. Survey research
- d. Computer-assisted survey information collection

Guidance: level 1

:: Job interview ::

A _____ is a job interview in which the applicant is presented with a challenging business scenario that he/she must investigate and propose a solution to. _____ s are designed to test the candidate's analytical skills and "soft" skills within a realistic business context. The case is often a business situation or a business case that the interviewer has worked on in real life.

Exam Probability: **Medium**

28. *Answer choices:*

(see index for correct answer)

- a. Case interview
- b. Mock interview
- c. Exit interview
- d. SOARA

Guidance: level 1

:: Belief ::

_____ is the ability to acquire knowledge without proof, evidence, or conscious reasoning, or without understanding how the knowledge was acquired. Different writers give the word " _____ " a great variety of different meanings, ranging from direct access to unconscious knowledge, unconscious cognition, inner sensing, inner insight to unconscious pattern-recognition and the ability to understand something instinctively, without the need for conscious reasoning.

Exam Probability: **High**

29. *Answer choices:*

(see index for correct answer)

- a. Doxa
- b. Cynicism
- c. Intuition
- d. Ideological assumption

Guidance: level 1

:: Labour relations ::

_____ is a field of study that can have different meanings depending on the context in which it is used. In an international context, it is a subfield of labor history that studies the human relations with regard to work – in its broadest sense – and how this connects to questions of social inequality. It explicitly encompasses unregulated, historical, and non-Western forms of labor. Here, _____ define "for or with whom one works and under what rules. These rules determine the type of work, type and amount of remuneration, working hours, degrees of physical and psychological strain, as well as the degree of freedom and autonomy associated with the work."

Exam Probability: **Low**

30. *Answer choices:*

(see index for correct answer)

- a. Big labor
- b. Passfield Memorandum
- c. Labor relations
- d. Jesse Simons

Guidance: level 1

:: Organizational behavior ::

Greenberg introduced the concept of _____ with regard to how an employee judges the behaviour of the organization and the employee's resulting attitude and behaviour.

Exam Probability: **Low**

31. *Answer choices:*

(see index for correct answer)

- a. Achievement Motivation Inventory

- b. Organizational storytelling
- c. Organizational justice
- d. Conformity

Guidance: level 1

:: Financial statements ::

In financial accounting, a _____ or statement of financial position or statement of financial condition is a summary of the financial balances of an individual or organization, whether it be a sole proprietorship, a business partnership, a corporation, private limited company or other organization such as Government or not-for-profit entity. Assets, liabilities and ownership equity are listed as of a specific date, such as the end of its financial year. A _____ is often described as a "snapshot of a company's financial condition". Of the four basic financial statements, the _____ is the only statement which applies to a single point in time of a business` calendar year.

Exam Probability: **High**

32. *Answer choices:*

(see index for correct answer)

- a. Balance sheet
- b. Statement on Auditing Standards No. 55
- c. Financial report
- d. Consolidated financial statement

Guidance: level 1

:: Human resource management ::

_____ or work sharing is an employment arrangement where typically two people are retained on a part-time or reduced-time basis to perform a job normally fulfilled by one person working full-time. Since all positions are shared thus leads to a net reduction in per-employee income. The people sharing the job work as a team to complete the job task and are equally responsible for the job workload. Compensation is apportioned between the workers. Working hours, pay and holidays are divided equally. The pay as you go system helps make deductions for national insurance and superannuations are made as a straightforward percentage.

Exam Probability: **Medium**

33. *Answer choices:*

(see index for correct answer)

- a. Vendor management system
- b. ABC Consultants
- c. Fresh tracks
- d. Job design

Guidance: level 1

:: Validity (statistics) ::

In psychometrics, criterion or concrete validity is the extent to which a measure is related to an outcome. _____ is often divided into concurrent and predictive validity. Concurrent validity refers to a comparison between the measure in question and an outcome assessed at the same time. In Standards for Educational & Psychological Tests, it states, "concurrent validity reflects only the status quo at a particular time." Predictive validity, on the other hand, compares the measure in question with an outcome assessed at a later time. Although concurrent and predictive validity are similar, it is cautioned to keep the terms and findings separated. "Concurrent validity should not be used as a substitute for predictive validity without an appropriate supporting rationale."

Exam Probability: **Low**

34. *Answer choices:*

(see index for correct answer)

- a. Content validity
- b. Construct validity
- c. Incremental validity
- d. Verification and validation

Guidance: level 1

:: Hazard analysis ::

A _____ is an agent which has the potential to cause harm to a vulnerable target. The terms "_____" and "risk" are often used interchangeably. However, in terms of risk assessment, they are two very distinct terms. A _____ is any agent that can cause harm or damage to humans, property, or the environment. Risk is defined as the probability that exposure to a _____ will lead to a negative consequence, or more simply, a _____ poses no risk if there is no exposure to that _____ .

Exam Probability: **Low**

35. *Answer choices:*
(see index for correct answer)

- a. Risk assessment
- b. Hazard
- c. Hazardous Materials Identification System
- d. Swiss cheese model

Guidance: level 1

:: Human resource management ::

_____ is a continual process used to align the needs and priorities of the organization with those of its workforce to ensure it can meet its legislative, regulatory, service and production requirements and organizational objectives. _____ enables evidence based workforce development strategies.

Exam Probability: **Low**

36. *Answer choices:*
(see index for correct answer)

- a. Parallel running
- b. Domestic inquiry
- c. Workforce planning
- d. Co-determination

Guidance: level 1

:: Human resource management ::

_____ is a process for identifying and developing new leaders who can replace old leaders when they leave, retire or die. _____ increases the availability of experienced and capable employees that are prepared to assume these roles as they become available. Taken narrowly, "replacement planning" for key roles is the heart of _____ .

Exam Probability: **High**

37. *Answer choices:*

(see index for correct answer)

- a. Voluntary redundancy
- b. ROWE
- c. Compensation and benefits
- d. Succession planning

Guidance: level 1

:: Types of marketing ::

In microeconomics and management, _____ is an arrangement in which the supply chain of a company is owned by that company. Usually each member of the supply chain produces a different product or service, and the products combine to satisfy a common need. It is contrasted with horizontal integration, wherein a company produces several items which are related to one another. _____ has also described management styles that bring large portions of the supply chain not only under a common ownership, but also into one corporation.

Exam Probability: **Low**

38. *Answer choices:*

(see index for correct answer)

- a. Consumer Generated Advertising
- b. Vertical integration
- c. Secret brand
- d. Limited edition candy

Guidance: level 1

:: ::

_____ is defined by sociologist John R. Schermerhorn as the "...degree to which the people affected by decision are treated by dignity and respect. The theory focuses on the interpersonal treatment people receive when procedures are implemented.

Exam Probability: **High**

39. *Answer choices:*
(see index for correct answer)

- a. co-culture
- b. Interactional justice
- c. information systems assessment
- d. surface-level diversity

Guidance: level 1

:: Industrial agreements ::

A _____, in labor relations, is a group of employees with a clear and identifiable community of interests who are represented by a single labor union in collective bargaining and other dealings with management. Examples would be non-management professors, law enforcement professionals, blue-collar workers, clerical and administrative employees, etc. Geographic location as well as the number of facilities included in _____ s can be at issue during representation cases.

Exam Probability: **Low**

40. *Answer choices:*
(see index for correct answer)

- a. Federal Labor Relations Act
- b. Common rule awards
- c. In Place of Strife
- d. Conciliation and Arbitration Act 1904

Guidance: level 1

:: Occupational safety and health organizations ::

The _____ is the United States federal agency responsible for conducting research and making recommendations for the prevention of work-related injury and illness. NIOSH is part of the Centers for Disease Control and Prevention within the U.S. Department of Health and Human Services.

Exam Probability: **Medium**

41. *Answer choices:*
(see index for correct answer)

- a. Basic Occupational Health Services
- b. National Occupational Research Agenda
- c. National Institute for Occupational Safety and Health
- d. Federal Institute for Occupational Safety and Health

Guidance: level 1

:: Television terminology ::

Distance education or long-_____ is the education of students who may not always be physically present at a school. Traditionally, this usually involved correspondence courses wherein the student corresponded with the school via post. Today it involves online education. Courses that are conducted are either hybrid, blended or 100% _____. Massive open online courses, offering large-scale interactive participation and open access through the World Wide Web or other network technologies, are recent developments in distance education. A number of other terms are used roughly synonymously with distance education.

Exam Probability: **Low**

42. *Answer choices:*
(see index for correct answer)

- a. nonprofit
- b. multiplexing
- c. Satellite television
- d. Distance learning

Guidance: level 1

:: Validity (statistics) ::

_____ is "the degree to which a test measures what it claims, or purports, to be measuring." In the classical model of test validity, _____ is one of three main types of validity evidence, alongside content validity and criterion validity. Modern validity theory defines _____ as the overarching concern of validity research, subsuming all other types of validity evidence.

Exam Probability: **Medium**

43. *Answer choices:*
(see index for correct answer)

- a. Construct validity
- b. Predictive validity
- c. Test validity
- d. Nomological network

Guidance: level 1

:: Sociological theories ::

A _____ is a systematic process for determining and addressing needs, or "gaps" between current conditions and desired conditions or "wants". The discrepancy between the current condition and wanted condition must be measured to appropriately identify the need. The need can be a desire to improve current performance or to correct a deficiency.

Exam Probability: **Medium**

44. *Answer choices:*
(see index for correct answer)

- a. resource mobilization
- b. social construction
- c. comfort zone
- d. Needs assessment

Guidance: level 1

:: Employment ::

_____ is a relationship between two parties, usually based on a contract where work is paid for, where one party, which may be a corporation, for profit, not-for-profit organization, co-operative or other entity is the employer and the other is the employee. Employees work in return for payment, which may be in the form of an hourly wage, by piecework or an annual salary, depending on the type of work an employee does or which sector she or he is working in. Employees in some fields or sectors may receive gratuities, bonus payment or stock options. In some types of _____ , employees may receive benefits in addition to payment. Benefits can include health insurance, housing, disability insurance or use of a gym. _____ is typically governed by _____ laws, regulations or legal contracts.

Exam Probability: **High**

45. *Answer choices:*
(see index for correct answer)

- a. Gold-collar worker
- b. Supernumerary
- c. Work experience
- d. Dead-end job

Guidance: level 1

:: Management ::

In the field of management, _____ involves the formulation and implementation of the major goals and initiatives taken by an organization's top management on behalf of owners, based on consideration of resources and an assessment of the internal and external environments in which the organization operates.

Exam Probability: **Low**

46. *Answer choices:*
(see index for correct answer)

- a. Management cockpit
- b. Business rule
- c. Operations management
- d. Law practice management

Guidance: level 1

:: Human resource management ::

_____ is the application of information technology for both networking and supporting at least two individual or collective actors in their shared performing of HR activities.

Exam Probability: **High**

47. *Answer choices:*
(see index for correct answer)

- a. Salary
- b. Job enlargement
- c. Mentorship
- d. E-HRM

Guidance: level 1

:: Validity (statistics) ::

_____ is the extent to which a test accurately measures what it is supposed to measure. In the fields of psychological testing and educational testing, "validity refers to the degree to which evidence and theory support the interpretations of test scores entailed by proposed uses of tests". Although classical models divided the concept into various "validities", the currently dominant view is that validity is a single unitary construct.

Exam Probability: **High**

48. *Answer choices:*
(see index for correct answer)

- a. Predictive validity
- b. Construct validity
- c. Ecological validity
- d. Incremental validity

Guidance: level 1

:: Occupations ::

An _____ is a person who has a position of authority in a hierarchical organization. The term derives from the late Latin from officiarius, meaning "official".

Exam Probability: **High**

49. *Answer choices:*

(see index for correct answer)

- a. Securities research
- b. Operator
- c. Officer
- d. Archivist

Guidance: level 1

:: Cognitive biases ::

In personality psychology, _____ is the degree to which people believe that they have control over the outcome of events in their lives, as opposed to external forces beyond their control. Understanding of the concept was developed by Julian B. Rotter in 1954, and has since become an aspect of personality studies. A person's "locus" is conceptualized as internal or external.

Exam Probability: **High**

50. *Answer choices:*

(see index for correct answer)

- a. Curse of knowledge
- b. Mistakes Were Made
- c. Pseudocertainty effect
- d. Locus of control

Guidance: level 1

:: Employment ::

_____ is measuring the output of a particular business process or procedure, then modifying the process or procedure to increase the output, increase efficiency, or increase the effectiveness of the process or procedure. _____ can be applied to either individual performance such as an athlete or organizational performance such as a racing team or a commercial business.

Exam Probability: **Medium**

51. *Answer choices:*

(see index for correct answer)

- a. Performance improvement
- b. Spatial mismatch
- c. Alternative employment arrangements
- d. Local hiring

Guidance: level 1

:: Production and manufacturing ::

_____ is a set of techniques and tools for process improvement. Though as a shortened form it may be found written as 6S, it should not be confused with the methodology known as 6S.

Exam Probability: **Medium**

52. *Answer choices:*

(see index for correct answer)

- a. Low rate initial production
- b. Value engineering
- c. Six Sigma
- d. Copacker

Guidance: level 1

:: Business ethics ::

_____ is a pejorative term for a workplace that has very poor, socially unacceptable working conditions. The work may be difficult, dangerous, climatically challenged or underpaid. Workers in _____ s may work long hours with low pay, regardless of laws mandating overtime pay or a minimum wage; child labor laws may also be violated. The Fair Labor Association's "2006 Annual Public Report" inspected factories for FLA compliance in 18 countries including Bangladesh, El Salvador, Colombia, Guatemala, Malaysia, Thailand, Tunisia, Turkey, China, India, Vietnam, Honduras, Indonesia, Brazil, Mexico, and the US. The U.S. Department of Labor's "2015 Findings on the Worst Forms of Child Labor" found that "18 countries did not meet the International Labour Organization's recommendation for an adequate number of inspectors."

Exam Probability: **Low**

53. *Answer choices:*

(see index for correct answer)

- a. Sweatshop
- b. Interfaith Center on Corporate Responsibility
- c. Centre for Research on Multinational Corporations
- d. Corporate Knights

Guidance: level 1

:: Employment ::

A _____ , a concept developed in contemporary research by organizational scholar Denise Rousseau, represents the mutual beliefs, perceptions and informal obligations between an employer and an employee. It sets the dynamics for the relationship and defines the detailed practicality of the work to be done. It is distinguishable from the formal written contract of employment which, for the most part, only identifies mutual duties and responsibilities in a generalized form.

Exam Probability: **Medium**

54. *Answer choices:*

(see index for correct answer)

- a. Psychological contract
- b. PATCOB
- c. BA-X
- d. Blue-collar worker

Guidance: level 1

:: Management ::

A _____ describes the rationale of how an organization creates, delivers, and captures value, in economic, social, cultural or other contexts. The process of _____ construction and modification is also called _____ innovation and forms a part of business strategy.

Exam Probability: **Low**

55. *Answer choices:*
(see index for correct answer)

- a. Force-field analysis
- b. Shamrock Organization
- c. Mushroom management
- d. Omnex

Guidance: level 1

:: Trade union legislation ::

The _____ is the name for several legislative bills on US labor law which have been proposed and sometimes introduced into one or both chambers of the U.S. Congress.

Exam Probability: **High**

56. *Answer choices:*
(see index for correct answer)

- a. Employment Act 1982
- b. Trade Disputes and Trade Unions Act 1927
- c. National Labor Relations Act
- d. Trade Disputes Act 1906

Guidance: level 1

:: Recruitment ::

_____ is a tool companies and organizations use as a way to communicate the good and the bad characteristics of the job during the hiring process of new employees, or as a tool to reestablish job specificity for existing employees. _____ s should provide the individuals with a well-rounded description that details what obligations the individual can expect to perform while working for that specific company. Descriptions may include, but are not limited to, work environment, expectations, and Company policies.

Exam Probability: **Low**

57. *Answer choices:*
(see index for correct answer)

- a. Probation
- b. contract of employment
- c. Employment agency
- d. Realistic job preview

Guidance: level 1

:: ::

On December 31, 2016, Xerox separated its business process service operations into a new publicly traded company, Conduent. Xerox focuses on its document technology and document outsourcing business, and continues to trade on the NYSE. On January 31, 2018, Xerox announced that it would sell a controlling stake to Fujifilm, which has maintained a joint venture in the Asia-Pacific region known as Fuji Xerox.

Exam Probability: **High**

58. *Answer choices:*
(see index for correct answer)

- a. Sarbanes-Oxley act of 2002
- b. co-culture
- c. empathy
- d. Xerox Corporation

Guidance: level 1

:: Ethically disputed business practices ::

An _____ in US labor law refers to certain actions taken by employers or unions that violate the National Labor Relations Act of 1935 29 U.S.C. § 151–169 and other legislation. Such acts are investigated by the National Labor Relations Board.

Exam Probability: **High**

59. *Answer choices:*

(see index for correct answer)

- a. Tobashi scheme
- b. False economy
- c. Unfair labor practice
- d. Two sets of books

Guidance: level 1

Information systems

Information systems (IS) are formal, sociotechnical, organizational systems designed to collect, process, store, and distribute information. In a sociotechnical perspective Information Systems are composed by four components: technology, process, people and organizational structure.

:: Internet governance ::

A _____ is one of the domains at the highest level in the hierarchical Domain Name System of the Internet. The _____ names are installed in the root zone of the name space. For all domains in lower levels, it is the last part of the domain name, that is, the last label of a fully qualified domain name. For example, in the domain name www.example.com, the _____ is com. Responsibility for management of most _____ s is delegated to specific organizations by the Internet Corporation for Assigned Names and Numbers , which operates the Internet Assigned Numbers Authority , and is in charge of maintaining the DNS root zone.

Exam Probability: **Low**

1. *Answer choices:*
(see index for correct answer)

- a. Chris Disspain
- b. Domain name registry
- c. Top-level domain
- d. IETF language tag

Guidance: level 1

:: Virtual reality ::

_____ is an experience taking place within simulated and immersive environments that can be similar to or completely different from the real world. Applications of _____ can include entertainment and educational purposes. Other, distinct types of VR style technology include augmented reality and mixed reality.

Exam Probability: **Low**

2. *Answer choices:*
(see index for correct answer)

- a. Graphics Turing Test
- b. Outernet
- c. OpenGL
- d. Virtual reality

Guidance: level 1

:: User interfaces ::

The _____, in the industrial design field of human–computer interaction, is the space where interactions between humans and machines occur. The goal of this interaction is to allow effective operation and control of the machine from the human end, whilst the machine simultaneously feeds back information that aids the operators' decision-making process. Examples of this broad concept of _____ s include the interactive aspects of computer operating systems, hand tools, heavy machinery operator controls, and process controls. The design considerations applicable when creating _____ s are related to or involve such disciplines as ergonomics and psychology.

Exam Probability: **Medium**

3. *Answer choices:*
(see index for correct answer)

- a. Interface apparency
- b. Multi-monitor
- c. Pointman
- d. H-Sphere

Guidance: level 1

:: ::

A _____ is a system designed to capture, store, manipulate, analyze, manage, and present spatial or geographic data. GIS applications are tools that allow users to create interactive queries, analyze spatial information, edit data in maps, and present the results of all these operations. GIS sometimes refers to geographic information science, the science underlying geographic concepts, applications, and systems.

Exam Probability: **Low**

4. *Answer choices:*
(see index for correct answer)

- a. personal values
- b. similarity-attraction theory
- c. Geographic information system
- d. corporate values

Guidance: level 1

:: Data collection ::

_____ is the application of data mining techniques to discover patterns from the World Wide Web. As the name proposes, this is information gathered by mining the web. It makes utilization of automated apparatuses to reveal and extricate data from servers and web2 reports, and it permits organizations to get to both organized and unstructured information from browser activities, server logs, website and link structure, page content and different sources.

Exam Probability: **High**

5. *Answer choices:*
(see index for correct answer)

- a. Web mining
- b. IPUMS
- c. North Atlantic Population Project
- d. Unstructured data

Guidance: level 1

:: ::

_____, Inc. is an American online social media and social networking service company based in Menlo Park, California. It was founded by Mark Zuckerberg, along with fellow Harvard College students and roommates Eduardo Saverin, Andrew McCollum, Dustin Moskovitz and Chris Hughes. It is considered one of the Big Four technology companies along with Amazon, Apple, and Google.

Exam Probability: **Medium**

6. *Answer choices:*

(see index for correct answer)

- a. cultural
- b. Character
- c. interpersonal communication
- d. hierarchical

Guidance: level 1

:: Market research ::

_____ s are many different distantly related animals that typically have a long cylindrical tube-like body and no limbs. _____ s vary in size from microscopic to over 1 metre in length for marine polychaete _____ s , 6.7 metres for the African giant earth _____ , Microchaetus rappi, and 58 metres for the marine nemertean _____ , Lineus longissimus. Various types of _____ occupy a small variety of parasitic niches, living inside the bodies of other animals. Free-living _____ species do not live on land, but instead, live in marine or freshwater environments, or underground by burrowing. In biology, "_____" refers to an obsolete taxon, vermes, used by Carolus Linnaeus and Jean-Baptiste Lamarck for all non-arthropod invertebrate animals, now seen to be paraphyletic. The name stems from the Old English word wyrm. Most animals called "_____ s" are invertebrates, but the term is also used for the amphibian caecilians and the slow _____ Anguis, a legless burrowing lizard. Invertebrate animals commonly called "_____ s" include annelids , nematodes , platyhelminthes , marine nemertean _____ s , marine Chaetognatha , priapulid _____ s, and insect larvae such as grubs and maggots.

Exam Probability: **High**

7. *Answer choices:*

(see index for correct answer)

- a. A/B testing
- b. Computer-assisted web interviewing
- c. Sociomapping
- d. Eddie Chung

Guidance: level 1

:: Computer data ::

In computer science, _____ is the ability to access an arbitrary element of a sequence in equal time or any datum from a population of addressable elements roughly as easily and efficiently as any other, no matter how many elements may be in the set. It is typically contrasted to sequential access.

Exam Probability: **High**

8. *Answer choices:*

(see index for correct answer)

- a. DataPortability
- b. Energy Logic
- c. Random access
- d. Data in Use

Guidance: level 1

:: Computer access control protocols ::

An _____ is a type of computer communications protocol or cryptographic protocol specifically designed for transfer of authentication data between two entities. It allows the receiving entity to authenticate the connecting entity as well as authenticate itself to the connecting entity by declaring the type of information needed for authentication as well as syntax. It is the most important layer of protection needed for secure communication within computer networks.

Exam Probability: **Low**

9. *Answer choices:*

(see index for correct answer)

- a. Central Authentication Service
- b. Protected Extensible Authentication Protocol
- c. Authentication protocol

- d. Kerberos

Guidance: level 1

:: Commercial item transport and distribution ::

In commerce, supply-chain management, the management of the flow of goods and services, involves the movement and storage of raw materials, of work-in-process inventory, and of finished goods from point of origin to point of consumption. Interconnected or interlinked networks, channels and node businesses combine in the provision of products and services required by end customers in a supply chain. Supply-chain management has been defined as the "design, planning, execution, control, and monitoring of supply-chain activities with the objective of creating net value, building a competitive infrastructure, leveraging worldwide logistics, synchronizing supply with demand and measuring performance globally."SCM practice draws heavily from the areas of industrial engineering, systems engineering, operations management, logistics, procurement, information technology, and marketing and strives for an integrated approach. Marketing channels play an important role in supply-chain management. Current research in supply-chain management is concerned with topics related to sustainability and risk management, among others. Some suggest that the "people dimension" of SCM, ethical issues, internal integration, transparency/visibility, and human capital/talent management are topics that have, so far, been underrepresented on the research agenda.

Exam Probability: **Medium**

10. *Answer choices:*

(see index for correct answer)

- a. Cross-docking
- b. EPCglobal Network
- c. Supply chain management
- d. Outsize cargo

Guidance: level 1

:: Data security ::

In information technology, a _____ , or data _____ , or the process of backing up, refers to the copying into an archive file of computer data that is already in secondary storage—so that it may be used to restore the original after a data loss event. The verb form is "back up", whereas the noun and adjective form is " _____ ".

Exam Probability: **Low**

11. *Answer choices:*

(see index for correct answer)

- a. Backup
- b. Salami slicing
- c. Security information management
- d. Crypto cloud computing

Guidance: level 1

:: Content management systems ::

_____ is the textual, visual, or aural content that is encountered as part of the user experience on websites. It may include—among other things—text, images, sounds, videos, and animations.

Exam Probability: **Medium**

12. *Answer choices:*

(see index for correct answer)

- a. Web content
- b. Omeka
- c. MotoCMS
- d. PHP-Nuke

Guidance: level 1

:: E-commerce ::

A _____ is a plastic payment card that can be used instead of cash when making purchases. It is similar to a credit card, but unlike a credit card, the money is immediately transferred directly from the cardholder's bank account when performing a transaction.

Exam Probability: **High**

13. *Answer choices:*

(see index for correct answer)

- a. Electronic Payment Services
- b. Types of E-commerce
- c. Debit card
- d. Mobile ticketing

Guidance: level 1

:: E-commerce ::

Customer to customer markets provide an innovative way to allow customers to interact with each other. Traditional markets require business to customer relationships, in which a customer goes to the business in order to purchase a product or service. In customer to customer markets, the business facilitates an environment where customers can sell goods or services to each other. Other types of markets include business to business and business to customer.

Exam Probability: **High**

14. *Answer choices:*

(see index for correct answer)

- a. Consumer-to-consumer
- b. Inventory Information Approval System
- c. Mobile commerce
- d. Public key certificate

Guidance: level 1

:: Information technology management ::

_____ concerns a cycle of organizational activity: the acquisition of information from one or more sources, the custodianship and the distribution of that information to those who need it, and its ultimate disposition through archiving or deletion.

Exam Probability: **Low**

15. *Answer choices:*

(see index for correct answer)

- a. Information management
- b. Information protection policy
- c. Piazza telematica
- d. Capability Maturity Model

Guidance: level 1

:: Network analyzers ::

A _____ , meaning "meat eater" , is an organism that derives its energy and nutrient requirements from a diet consisting mainly or exclusively of animal tissue, whether through predation or scavenging. Animals that depend solely on animal flesh for their nutrient requirements are called obligate _____ s while those that also consume non-animal food are called facultative _____ s. Omnivores also consume both animal and non-animal food, and, apart from the more general definition, there is no clearly defined ratio of plant to animal material that would distinguish a facultative _____ from an omnivore. A _____ at the top of the food chain, not preyed upon by other animals, is termed an apex predator.

Exam Probability: **High**

16. *Answer choices:*
(see index for correct answer)

- a. MTR
- b. Carnivore
- c. Aircrack-ng
- d. Ntopng

Guidance: level 1

:: Marketing by medium ::

_____ , also called online marketing or Internet advertising or web advertising, is a form of marketing and advertising which uses the Internet to deliver promotional marketing messages to consumers. Many consumers find _____ disruptive and have increasingly turned to ad blocking for a variety of reasons. When software is used to do the purchasing, it is known as programmatic advertising.

Exam Probability: **Low**

17. *Answer choices:*

(see index for correct answer)

- a. Social video marketing
- b. Viral marketing
- c. New media marketing
- d. Online advertising

Guidance: level 1

:: Remote administration software ::

_____ is a protocol used on the Internet or local area network to provide a bidirectional interactive text-oriented communication facility using a virtual terminal connection. User data is interspersed in-band with _____ control information in an 8-bit byte oriented data connection over the Transmission Control Protocol .

Exam Probability: **Medium**

18. *Answer choices:*

(see index for correct answer)

- a. GoToMyPC
- b. Virtual Machine Manager
- c. Bomgar
- d. RealVNC

Guidance: level 1

:: Information science ::

_____ has been defined as "the branch of ethics that focuses on the relationship between the creation, organization, dissemination, and use of information, and the ethical standards and moral codes governing human conduct in society". It examines the morality that comes from information as a resource, a product, or as a target. It provides a critical framework for considering moral issues concerning informational privacy, moral agency , new environmental issues , problems arising from the life-cycle of information . It is very vital to understand that librarians, archivists, information professionals among others, really understand the importance of knowing how to disseminate proper information as well as being responsible with their actions when addressing information.

Exam Probability: **Medium**

19. *Answer choices:*

(see index for correct answer)

- a. POSC Caesar
- b. Information ethics
- c. Transliteracy
- d. Subject indexing

Guidance: level 1

:: Critical thinking ::

In psychology, _____ is regarded as the cognitive process resulting in the selection of a belief or a course of action among several alternative possibilities. Every _____ process produces a final choice, which may or may not prompt action.

Exam Probability: **High**

20. *Answer choices:*

(see index for correct answer)

- a. Moral reasoning
- b. Ad hoc hypothesis
- c. Informal logic
- d. Decision-making

Guidance: level 1

:: Knowledge engineering ::

The _____ is an extension of the World Wide Web through standards by the World Wide Web Consortium . The standards promote common data formats and exchange protocols on the Web, most fundamentally the Resource Description Framework . According to the W3C, "The _____ provides a common framework that allows data to be shared and reused across application, enterprise, and community boundaries". The _____ is therefore regarded as an integrator across different content, information applications and systems.

Exam Probability: **High**

21. *Answer choices:*

(see index for correct answer)

- a. Subject-matter expert
- b. Knowledge Engineering Environment
- c. Knowledge-based engineering
- d. Semantic Web

Guidance: level 1

:: Information systems ::

_____ is the process of creating, sharing, using and managing the knowledge and information of an organisation. It refers to a multidisciplinary approach to achieving organisational objectives by making the best use of knowledge.

Exam Probability: **Low**

22. *Answer choices:*
(see index for correct answer)

- a. Data flow diagram
- b. Control flow diagram
- c. Knowledge management
- d. Connectionist expert system

Guidance: level 1

:: Data privacy ::

The _____ is an information security standard for organizations that handle branded credit cards from the major card schemes.

Exam Probability: **Low**

23. *Answer choices:*
(see index for correct answer)

- a. Statewatch
- b. Declassification
- c. Information Commissioner
- d. Payment Card Industry Data Security Standard

Guidance: level 1

:: Data management ::

_____ is a set of processes and technologies that supports the collection, managing, and publishing of information in any form or medium. When stored and accessed via computers, this information may be more specifically referred to as digital content, or simply as content.

Exam Probability: **Low**

24. *Answer choices:*
(see index for correct answer)

- a. Data aggregator
- b. Locks with ordered sharing
- c. Content management
- d. Navigational database

Guidance: level 1

:: Data quality ::

_____ is the maintenance of, and the assurance of the accuracy and consistency of, data over its entire life-cycle, and is a critical aspect to the design, implementation and usage of any system which stores, processes, or retrieves data. The term is broad in scope and may have widely different meanings depending on the specific context even under the same general umbrella of computing. It is at times used as a proxy term for data quality, while data validation is a pre-requisite for _____ . _____ is the opposite of data corruption. The overall intent of any _____ technique is the same: ensure data is recorded exactly as intended and upon later retrieval, ensure the data is the same as it was when it was originally recorded. In short, _____ aims to prevent unintentional changes to information. _____ is not to be confused with data security, the discipline of protecting data from unauthorized parties.

Exam Probability: **High**

25. *Answer choices:*
(see index for correct answer)

- a. Declarative Referential Integrity
- b. Soft error
- c. Data quality assessment
- d. Data integrity

Guidance: level 1

:: Information science ::

In discourse-based grammatical theory, _____ is any tracking of referential information by speakers. Information may be new, just introduced into the conversation; given, already active in the speakers' consciousness; or old, no longer active. The various types of activation, and how these are defined, are model-dependent.

Exam Probability: **High**

26. *Answer choices:*
(see index for correct answer)

- a. Knowledge organization
- b. Information flow
- c. Recording format
- d. Legal informatics

Guidance: level 1

:: Ethically disputed business practices ::

_____ is the use of messaging systems to send an unsolicited message, especially advertising, as well as sending messages repeatedly on the same site. While the most widely recognized form of spam is email spam, the term is applied to similar abuses in other media: instant messaging spam, Usenet newsgroup spam, Web search engine spam, spam in blogs, wiki spam, online classified ads spam, mobile phone messaging spam, Internet forum spam, junk fax transmissions, social spam, spam mobile apps, television advertising and file sharing spam. It is named after Spam, a luncheon meat, by way of a Monty Python sketch about a restaurant that has Spam in every dish and where patrons annoyingly chant "Spam!" over and over again.

Exam Probability: **Low**

27. *Answer choices:*
(see index for correct answer)

- a. Operation Red Spider
- b. Maya ICBG bioprospecting controversy
- c. Copyright troll
- d. Two sets of books

Guidance: level 1

:: ::

An _____ is system software that manages computer hardware and software resources and provides common services for computer programs.

Exam Probability: **Medium**

28. *Answer choices:*

(see index for correct answer)

- a. deep-level diversity
- b. levels of analysis
- c. imperative
- d. Operating system

Guidance: level 1

:: Data collection ::

_____ is information that either does not have a pre-defined data model or is not organized in a pre-defined manner. Unstructured information is typically text-heavy, but may contain data such as dates, numbers, and facts as well. This results in irregularities and ambiguities that make it difficult to understand using traditional programs as compared to data stored in fielded form in databases or annotated in documents.

Exam Probability: **High**

29. *Answer choices:*

(see index for correct answer)

- a. Surveylab
- b. Concrete slump test
- c. Unstructured data
- d. ScraperWiki

Guidance: level 1

:: Google services ::

_____ is a time-management and scheduling calendar service developed by Google. It became available in beta release April 13, 2006, and in general release in July 2009, on the web and as mobile apps for the Android and iOS platforms.

Exam Probability: **Medium**

30. *Answer choices:*

(see index for correct answer)

- a. Google Plugin for Eclipse
- b. Google Calendar
- c. Google Apps for Business
- d. Google Personalized Search

Guidance: level 1

:: ::

A _____ is a knowledge base website on which users collaboratively modify content and structure directly from the web browser. In a typical _____, text is written using a simplified markup language and often edited with the help of a rich-text editor.

Exam Probability: **Low**

31. *Answer choices:*

(see index for correct answer)

- a. information systems assessment
- b. co-culture
- c. deep-level diversity
- d. Wiki

Guidance: level 1

:: ::

A _____ is the event in which two or more bodies exert forces on each other in about a relatively short time. Although the most common use of the word _____ refers to incidents in which two or more objects collide with great force, the scientific use of the term implies nothing about the magnitude of the force.

Exam Probability: **Low**

32. *Answer choices:*

(see index for correct answer)

- a. corporate values
- b. co-culture
- c. Collision
- d. similarity-attraction theory

Guidance: level 1

:: Business planning ::

_____ is an organization's process of defining its strategy, or direction, and making decisions on allocating its resources to pursue this strategy. It may also extend to control mechanisms for guiding the implementation of the strategy. _____ became prominent in corporations during the 1960s and remains an important aspect of strategic management. It is executed by strategic planners or strategists, who involve many parties and research sources in their analysis of the organization and its relationship to the environment in which it competes.

Exam Probability: **Medium**

33. *Answer choices:*

(see index for correct answer)

- a. Stakeholder management
- b. Business war games
- c. Open Options Corporation
- d. Strategic planning

Guidance: level 1

:: Enterprise modelling ::

_____ are large-scale application software packages that support business processes, information flows, reporting, and data analytics in complex organizations. While ES are generally packaged enterprise application software systems they can also be bespoke, custom developed systems created to support a specific organization's needs.

Exam Probability: **High**

34. *Answer choices:*

(see index for correct answer)

- a. Enterprise systems
- b. ISO 19439
- c. Application Portability Profile
- d. Integrated enterprise modeling

Guidance: level 1

:: Information systems ::

_____ are formal, sociotechnical, organizational systems designed to collect, process, store, and distribute information. In a sociotechnical perspective, _____ are composed by four components: task, people, structure, and technology.

Exam Probability: **High**

35. *Answer choices:*

(see index for correct answer)

- a. CGA
- b. Electronic markets
- c. Hybrid positioning system
- d. Expert systems for mortgages

Guidance: level 1

:: Security compliance ::

_____ refers to the inability to withstand the effects of a hostile environment. A window of _____ is a time frame within which defensive measures are diminished, compromised or lacking.

Exam Probability: **Medium**

36. *Answer choices:*

(see index for correct answer)

- a. Federal Information Security Management Act of 2002
- b. 201 CMR 17.00
- c. Vulnerability
- d. Vulnerability management

Guidance: level 1

:: Data management ::

" _____ " is a field that treats ways to analyze, systematically extract information from, or otherwise deal with data sets that are too large or complex to be dealt with by traditional data-processing application software. Data with many cases offer greater statistical power, while data with higher complexity may lead to a higher false discovery rate. _____ challenges include capturing data, data storage, data analysis, search, sharing, transfer, visualization, querying, updating, information privacy and data source. _____ was originally associated with three key concepts: volume, variety, and velocity. Other concepts later attributed with _____ are veracity and value.

Exam Probability: **Medium**

37. *Answer choices:*

(see index for correct answer)

- a. ADO.NET
- b. Tagsistant
- c. Content-oriented workflow models
- d. Reference table

Guidance: level 1

:: Computer memory ::

_____ is an electronic non-volatile computer storage medium that can be electrically erased and reprogrammed.

Exam Probability: **Low**

38. *Answer choices:*

(see index for correct answer)

- a. Interleaved memory
- b. Memory timings
- c. Memory ordering
- d. Delay line memory

Guidance: level 1

:: Information science ::

The United States National Forum on _____ defines _____ as "... the hyper ability to know when there is a need for information, to be able to identify, locate, evaluate, and effectively use that information for the issue or problem at hand." The American Library Association defines "_____" as a set of abilities requiring individuals to "recognize when information is needed and have the ability to locate, evaluate, and use effectively the needed information. Other definitions incorporate aspects of "skepticism, judgement, free thinking, questioning, and understanding..." or incorporate competencies that an informed citizen of an information society ought to possess to participate intelligently and actively in that society.

Exam Probability: **Medium**

39. *Answer choices:*

(see index for correct answer)

- a. Media ecology
- b. Pearl growing
- c. Information processing theory
- d. Jason Farradane

Guidance: level 1

:: Data modeling languages ::

An entity–relationship model describes interrelated things of interest in a specific domain of knowledge. A basic ER model is composed of entity types and specifies relationships that can exist between entities.

Exam Probability: **High**

40. *Answer choices:*

(see index for correct answer)

- a. Data Base Task Group
- b. Entity-relationship
- c. IDEF4
- d. OGML

Guidance: level 1

:: World Wide Web Consortium standards ::

_____ is a markup language that defines a set of rules for encoding documents in a format that is both human-readable and machine-readable. The W3C's XML 1.0 Specification and several other related specifications—all of them free open standards—define XML.

Exam Probability: **Low**

41. *Answer choices:*
(see index for correct answer)

- a. Extensible Markup Language
- b. Hyper Text Markup Language

Guidance: level 1

:: Information and communication technologies for development ::

_____ is a non-profit initiative established with the goal of transforming education for children around the world; this goal was to be achieved by creating and distributing educational devices for the developing world, and by creating software and content for those devices.

Exam Probability: **Medium**

42. *Answer choices:*
(see index for correct answer)

- a. Wamani
- b. Arid Lands Information Network
- c. Geekcorps
- d. One Laptop per Child

Guidance: level 1

:: Systems theory ::

A _____ is a group of interacting or interrelated entities that form a unified whole. A _____ is delineated by its spatial and temporal boundaries, surrounded and influenced by its environment, described by its structure and purpose and expressed in its functioning.

Exam Probability: **High**

43. *Answer choices:*
(see index for correct answer)

- a. transient state
- b. Black box
- c. Viable System Model
- d. System

Guidance: level 1

:: Data management ::

_____ s or data _____ s are computer languages used to make queries in databases and information systems.

Exam Probability: **Medium**

44. *Answer choices:*
(see index for correct answer)

- a. Metadata
- b. Global concurrency control
- c. Australian National Data Service
- d. Query language

Guidance: level 1

:: Database management systems ::

A _____ is a type of data model that determines the logical structure of a database and fundamentally determines in which manner data can be stored, organized and manipulated. The most popular example of a _____ is the relational model, which uses a table-based format.

Exam Probability: **Medium**

45. *Answer choices:*

(see index for correct answer)

- a. Database model
- b. Query plan
- c. Data definition language
- d. Pool

Guidance: level 1

:: Data management ::

An _____ is any kind of information system which improves the functions of enterprise business processes by integration. This means typically offering high quality of service, dealing with large volumes of data and capable of supporting some large and possibly complex organization or enterprise. An EIS must be able to be used by all parts and all levels of an enterprise.

Exam Probability: **Low**

46. *Answer choices:*

(see index for correct answer)

- a. Physical schema
- b. Cloud Data Management Interface
- c. Learning object
- d. CommVault Systems

Guidance: level 1

:: Search engine optimization ::

_____ is an algorithm used by Google Search to rank web pages in their search engine results. _____ was named after Larry Page, one of the founders of Google. _____ is a way of measuring the importance of website pages. According to Google.

Exam Probability: **Medium**

47. *Answer choices:*

(see index for correct answer)

- a. Ultimate Research Assistant
- b. Google penalty

- c. Link farm
- d. WPromote

Guidance: level 1

:: ::

A _____ is a discussion or informational website published on the World Wide Web consisting of discrete, often informal diary-style text entries . Posts are typically displayed in reverse chronological order, so that the most recent post appears first, at the top of the web page. Until 2009, _____ s were usually the work of a single individual, occasionally of a small group, and often covered a single subject or topic. In the 2010s, "multi-author _____ s" emerged, featuring the writing of multiple authors and sometimes professionally edited. MABs from newspapers, other media outlets, universities, think tanks, advocacy groups, and similar institutions account for an increasing quantity of _____ traffic. The rise of Twitter and other "micro _____ ging" systems helps integrate MABs and single-author _____ s into the news media. _____ can also be used as a verb, meaning to maintain or add content to a _____ .

Exam Probability: **Low**

48. *Answer choices:*

(see index for correct answer)

- a. levels of analysis
- b. deep-level diversity
- c. corporate values
- d. information systems assessment

Guidance: level 1

:: Information technology management ::

_____ s or pop-ups are forms of online advertising on the World Wide Web. A pop-up is a graphical user interface display area, usually a small window, that suddenly appears in the foreground of the visual interface. The pop-up window containing an advertisement is usually generated by JavaScript that uses cross-site scripting , sometimes with a secondary payload that uses Adobe Flash. They can also be generated by other vulnerabilities/security holes in browser security.

Exam Probability: **Low**

49. *Answer choices:*

(see index for correct answer)

- a. ITIL security management
- b. Pop-up ad
- c. Information Lifecycle Management
- d. Information model

Guidance: level 1

:: Data management ::

_____ represents the business objects that contain the most valuable, agreed upon information shared across an organization. It can cover relatively static reference data, transactional, unstructured, analytical, hierarchical and metadata. It is the primary focus of the information technology discipline of _____ management .

Exam Probability: **High**

50. *Answer choices:*

(see index for correct answer)

- a. UI data binding
- b. Data binding
- c. CA Gen
- d. Secure electronic delivery service

Guidance: level 1

:: ::

A _____ is a telecommunications network that extends over a large geographical distance for the primary purpose of computer networking. _____ s are often established with leased telecommunication circuits.

Exam Probability: **Medium**

51. *Answer choices:*

(see index for correct answer)

- a. personal values
- b. interpersonal communication
- c. functional perspective

- d. Wide Area Network

Guidance: level 1

:: Management ::

_____ is the kind of knowledge that is difficult to transfer to another person by means of writing it down or verbalizing it. For example, that London is in the United Kingdom is a piece of explicit knowledge that can be written down, transmitted, and understood by a recipient. However, the ability to speak a language, ride a bicycle, knead dough, play a musical instrument, or design and use complex equipment requires all sorts of knowledge that is not always known explicitly, even by expert practitioners, and which is difficult or impossible to explicitly transfer to other people.

Exam Probability: **Low**

52. *Answer choices:*
(see index for correct answer)

- a. I-VMS
- b. Tacit knowledge
- c. Automated decision support
- d. Financial planning

Guidance: level 1

:: Strategic management ::

In marketing strategy, first-mover advantage is the advantage gained by the initial significant occupant of a market segment. First-mover advantage may be gained by technological leadership, or early purchase of resources.

Exam Probability: **High**

53. *Answer choices:*
(see index for correct answer)

- a. First mover advantage
- b. Complementors
- c. Core product
- d. Operational responsiveness

Guidance: level 1

:: Online companies ::

_____ is a business directory service and crowd-sourced review forum, and a public company of the same name that is headquartered in San Francisco, California. The company develops, hosts and markets the _____.com website and the _____ mobile app, which publish crowd-sourced reviews about businesses. It also operates an online reservation service called _____ Reservations.

Exam Probability: **Low**

54. *Answer choices:*
(see index for correct answer)

- a. Logosportswear
- b. RateMyTeachers
- c. Indieflix
- d. Outalot

Guidance: level 1

:: Commerce ::

_____, Inc. is an American media-services provider headquartered in Los Gatos, California, founded in 1997 by Reed Hastings and Marc Randolph in Scotts Valley, California. The company's primary business is its subscription-based streaming OTT service which offers online streaming of a library of films and television programs, including those produced in-house. As of April 2019, _____ had over 148 million paid subscriptions worldwide, including 60 million in the United States, and over 154 million subscriptions total including free trials. It is available almost worldwide except in mainland China as well as Syria, North Korea, and Crimea . The company also has offices in the Netherlands, Brazil, India, Japan, and South Korea. _____ is a member of the Motion Picture Association of America .

Exam Probability: **Medium**

55. *Answer choices:*
(see index for correct answer)

- a. Netflix
- b. TradeCard
- c. Export restriction
- d. Perfect tender rule

:: ::

_____ is a free email service developed by Google. Users can access _____ on the web and using third-party programs that synchronize email content through POP or IMAP protocols. _____ started as a limited beta release on April 1, 2004 and ended its testing phase on July 7, 2009.

Exam Probability: **Medium**

56. *Answer choices:*
(see index for correct answer)

- a. Gmail
- b. similarity-attraction theory
- c. personal values
- d. process perspective

Guidance: level 1

:: ::

A web _____ or Internet _____ is a software system that is designed to carry out web search , which means to search the World Wide Web in a systematic way for particular information specified in a web search query. The search results are generally presented in a line of results, often referred to as _____ results pages . The information may be a mix of web pages, images, videos, infographics, articles, research papers and other types of files. Some _____ s also mine data available in databases or open directories. Unlike web directories, which are maintained only by human editors, _____ s also maintain real-time information by running an algorithm on a web crawler. Internet content that is not capable of being searched by a web _____ is generally described as the deep web.

Exam Probability: **Low**

57. *Answer choices:*
(see index for correct answer)

- a. open system
- b. cultural
- c. co-culture

- d. surface-level diversity

Guidance: level 1

:: Marketing ::

_____ is the percentage of a market accounted for by a specific entity. In a survey of nearly 200 senior marketing managers, 67% responded that they found the revenue- "dollar _____ " metric very useful, while 61% found "unit _____ " very useful.

Exam Probability: **Medium**

58. *Answer choices:*
(see index for correct answer)

- a. Negotiation
- b. Market share
- c. societal marketing
- d. Content creation

Guidance: level 1

:: Information systems ::

In artificial intelligence, an _____ is a computer system that emulates the decision-making ability of a human expert. _____ s are designed to solve complex problems by reasoning through bodies of knowledge, represented mainly as if–then rules rather than through conventional procedural code. The first _____ s were created in the 1970s and then proliferated in the 1980s. _____ s were among the first truly successful forms of artificial intelligence software. However, some experts point out that _____ s were not part of true artificial intelligence since they lack the ability to learn autonomously from external data. An _____ is divided into two subsystems: the inference engine and the knowledge base. The knowledge base represents facts and rules. The inference engine applies the rules to the known facts to deduce new facts. Inference engines can also include explanation and debugging abilities.

Exam Probability: **Low**

59. *Answer choices:*
(see index for correct answer)

- a. DigitalFusion Platform
- b. MES Hybrid Document Systems
- c. Expert system
- d. Resistance Database Initiative

Guidance: level 1

Marketing

Marketing is the study and management of exchange relationships. Marketing is the business process of creating relationships with and satisfying customers. With its focus on the customer, marketing is one of the premier components of business management.

Marketing is defined by the American Marketing Association as "the activity, set of institutions, and processes for creating, communicating, delivering, and exchanging offerings that have value for customers, clients, partners, and society at large."

In business and engineering, new _____ covers the complete process of bringing a new product to market. A central aspect of NPD is product design, along with various business considerations. New _____ is described broadly as the transformation of a market opportunity into a product available for sale. The product can be tangible or intangible, though sometimes services and other processes are distinguished from "products." NPD requires an understanding of customer needs and wants, the competitive environment, and the nature of the market. Cost, time and quality are the main variables that drive customer needs. Aiming at these three variables, innovative companies develop continuous practices and strategies to better satisfy customer requirements and to increase their own market share by a regular development of new products. There are many uncertainties and challenges which companies must face throughout the process. The use of best practices and the elimination of barriers to communication are the main concerns for the management of the NPD.

Exam Probability: **High**

1. *Answer choices:*
(see index for correct answer)

- a. corporate values
- b. deep-level diversity
- c. imperative
- d. Product development

Guidance: level 1

:: Direct marketing ::

_____ is a form of advertising where organizations communicate directly to customers through a variety of media including cell phone text messaging, email, websites, online adverts, database marketing, fliers, catalog distribution, promotional letters, targeted television, newspapers, magazine advertisements, and outdoor advertising. Among practitioners, it is also known as direct response marketing.

Exam Probability: **Low**

2. *Answer choices:*
(see index for correct answer)

- a. Direct marketing
- b. American Family Publishers
- c. Alticor
- d. Mailing list

Guidance: level 1

:: Marketing ::

_____ uses different marketing channels and tools in combination: Marketing communication channels focus on any way a business communicates a message to its desired market, or the market in general. A marketing communication tool can be anything from: advertising, personal selling, direct marketing, sponsorship, communication, and promotion to public relations.

Exam Probability: **Low**

3. *Answer choices:*
(see index for correct answer)

- a. Profit chart
- b. Gift suite
- c. Marketing communications
- d. Performance-based advertising

Guidance: level 1

:: Monopoly (economics) ::

_____ is a category of property that includes intangible creations of the human intellect. _____ encompasses two types of rights: industrial property rights and copyright. It was not until the 19th century that the term " _____ " began to be used, and not until the late 20th century that it became commonplace in the majority of the world.

Exam Probability: **Low**

4. *Answer choices:*

(see index for correct answer)

- a. Wartime Law on Industrial Property
- b. Demonopolization
- c. Contestable market
- d. Trust

Guidance: level 1

:: ::

_____ refers to a diverse array of media technologies that reach a large audience via mass communication. The technologies through which this communication takes place include a variety of outlets.

Exam Probability: **Medium**

5. *Answer choices:*

(see index for correct answer)

- a. co-culture
- b. Mass media
- c. hierarchical
- d. empathy

Guidance: level 1

:: Information technology management ::

B2B is often contrasted with business-to-consumer. In B2B commerce, it is often the case that the parties to the relationship have comparable negotiating power, and even when they do not, each party typically involves professional staff and legal counsel in the negotiation of terms, whereas B2C is shaped to a far greater degree by economic implications of information asymmetry. However, within a B2B context, large companies may have many commercial, resource and information advantages over smaller businesses. The United Kingdom government, for example, created the post of Small Business Commissioner under the Enterprise Act 2016 to "enable small businesses to resolve disputes" and "consider complaints by small business suppliers about payment issues with larger businesses that they supply."

Exam Probability: **High**

6. *Answer choices:*

(see index for correct answer)

- a. Virtual filing cabinet
- b. Network configuration and change management
- c. Intelligent workload management
- d. Data warehouse appliance

Guidance: level 1

:: ::

Management is the administration of an organization, whether it is a business, a not-for-profit organization, or government body. Management includes the activities of setting the strategy of an organization and coordinating the efforts of its employees to accomplish its objectives through the application of available resources, such as financial, natural, technological, and human resources. The term "management" may also refer to those people who manage an organization.

Exam Probability: **High**

7. *Answer choices:*

(see index for correct answer)

- a. empathy
- b. similarity-attraction theory
- c. Manager
- d. corporate values

Guidance: level 1

:: ::

_____ is a term frequently used in marketing. It is a measure of how products and services supplied by a company meet or surpass customer expectation. _____ is defined as "the number of customers, or percentage of total customers, whose reported experience with a firm, its products, or its services exceeds specified satisfaction goals."

Exam Probability: **Medium**

8. *Answer choices:*

(see index for correct answer)

- a. deep-level diversity
- b. Customer satisfaction
- c. open system
- d. information systems assessment

Guidance: level 1

:: ::

In law, an _____ is the process in which cases are reviewed, where parties request a formal change to an official decision. _____ s function both as a process for error correction as well as a process of clarifying and interpreting law. Although appellate courts have existed for thousands of years, common law countries did not incorporate an affirmative right to _____ into their jurisprudence until the 19th century.

Exam Probability: **High**

9. *Answer choices:*

(see index for correct answer)

- a. hierarchical
- b. Appeal
- c. empathy
- d. personal values

Guidance: level 1

:: ::

_____ is the production of products for use or sale using labour and machines, tools, chemical and biological processing, or formulation. The term may refer to a range of human activity, from handicraft to high tech, but is most commonly applied to industrial design, in which raw materials are transformed into finished goods on a large scale. Such finished goods may be sold to other manufacturers for the production of other, more complex products, such as aircraft, household appliances, furniture, sports equipment or automobiles, or sold to wholesalers, who in turn sell them to retailers, who then sell them to end users and consumers.

Exam Probability: **Medium**

10. *Answer choices:*

(see index for correct answer)

- a. hierarchical
- b. Manufacturing
- c. Sarbanes-Oxley act of 2002
- d. co-culture

Guidance: level 1

:: bad_topic ::

Sponsoring something is the act of supporting an event, activity, person, or organization financially or through the provision of products or services. The individual or group that provides the support, similar to a benefactor, is known as sponsor.

Exam Probability: **High**

11. *Answer choices:*

(see index for correct answer)

- a. Inept
- b. Esperanto
- c. Northwest Air
- d. Sponsorship

Guidance: level 1

:: ::

_____, known in Europe as research and technological development, refers to innovative activities undertaken by corporations or governments in developing new services or products, or improving existing services or products. _____ constitutes the first stage of development of a potential new service or the production process.

Exam Probability: **Medium**

12. *Answer choices:*

<small>(see index for correct answer)</small>

- a. process perspective
- b. corporate values
- c. surface-level diversity
- d. Research and development

Guidance: level 1

:: ::

_____ Corporation is an American multinational technology company with headquarters in Redmond, Washington. It develops, manufactures, licenses, supports and sells computer software, consumer electronics, personal computers, and related services. Its best known software products are the _____ Windows line of operating systems, the _____ Office suite, and the Internet Explorer and Edge Web browsers. Its flagship hardware products are the Xbox video game consoles and the _____ Surface lineup of touchscreen personal computers. As of 2016, it is the world's largest software maker by revenue, and one of the world's most valuable companies. The word "_____" is a portmanteau of "microcomputer" and "software". _____ is ranked No. 30 in the 2018 Fortune 500 rankings of the largest United States corporations by total revenue.

Exam Probability: **Low**

13. *Answer choices:*

<small>(see index for correct answer)</small>

- a. hierarchical
- b. hierarchical perspective
- c. Microsoft
- d. process perspective

Guidance: level 1

:: Trade associations ::

A _____ , also known as an industry trade group, business association, sector association or industry body, is an organization founded and funded by businesses that operate in a specific industry. An industry _____ participates in public relations activities such as advertising, education, political donations, lobbying and publishing, but its focus is collaboration between companies. Associations may offer other services, such as producing conferences, networking or charitable events or offering classes or educational materials. Many associations are non-profit organizations governed by bylaws and directed by officers who are also members.

Exam Probability: **High**

14. *Answer choices:*

(see index for correct answer)

- a. National Federation of Coffee Growers of Colombia
- b. PCIA - The Wireless Infrastructure Association
- c. Trade association
- d. Seller agency

Guidance: level 1

:: ::

_____ LLC is an American multinational technology company that specializes in Internet-related services and products, which include online advertising technologies, search engine, cloud computing, software, and hardware. It is considered one of the Big Four technology companies, alongside Amazon, Apple and Facebook.

Exam Probability: **High**

15. *Answer choices:*

(see index for correct answer)

- a. levels of analysis
- b. empathy
- c. Google
- d. similarity-attraction theory

Guidance: level 1

:: Product management ::

A _____ is a professional role which is responsible for the development of products for an organization, known as the practice of product management. _____ s own the business strategy behind a product , specify its functional requirements and generally manage the launch of features. They coordinate work done by many other functions and are ultimately responsible for the business success of the product.

Exam Probability: **High**

16. *Answer choices:*

(see index for correct answer)

- a. Trademark distinctiveness
- b. Product manager
- c. Rapid prototyping
- d. Tipping point

Guidance: level 1

:: Consumer behaviour ::

Convenient procedures, products and services are those intended to increase ease in accessibility, save resources and decrease frustration. A modern _____ is a labor-saving device, service or substance which make a task easier or more efficient than a traditional method. _____ is a relative concept, and depends on context. For example, automobiles were once considered a _____ , yet today are regarded as a normal part of life.

Exam Probability: **High**

17. *Answer choices:*

(see index for correct answer)

- a. Conspicuous conservation
- b. Shopping while black
- c. Consumption smoothing
- d. Health consumerism

Guidance: level 1

:: Market research ::

_____ is the action of defining, gathering, analyzing, and distributing intelligence about products, customers, competitors, and any aspect of the environment needed to support executives and managers in strategic decision making for an organization.

Exam Probability: **High**

18. *Answer choices:*
(see index for correct answer)

- a. DigitalMR
- b. Mendelsohn Affluent Survey
- c. AQH Share
- d. Competitive intelligence

Guidance: level 1

:: Belief ::

_____ is an umbrella term of influence. _____ can attempt to influence a person's beliefs, attitudes, intentions, motivations, or behaviors. In business, _____ is a process aimed at changing a person's attitude or behavior toward some event, idea, object, or other person, by using written, spoken words or visual tools to convey information, feelings, or reasoning, or a combination thereof. _____ is also an often used tool in the pursuit of personal gain, such as election campaigning, giving a sales pitch, or in trial advocacy. _____ can also be interpreted as using one's personal or positional resources to change people's behaviors or attitudes. Systematic _____ is the process through which attitudes or beliefs are leveraged by appeals to logic and reason. Heuristic _____ on the other hand is the process through which attitudes or beliefs are leveraged by appeals to habit or emotion.

Exam Probability: **Medium**

19. *Answer choices:*
(see index for correct answer)

- a. Eschatological verification
- b. Doctrine
- c. Urdoxa
- d. Persuasion

Guidance: level 1

:: ::

In legal terminology, a _____ is any formal legal document that sets out the facts and legal reasons that the filing party or parties believes are sufficient to support a claim against the party or parties against whom the claim is brought that entitles the plaintiff to a remedy. For example, the Federal Rules of Civil Procedure that govern civil litigation in United States courts provide that a civil action is commenced with the filing or service of a pleading called a _____ . Civil court rules in states that have incorporated the Federal Rules of Civil Procedure use the same term for the same pleading.

Exam Probability: **Low**

20. *Answer choices:*

(see index for correct answer)

- a. Complaint
- b. process perspective
- c. personal values
- d. interpersonal communication

Guidance: level 1

:: Network theory ::

A _____ is a social structure made up of a set of social actors, sets of dyadic ties, and other social interactions between actors. The _____ perspective provides a set of methods for analyzing the structure of whole social entities as well as a variety of theories explaining the patterns observed in these structures. The study of these structures uses _____ analysis to identify local and global patterns, locate influential entities, and examine network dynamics.

Exam Probability: **High**

21. *Answer choices:*

(see index for correct answer)

- a. Network formation
- b. Network Description Language
- c. Complex network
- d. NodeXL

:: ::

_____ is the administration of an organization, whether it is a business, a not-for-profit organization, or government body. _____ includes the activities of setting the strategy of an organization and coordinating the efforts of its employees to accomplish its objectives through the application of available resources, such as financial, natural, technological, and human resources. The term "_____" may also refer to those people who manage an organization.

Exam Probability: **Medium**

22. *Answer choices:*
(see index for correct answer)

- a. Management
- b. open system
- c. levels of analysis
- d. personal values

Guidance: level 1

:: ::

A _____ is the process of presenting a topic to an audience. It is typically a demonstration, introduction, lecture, or speech meant to inform, persuade, inspire, motivate, or to build good will or to present a new idea or product. The term can also be used for a formal or ritualized introduction or offering, as with the _____ of a debutante. _____ s in certain formats are also known as keynote address.

Exam Probability: **Medium**

23. *Answer choices:*
(see index for correct answer)

- a. Presentation
- b. levels of analysis
- c. surface-level diversity
- d. open system

Guidance: level 1

:: Supply chain management ::

The _____ is a barcode symbology that is widely used in the United States, Canada, United Kingdom, Australia, New Zealand, in Europe and other countries for tracking trade items in stores.

Exam Probability: **Medium**

24. *Answer choices:*

(see index for correct answer)

- a. Astra Resources Plc
- b. Netchain analysis
- c. Demand Solutions
- d. Universal Product Code

Guidance: level 1

:: ::

In regulatory jurisdictions that provide for it , _____ is a group of laws and organizations designed to ensure the rights of consumers as well as fair trade, competition and accurate information in the marketplace. The laws are designed to prevent the businesses that engage in fraud or specified unfair practices from gaining an advantage over competitors. They may also provides additional protection for those most vulnerable in society. _____ laws are a form of government regulation that aim to protect the rights of consumers. For example, a government may require businesses to disclose detailed information about products—particularly in areas where safety or public health is an issue, such as food.

Exam Probability: **Medium**

25. *Answer choices:*

(see index for correct answer)

- a. Consumer Protection
- b. open system
- c. process perspective
- d. levels of analysis

Guidance: level 1

:: Marketing ::

_____ comes from the Latin neg and otsia referring to businessmen who, unlike the patricians, had no leisure time in their industriousness; it held the meaning of business until the 17th century when it took on the diplomatic connotation as a dialogue between two or more people or parties intended to reach a beneficial outcome over one or more issues where a conflict exists with respect to at least one of these issues. Thus, _____ is a process of combining divergent positions into a joint agreement under a decision rule of unanimity.

Exam Probability: **Low**

26. *Answer choices:*
(see index for correct answer)

- a. Accreditation in Public Relations
- b. Configurator
- c. Negotiation
- d. Price war

Guidance: level 1

:: Data ::

Data has two ways of being created or generated. The first is what is called `captured data`, and is found through purposeful investigation or analysis. The second is called `exhaust data`, and is gathered usually by machines or terminals as a secondary function. For example, cash registers, smartphones, and speedometers serve a main function but may collect data as a secondary task. Exhaustive data is usually too large or of little use to process and becomes `transient` or thrown away.

Exam Probability: **High**

27. *Answer choices:*
(see index for correct answer)

- a. Data acquisition
- b. QUADRIGRAM
- c. Primary data
- d. Raw data

Guidance: level 1

:: Information technology ::

_____ is the use of computers to store, retrieve, transmit, and manipulate data, or information, often in the context of a business or other enterprise. IT is considered to be a subset of information and communications technology . An _____ system is generally an information system, a communications system or, more specifically speaking, a computer system – including all hardware, software and peripheral equipment – operated by a limited group of users.

Exam Probability: **High**

28. *Answer choices:*
<small>(see index for correct answer)</small>

- a. Mobile file management
- b. Computer surveillance in the workplace
- c. Information technology
- d. MobilEcho

Guidance: level 1

:: Monopoly (economics) ::

A _____ exists when a specific person or enterprise is the only supplier of a particular commodity. This contrasts with a monopsony which relates to a single entity`s control of a market to purchase a good or service, and with oligopoly which consists of a few sellers dominating a market. Monopolies are thus characterized by a lack of economic competition to produce the good or service, a lack of viable substitute goods, and the possibility of a high _____ price well above the seller`s marginal cost that leads to a high _____ profit. The verb monopolise or monopolize refers to the process by which a company gains the ability to raise prices or exclude competitors. In economics, a _____ is a single seller. In law, a _____ is a business entity that has significant market power, that is, the power to charge overly high prices. Although monopolies may be big businesses, size is not a characteristic of a _____ . A small business may still have the power to raise prices in a small industry .

Exam Probability: **Low**

29. *Answer choices:*

(see index for correct answer)

- a. Regulatory economics
- b. Practice of law
- c. Monopoly
- d. State monopoly capitalism

Guidance: level 1

:: Management ::

In economics and marketing, _____ is the process of distinguishing a product or service from others, to make it more attractive to a particular target market. This involves differentiating it from competitors' products as well as a firm's own products. The concept was proposed by Edward Chamberlin in his 1933 The Theory of Monopolistic Competition.

Exam Probability: **High**

30. *Answer choices:*

(see index for correct answer)

- a. Adhocracy
- b. Product differentiation
- c. Productive efficiency
- d. Opera management

Guidance: level 1

:: ::

An _____ is the production of goods or related services within an economy. The major source of revenue of a group or company is the indicator of its relevant _____ . When a large group has multiple sources of revenue generation, it is considered to be working in different industries. Manufacturing _____ became a key sector of production and labour in European and North American countries during the Industrial Revolution, upsetting previous mercantile and feudal economies. This came through many successive rapid advances in technology, such as the production of steel and coal.

Exam Probability: **Low**

31. *Answer choices:*

(see index for correct answer)

- a. Industry
- b. cultural
- c. interpersonal communication
- d. levels of analysis

Guidance: level 1

:: Marketing ::

A _____ is a group of customers within a business's serviceable available market at which a business aims its marketing efforts and resources. A _____ is a subset of the total market for a product or service. The _____ typically consists of consumers who exhibit similar characteristics and are considered most likely to buy a business's market offerings or are likely to be the most profitable segments for the business to service.

Exam Probability: **Low**

32. *Answer choices:*

(see index for correct answer)

- a. Digital omnivore
- b. Product naming convention
- c. Engagement marketing
- d. Gatefold

Guidance: level 1

:: Monopoly (economics) ::

A _____ is a form of intellectual property that gives its owner the legal right to exclude others from making, using, selling, and importing an invention for a limited period of years, in exchange for publishing an enabling public disclosure of the invention. In most countries _____ rights fall under civil law and the _____ holder needs to sue someone infringing the _____ in order to enforce his or her rights. In some industries _____ s are an essential form of competitive advantage; in others they are irrelevant.

Exam Probability: **High**

33. *Answer choices:*

(see index for correct answer)

- a. Patent
- b. Demonopolization
- c. Statute of Monopolies
- d. Tesco Town

Guidance: level 1

:: Investment ::

In finance, the benefit from an _____ is called a return. The return may consist of a gain realised from the sale of property or an _____, unrealised capital appreciation, or _____ income such as dividends, interest, rental income etc., or a combination of capital gain and income. The return may also include currency gains or losses due to changes in foreign currency exchange rates.

Exam Probability: **High**

34. *Answer choices:*

(see index for correct answer)

- a. Psychology of previous investment
- b. Advocis
- c. Share Incentive Plan
- d. Fund platform

Guidance: level 1

:: Competition (economics) ::

_____ arises whenever at least two parties strive for a goal which cannot be shared: where one's gain is the other's loss.

Exam Probability: **Low**

35. *Answer choices:*

(see index for correct answer)

- a. Competition
- b. Currency competition
- c. Level playing field
- d. Economic forces

Guidance: level 1

:: ::

A _____ is a person who trades in commodities produced by other people. Historically, a _____ is anyone who is involved in business or trade. _____ s have operated for as long as industry, commerce, and trade have existed. During the 16th-century, in Europe, two different terms for _____ s emerged: One term, meerseniers, described local traders such as bakers, grocers, etc.; while a new term, koopman (Dutch: koopman, described _____ s who operated on a global stage, importing and exporting goods over vast distances, and offering added-value services such as credit and finance.

Exam Probability: **Low**

36. *Answer choices:*

(see index for correct answer)

- a. functional perspective
- b. deep-level diversity
- c. Sarbanes-Oxley act of 2002
- d. Merchant

Guidance: level 1

:: ::

In communications and information processing, _____ is a system of rules to convert information—such as a letter, word, sound, image, or gesture—into another form or representation, sometimes shortened or secret, for communication through a communication channel or storage in a storage medium. An early example is the invention of language, which enabled a person, through speech, to communicate what they saw, heard, felt, or thought to others. But speech limits the range of communication to the distance a voice can carry, and limits the audience to those present when the speech is uttered. The invention of writing, which converted spoken language into visual symbols, extended the range of communication across space and time.

Exam Probability: **Low**

37. *Answer choices:*

(see index for correct answer)

- a. levels of analysis
- b. imperative
- c. Code
- d. co-culture

Guidance: level 1

:: Marketing ::

_____ is a pricing strategy where the price of a product is initially set low to rapidly reach a wide fraction of the market and initiate word of mouth. The strategy works on the expectation that customers will switch to the new brand because of the lower price. _____ is most commonly associated with marketing objectives of enlarging market share and exploiting economies of scale or experience.

Exam Probability: **High**

38. *Answer choices:*
(see index for correct answer)

- a. Lead generation
- b. Email production
- c. Promo
- d. Penetration pricing

Guidance: level 1

:: Business models ::

A _____, _____ company or daughter company is a company that is owned or controlled by another company, which is called the parent company, parent, or holding company. The _____ can be a company, corporation, or limited liability company. In some cases it is a government or state-owned enterprise. In some cases, particularly in the music and book publishing industries, subsidiaries are referred to as imprints.

Exam Probability: **Medium**

39. *Answer choices:*
(see index for correct answer)

- a. Business model pattern
- b. Subsidiary
- c. Defensive patent aggregation

- d. Micro-enterprise

Guidance: level 1

:: ::

In _____ relations and communication science, _____ s are groups of individual people, and the _____ is the totality of such groupings. This is a different concept to the sociological concept of the Öffentlichkeit or _____ sphere. The concept of a _____ has also been defined in political science, psychology, marketing, and advertising. In _____ relations and communication science, it is one of the more ambiguous concepts in the field. Although it has definitions in the theory of the field that have been formulated from the early 20th century onwards, it has suffered in more recent years from being blurred, as a result of conflation of the idea of a _____ with the notions of audience, market segment, community, constituency, and stakeholder.

Exam Probability: **Medium**

40. *Answer choices:*
(see index for correct answer)

- a. process perspective
- b. Public
- c. corporate values
- d. Sarbanes-Oxley act of 2002

Guidance: level 1

:: ::

In the broadest sense, _____ is any practice which contributes to the sale of products to a retail consumer. At a retail in-store level, _____ refers to the variety of products available for sale and the display of those products in such a way that it stimulates interest and entices customers to make a purchase.

Exam Probability: **Low**

41. *Answer choices:*
(see index for correct answer)

- a. interpersonal communication
- b. Merchandising
- c. personal values
- d. cultural

Guidance: level 1

:: ::

A _____ is a professional who provides expert advice in a particular area such as security, management, education, accountancy, law, human resources, marketing, finance, engineering, science or any of many other specialized fields.

Exam Probability: **High**

42. *Answer choices:*

(see index for correct answer)

- a. surface-level diversity
- b. similarity-attraction theory
- c. hierarchical
- d. levels of analysis

Guidance: level 1

:: Direct selling ::

_____ consists of two main business models: single-level marketing, in which a direct seller makes money by buying products from a parent organization and selling them directly to customers, and multi-level marketing, in which the direct seller may earn money from both direct sales to customers and by sponsoring new direct sellers and potentially earning a commission from their efforts.

Exam Probability: **High**

43. *Answer choices:*

(see index for correct answer)

- a. Direct Selling News
- b. The Longaberger Company
- c. Direct Selling Association
- d. Direct selling

Guidance: level 1

:: Project management ::

Contemporary business and science treat as a _____ any undertaking, carried out individually or collaboratively and possibly involving research or design, that is carefully planned to achieve a particular aim.

Exam Probability: **Medium**

44. *Answer choices:*
(see index for correct answer)

- a. Critical path drag
- b. Akihabara syndrome
- c. Project
- d. Project network

Guidance: level 1

:: Social psychology ::

_____ s is a qualitative methodology used to describe consumers on psychological attributes. _____ s have been applied to the study of personality, values, opinions, attitudes, interests, and lifestyles. While _____ s are often equated with lifestyle research, it has been argued that _____ s should apply to the study of cognitive attributes such as attitudes, interests, opinions, and beliefs while lifestyle should apply to the study of overt behavior. Because this area of research focuses on activities, interests, and opinions, _____ factors are sometimes abbreviated to `AIO variables`.

Exam Probability: **High**

45. *Answer choices:*
(see index for correct answer)

- a. Prosocial
- b. Psychographic
- c. Mutual engagement
- d. Social penetration

Guidance: level 1

:: Stock market ::

The _____ of a corporation is all of the shares into which ownership of the corporation is divided. In American English, the shares are commonly known as "_____ s". A single share of the _____ represents fractional ownership of the corporation in proportion to the total number of shares. This typically entitles the _____ holder to that fraction of the company's earnings, proceeds from liquidation of assets , or voting power, often dividing these up in proportion to the amount of money each _____ holder has invested. Not all _____ is necessarily equal, as certain classes of _____ may be issued for example without voting rights, with enhanced voting rights, or with a certain priority to receive profits or liquidation proceeds before or after other classes of shareholders.

Exam Probability: **High**

46. *Answer choices:*
(see index for correct answer)

- a. Indirect finance
- b. Small-order execution system
- c. Direct participation program
- d. Direct public offering

Guidance: level 1

:: ::

_____ or commercialisation is the process of introducing a new product or production method into commerce—making it available on the market. The term often connotes especially entry into the mass market , but it also includes a move from the laboratory into commerce. Many technologies begin in a research and development laboratory or in an inventor's workshop and may not be practical for commercial use in their infancy . The "development" segment of the "research and development" spectrum requires time and money as systems are engineered with a view to making the product or method a paying commercial proposition. The product launch of a new product is the final stage of new product development - at this point advertising, sales promotion, and other marketing efforts encourage commercial adoption of the product or method. Beyond _____ can lie consumerization .

Exam Probability: **Medium**

47. *Answer choices:*

(see index for correct answer)

- a. hierarchical perspective
- b. open system
- c. cultural
- d. Commercialization

Guidance: level 1

:: Behaviorism ::

In behavioral psychology, _____ is a consequence applied that will strengthen an organism's future behavior whenever that behavior is preceded by a specific antecedent stimulus. This strengthening effect may be measured as a higher frequency of behavior, longer duration, greater magnitude, or shorter latency. There are two types of _____, known as positive _____ and negative _____; positive is where by a reward is offered on expression of the wanted behaviour and negative is taking away an undesirable element in the persons environment whenever the desired behaviour is achieved.

Exam Probability: **Low**

48. *Answer choices:*

(see index for correct answer)

- a. contingency management
- b. social facilitation
- c. chaining
- d. Systematic desensitization

Guidance: level 1

:: ::

_____ Motor Company is an American multinational automaker that has its main headquarter in Dearborn, Michigan, a suburb of Detroit. It was founded by Henry _____ and incorporated on June 16, 1903. The company sells automobiles and commercial vehicles under the _____ brand and most luxury cars under the Lincoln brand. _____ also owns Brazilian SUV manufacturer Troller, an 8% stake in Aston Martin of the United Kingdom and a 32% stake in Jiangling Motors. It also has joint-ventures in China , Taiwan , Thailand , Turkey , and Russia . The company is listed on the New York Stock Exchange and is controlled by the _____ family; they have minority ownership but the majority of the voting power.

Exam Probability: **Medium**

49. *Answer choices:*

(see index for correct answer)

- a. cultural
- b. Ford
- c. hierarchical perspective
- d. surface-level diversity

Guidance: level 1

:: ::

_____ is the practice of deliberately managing the spread of information between an individual or an organization and the public. _____ may include an organization or individual gaining exposure to their audiences using topics of public interest and news items that do not require direct payment. This differentiates it from advertising as a form of marketing communications. _____ is the idea of creating coverage for clients for free, rather than marketing or advertising. But now, advertising is also a part of greater PR Activities. An example of good _____ would be generating an article featuring a client, rather than paying for the client to be advertised next to the article. The aim of _____ is to inform the public, prospective customers, investors, partners, employees, and other stakeholders and ultimately persuade them to maintain a positive or favorable view about the organization, its leadership, products, or political decisions. _____ professionals typically work for PR and marketing firms, businesses and companies, government, and public officials as PIOs and nongovernmental organizations, and nonprofit organizations. Jobs central to _____ include account coordinator, account executive, account supervisor, and media relations manager.

Exam Probability: **Low**

50. *Answer choices:*

(see index for correct answer)

- a. Character
- b. Sarbanes-Oxley act of 2002
- c. levels of analysis
- d. hierarchical

Guidance: level 1

:: Production economics ::

In microeconomics, _____ are the cost advantages that enterprises obtain due to their scale of operation, with cost per unit of output decreasing with increasing scale.

Exam Probability: **Low**

51. *Answer choices:*

(see index for correct answer)

- a. Economies of scale
- b. Producer's risk
- c. short run
- d. Value and Capital

Guidance: level 1

:: Brokered programming ::

An _____ is a form of television commercial, which generally includes a toll-free telephone number or website. Most often used as a form of direct response television, long-form _____ s are typically 28:30 or 58:30 minutes in length. _____ s are also known as paid programming. This phenomenon started in the United States, where _____ s were typically shown overnight, outside peak prime time hours for commercial broadcasters. Some television stations chose to air _____ s as an alternative to the former practice of signing off. Some channels air _____ s 24 hours. Some stations also choose to air _____ s during the daytime hours mostly on weekends to fill in for unscheduled network or syndicated programming. By 2009, most _____ spending in the U.S. occurred during the early morning, daytime and evening hours, or in the afternoon. Stations in most countries around the world have instituted similar media structures. The _____ industry is worth over $200 billion.

Exam Probability: **Low**

52. *Answer choices:*
(see index for correct answer)

- a. Leased access
- b. Brokered programming
- c. One Magnificent Morning
- d. Infomercial

Guidance: level 1

:: Project management ::

A _____ is a source or supply from which a benefit is produced and it has some utility. _____ s can broadly be classified upon their availability—they are classified into renewable and non-renewable _____ s.Examples of non renewable _____ s are coal ,crude oil natural gas nuclear energy etc. Examples of renewable _____ s are air,water,wind,solar energy etc. They can also be classified as actual and potential on the basis of level of development and use, on the basis of origin they can be classified as biotic and abiotic, and on the basis of their distribution, as ubiquitous and localized . An item becomes a _____ with time and developing technology. Typically, _____ s are materials, energy, services, staff, knowledge, or other assets that are transformed to produce benefit and in the process may be consumed or made unavailable. Benefits of _____ utilization may include increased wealth, proper functioning of a system, or enhanced well-being. From a human perspective a natural _____ is anything obtained from the environment to satisfy human needs and wants. From a broader biological or ecological perspective a _____ satisfies the needs of a living organism .

Exam Probability: **Medium**

53. *Answer choices:*

(see index for correct answer)

- a. The Goal
- b. Organizational project management
- c. Resource
- d. SQEP

Guidance: level 1

:: Consumer behaviour ::

_____ refers to the ability of a company or product to retain its customers over some specified period. High _____ means customers of the product or business tend to return to, continue to buy or in some other way not defect to another product or business, or to non-use entirely. Selling organizations generally attempt to reduce customer defections. _____ starts with the first contact an organization has with a customer and continues throughout the entire lifetime of a relationship and successful retention efforts take this entire lifecycle into account. A company's ability to attract and retain new customers is related not only to its product or services, but also to the way it services its existing customers, the value the customers actually generate as a result of utilizing the solutions, and the reputation it creates within and across the marketplace.

Exam Probability: **Medium**

54. *Answer choices:*

(see index for correct answer)

- a. Angel and demon customers
- b. Homo consumericus
- c. Customer retention
- d. Behavioral clustering

Guidance: level 1

:: Marketing ::

A _____ is something that is necessary for an organism to live a healthy life. _____ s are distinguished from wants in that, in the case of a _____, a deficiency causes a clear adverse outcome: a dysfunction or death. In other words, a _____ is something required for a safe, stable and healthy life while a want is a desire, wish or aspiration. When _____ s or wants are backed by purchasing power, they have the potential to become economic demands.

Exam Probability: **High**

55. *Answer choices:*

(see index for correct answer)

- a. European Information Technology Observatory
- b. Boston matrix
- c. Marketing activation

- d. Earned media

Guidance: level 1

:: ::

In marketing, a _____ is a ticket or document that can be redeemed for a financial discount or rebate when purchasing a product.

Exam Probability: **Low**

56. *Answer choices:*
(see index for correct answer)

- a. open system
- b. deep-level diversity
- c. Sarbanes-Oxley act of 2002
- d. Coupon

Guidance: level 1

:: Commercial item transport and distribution ::

Wholesaling or distributing is the sale of goods or merchandise to retailers; to industrial, commercial, institutional, or other professional business users; or to other _____ rs and related subordinated services. In general, it is the sale of goods to anyone other than a standard consumer.

Exam Probability: **Medium**

57. *Answer choices:*
(see index for correct answer)

- a. Break bulk cargo
- b. International Road Transport Union
- c. Haulage
- d. Wholesale

Guidance: level 1

:: Management ::

In business, a _____ is the attribute that allows an organization to outperform its competitors. A _____ may include access to natural resources, such as high-grade ores or a low-cost power source, highly skilled labor, geographic location, high entry barriers, and access to new technology.

Exam Probability: **High**

58. *Answer choices:*

(see index for correct answer)

- a. Managerial hubris
- b. Corporate foresight
- c. Scrum
- d. Local management board

Guidance: level 1

:: Contract law ::

In contract law, a _____ is a promise which is not a condition of the contract or an innominate term: it is a term "not going to the root of the contract", and which only entitles the innocent party to damages if it is breached: i.e. the _____ is not true or the defaulting party does not perform the contract in accordance with the terms of the _____ . A _____ is not guarantee. It is a mere promise. It may be enforced if it is breached by an award for the legal remedy of damages.

Exam Probability: **High**

59. *Answer choices:*

(see index for correct answer)

- a. Collateral assurance
- b. Neo-classical contract
- c. Warranty
- d. The Death of Contract

Guidance: level 1

Manufacturing

Manufacturing is the production of merchandise for use or sale using labor and machines, tools, chemical and biological processing, or formulation. The term may refer to a range of human activity, from handicraft to high tech, but is most commonly applied to industrial design , in which raw materials are transformed into finished goods on a large scale. Such finished goods may be sold to other manufacturers for the production of other, more complex products, such as aircraft, household appliances, furniture, sports equipment or automobiles, or sold to wholesalers, who in turn sell them to retailers, who then sell them to end users and consumers.

:: Industries ::

The _____ comprises the companies that produce industrial chemicals. Central to the modern world economy, it converts raw materials into more than 70,000 different products. The plastics industry contains some overlap, as most chemical companies produce plastic as well as other chemicals.

Exam Probability: **Medium**

1. *Answer choices:*
(see index for correct answer)

- a. Chemical industry
- b. Tobacco industry
- c. Software industry
- d. Arms industry

Guidance: level 1

:: Costs ::

The _____ is computed by dividing the total cost of goods available for sale by the total units available for sale. This gives a weighted-average unit cost that is applied to the units in the ending inventory.

Exam Probability: **Low**

2. *Answer choices:*
(see index for correct answer)

- a. Khozraschyot
- b. Total cost of acquisition
- c. Average cost
- d. Sliding scale

Guidance: level 1

:: Quality assurance ::

Organizations that issue credentials or certify third parties against official standards are themselves formally accredited by _____ bodies ; hence they are sometimes known as "accredited certification bodies". The _____ process ensures that their certification practices are acceptable, typically meaning that they are competent to test and certify third parties, behave ethically and employ suitable quality assurance.

Exam Probability: **High**

3. *Answer choices:*
(see index for correct answer)

- a. Strengthening the reporting of observational studies in epidemiology
- b. Accreditation
- c. Community Health Accreditation Program
- d. Trent Accreditation Scheme

Guidance: level 1

:: Packaging ::

In work place, _____ or job _____ means good ranking with the hypothesized conception of requirements of a role. There are two types of job _____ s: contextual and task. Task _____ is related to cognitive ability while contextual _____ is dependent upon personality. Task _____ are behavioral roles that are recognized in job descriptions and by remuneration systems, they are directly related to organizational _____ , whereas, contextual _____ are value based and additional behavioral roles that are not recognized in job descriptions and covered by compensation; they are extra roles that are indirectly related to organizational _____ . Citizenship _____ like contextual _____ means a set of individual activity/contribution that supports the organizational culture.

Exam Probability: **Low**

4. *Answer choices:*
(see index for correct answer)

- a. Punnet
- b. Performance
- c. Tetra Brik
- d. Amaray case

Guidance: level 1

:: Information technology management ::

_____ is a collective term for all approaches to prepare, support and help individuals, teams, and organizations in making organizational change. The most common change drivers include: technological evolution, process reviews, crisis, and consumer habit changes; pressure from new business entrants, acquisitions, mergers, and organizational restructuring. It includes methods that redirect or redefine the use of resources, business process, budget allocations, or other modes of operation that significantly change a company or organization. Organizational _____ considers the full organization and what needs to change, while _____ may be used solely to refer to how people and teams are affected by such organizational transition. It deals with many different disciplines, from behavioral and social sciences to information technology and business solutions.

Exam Probability: **Low**

5. *Answer choices:*
(see index for correct answer)

- a. Global Information Governance Day
- b. Change management
- c. Storage hypervisor
- d. ServiceNow

Guidance: level 1

:: Information systems ::

_____ is the process of creating, sharing, using and managing the knowledge and information of an organisation. It refers to a multidisciplinary approach to achieving organisational objectives by making the best use of knowledge.

Exam Probability: **Medium**

6. *Answer choices:*
(see index for correct answer)

- a. Railway costing
- b. Knowledge management
- c. Notification system
- d. Master of Business Systems

Guidance: level 1

:: Process management ::

A _____ is a diagram commonly used in chemical and process engineering to indicate the general flow of plant processes and equipment. The PFD displays the relationship between major equipment of a plant facility and does not show minor details such as piping details and designations. Another commonly used term for a PFD is a flowsheet.

Exam Probability: **Low**

7. *Answer choices:*
(see index for correct answer)

- a. Business triage
- b. Throughput
- c. Planning horizon
- d. Process specification

Guidance: level 1

:: Project management ::

In economics, _____ is the assignment of available resources to various uses. In the context of an entire economy, resources can be allocated by various means, such as markets or central planning.

Exam Probability: **Medium**

8. *Answer choices:*

(see index for correct answer)

- a. Master of Science in Project Management
- b. Resource allocation
- c. Theory Z
- d. Code name

Guidance: level 1

:: Business planning ::

_____ is a critical component to the successful delivery of any project, programme or activity. A stakeholder is any individual, group or organization that can affect, be affected by, or perceive itself to be affected by a programme.

Exam Probability: **High**

9. *Answer choices:*

(see index for correct answer)

- a. Business war games
- b. Stakeholder management
- c. Gap analysis
- d. Customer Demand Planning

Guidance: level 1

:: Production economics ::

_____ is the joint use of a resource or space. It is also the process of dividing and distributing. In its narrow sense, it refers to joint or alternating use of inherently finite goods, such as a common pasture or a shared residence. Still more loosely, "_____" can actually mean giving something as an outright gift: for example, to "share" one's food really means to give some of it as a gift. _____ is a basic component of human interaction, and is responsible for strengthening social ties and ensuring a person's well-being.

Exam Probability: **Medium**

10. *Answer choices:*

(see index for correct answer)

- a. Marginal cost
- b. Robinson Crusoe economy
- c. Marginal cost of capital schedule
- d. Learning-by-doing

Guidance: level 1

:: Distribution, retailing, and wholesaling ::

The _____ is a distribution channel phenomenon in which forecasts yield supply chain inefficiencies. It refers to increasing swings in inventory in response to shifts in customer demand as one moves further up the supply chain. The concept first appeared in Jay Forrester's Industrial Dynamics and thus it is also known as the Forrester effect. The _____ was named for the way the amplitude of a whip increases down its length. The further from the originating signal, the greater the distortion of the wave pattern. In a similar manner, forecast accuracy decreases as one moves upstream along the supply chain. For example, many consumer goods have fairly consistent consumption at retail but this signal becomes more chaotic and unpredictable as the focus moves away from consumer purchasing behavior.

Exam Probability: **Medium**

11. *Answer choices:*

(see index for correct answer)

- a. Cycle count
- b. Demand modeling
- c. Distribution center management system

- d. Bullwhip effect

Guidance: level 1

:: Quality ::

The _____ , formerly the _____ Control , is a knowledge-based global community of quality professionals, with nearly 80,000 members dedicated to promoting and advancing quality tools, principles, and practices in their workplaces and communities.

Exam Probability: **Low**

12. *Answer choices:*

(see index for correct answer)

- a. Root cause analysis
- b. Customer Service Excellence
- c. American Society for Quality
- d. Dualistic Petri nets

Guidance: level 1

:: Inventory ::

The _____ is the level of inventory which triggers an action to replenish that particular inventory stock. It is a minimum amount of an item which a firm holds in stock, such that, when stock falls to this amount, the item must be reordered. It is normally calculated as the forecast usage during the replenishment lead time plus safety stock. In the EOQ model, it was assumed that there is no time lag between ordering and procuring of materials. Therefore the _____ for replenishing the stocks occurs at that level when the inventory level drops to zero and because instant delivery by suppliers, the stock level bounce back.

Exam Probability: **Medium**

13. *Answer choices:*

(see index for correct answer)

- a. Phantom inventory
- b. Reorder point
- c. Perpetual inventory
- d. Stock demands

Guidance: level 1

:: Management ::

_____ is the process of thinking about the activities required to achieve a desired goal. It is the first and foremost activity to achieve desired results. It involves the creation and maintenance of a plan, such as psychological aspects that require conceptual skills. There are even a couple of tests to measure someone's capability of _____ well. As such, _____ is a fundamental property of intelligent behavior. An important further meaning, often just called "_____" is the legal context of permitted building developments.

Exam Probability: **Low**

14. *Answer choices:*
(see index for correct answer)

- a. Planning
- b. Quick response manufacturing
- c. Meeting system
- d. Corporate recovery

Guidance: level 1

:: Manufacturing ::

_____ or lean production, often simply "lean", is a systematic method for the minimization of waste within a manufacturing system without sacrificing productivity, which can cause problems. Lean also takes into account waste created through overburden and waste created through unevenness in work loads. Working from the perspective of the client who consumes a product or service, "value" is any action or process that a customer would be willing to pay for.

Exam Probability: **Low**

15. *Answer choices:*
(see index for correct answer)

- a. Nanofoundry
- b. Ashery
- c. Form, fit and function
- d. Lean manufacturing

Guidance: level 1

:: Industrial engineering ::

_____ , in its contemporary conceptualisation, is a comparison of perceived expectations of a service with perceived performance, giving rise to the equation SQ=P-E. This conceptualistion of _____ has its origins in the expectancy-disconfirmation paradigm.

Exam Probability: **High**

16. *Answer choices:*

(see index for correct answer)

- a. Needs analysis
- b. Flow process chart
- c. Service quality
- d. Continuous emissions monitoring system

Guidance: level 1

:: Industrial processes ::

A _____ is a device used for high-temperature heating. The name derives from Latin word fornax, which means oven. The heat energy to fuel a _____ may be supplied directly by fuel combustion, by electricity such as the electric arc _____ , or through induction heating in induction _____ s.

Exam Probability: **Medium**

17. *Answer choices:*

(see index for correct answer)

- a. Crystal bar process
- b. Mass finishing
- c. Furnace
- d. Process chemistry

Guidance: level 1

:: Risk analysis ::

Supply-chain risk management is "the implementation of strategies to manage both everyday and exceptional risks along the supply chain based on continuous risk assessment with the objective of reducing vulnerability and ensuring continuity".

Exam Probability: **Medium**

18. *Answer choices:*
(see index for correct answer)

- a. Supply chain risk management
- b. Criticality index
- c. Qualitative risk analysis
- d. Collateral consequence

Guidance: level 1

:: Production and manufacturing ::

_____ is the production under license of technology developed elsewhere. It is an especially prominent commercial practice in developing nations, which often approach _____ as a starting point for indigenous industrial development.

Exam Probability: **Low**

19. *Answer choices:*
(see index for correct answer)

- a. Highly accelerated stress audit
- b. WorkPLAN
- c. Remanufacturing
- d. Licensed production

Guidance: level 1

:: Mereology ::

_____ , in the abstract, is what belongs to or with something, whether as an attribute or as a component of said thing. In the context of this article, it is one or more components , whether physical or incorporeal, of a person's estate; or so belonging to, as in being owned by, a person or jointly a group of people or a legal entity like a corporation or even a society. Depending on the nature of the _____ , an owner of _____ has the right to consume, alter, share, redefine, rent, mortgage, pawn, sell, exchange, transfer, give away or destroy it, or to exclude others from doing these things, as well as to perhaps abandon it; whereas regardless of the nature of the _____ , the owner thereof has the right to properly use it , or at the very least exclusively keep it.

Exam Probability: **Low**

20. *Answer choices:*

(see index for correct answer)

- a. Mereological essentialism
- b. Mereological nihilism
- c. Simple
- d. Mereology

Guidance: level 1

:: Management ::

_____ , also known as natural process limits, are horizontal lines drawn on a statistical process control chart, usually at a distance of ±3 standard deviations of the plotted statistic from the statistic's mean.

Exam Probability: **Medium**

21. *Answer choices:*

(see index for correct answer)

- a. Productive efficiency
- b. Nonconformity
- c. Control limits
- d. Millennium software

Guidance: level 1

:: Industrial organization ::

In economics, specifically general equilibrium theory, a perfect market is defined by several idealizing conditions, collectively called _____ . In theoretical models where conditions of _____ hold, it has been theoretically demonstrated that a market will reach an equilibrium in which the quantity supplied for every product or service, including labor, equals the quantity demanded at the current price. This equilibrium would be a Pareto optimum.

Exam Probability: **High**

22. *Answer choices:*
(see index for correct answer)

- a. Quaternary sector of the economy
- b. Perfect competition
- c. Worldwide Responsible Accredited Production
- d. Organizational studies

Guidance: level 1

:: Production and manufacturing ::

_____ is a concept in purchasing and project management for securing the quality and timely delivery of goods and components.

Exam Probability: **Medium**

23. *Answer choices:*
(see index for correct answer)

- a. Expediting
- b. Equipment service management and rental
- c. Digital materialization
- d. Zero Defects

Guidance: level 1

:: Production and manufacturing ::

_____ consists of organization-wide efforts to "install and make permanent climate where employees continuously improve their ability to provide on demand products and services that customers will find of particular value." "Total" emphasizes that departments in addition to production are obligated to improve their operations; "management" emphasizes that executives are obligated to actively manage quality through funding, training, staffing, and goal setting. While there is no widely agreed-upon approach, TQM efforts typically draw heavily on the previously developed tools and techniques of quality control. TQM enjoyed widespread attention during the late 1980s and early 1990s before being overshadowed by ISO 9000, Lean manufacturing, and Six Sigma.

Exam Probability: **High**

24. *Answer choices:*
(see index for correct answer)

- a. Engineering validation test
- b. Industrial engineering
- c. Foundation Fieldbus H1
- d. Report generator

Guidance: level 1

:: Data interchange standards ::

_____ is the concept of businesses electronically communicating information that was traditionally communicated on paper, such as purchase orders and invoices. Technical standards for EDI exist to facilitate parties transacting such instruments without having to make special arrangements.

Exam Probability: **Medium**

25. *Answer choices:*
(see index for correct answer)

- a. Electronic data interchange
- b. Uniform Communication Standard
- c. Domain Application Protocol
- d. Data Interchange Standards Association

Guidance: level 1

:: Natural resources ::

_____s are resources that exist without actions of humankind. This includes all valued characteristics such as magnetic, gravitational, electrical properties and forces etc. On Earth it includes sunlight, atmosphere, water, land along with all vegetation, crops and animal life that naturally subsists upon or within the heretofore identified characteristics and substances.

Exam Probability: **High**

26. *Answer choices:*

(see index for correct answer)

- a. Natural resource
- b. Land cover
- c. Dryland salinity
- d. Consolidated Natural Resources Act of 2008

Guidance: level 1

:: Infographics ::

The _____ is a form used to collect data in real time at the location where the data is generated. The data it captures can be quantitative or qualitative. When the information is quantitative, the _____ is sometimes called a tally sheet.

Exam Probability: **Medium**

27. *Answer choices:*

(see index for correct answer)

- a. Archaeological illustration
- b. Nautical chart
- c. Staircase model
- d. Harvey Balls

Guidance: level 1

:: Chemical reactions ::

A _____ is a process that leads to the chemical transformation of one set of chemical substances to another. Classically, _____ s encompass changes that only involve the positions of electrons in the forming and breaking of chemical bonds between atoms, with no change to the nuclei, and can often be described by a chemical equation. Nuclear chemistry is a sub-discipline of chemistry that involves the _____ s of unstable and radioactive elements where both electronic and nuclear changes can occur.

Exam Probability: **High**

28. *Answer choices:*

(see index for correct answer)

- a. Substrate
- b. Captodative effect
- c. Photoelectrochemical process
- d. Scavenger resin

Guidance: level 1

:: Business process ::

A committee is a body of one or more persons that is subordinate to a deliberative assembly. Usually, the assembly sends matters into a committee as a way to explore them more fully than would be possible if the assembly itself were considering them. Committees may have different functions and their type of work differ depending on the type of the organization and its needs.

Exam Probability: **Medium**

29. *Answer choices:*

(see index for correct answer)

- a. Social BPM
- b. Process mining
- c. Software ecosystem
- d. Steering committee

Guidance: level 1

:: Project management ::

A _____ is a team whose members usually belong to different groups, functions and are assigned to activities for the same project. A team can be divided into sub-teams according to need. Usually _____ s are only used for a defined period of time. They are disbanded after the project is deemed complete. Due to the nature of the specific formation and disbandment, _____ s are usually in organizations.

Exam Probability: **High**

30. *Answer choices:*

(see index for correct answer)

- a. Goodwerp
- b. Risk register
- c. TargetProcess
- d. Project team

Guidance: level 1

:: Fault-tolerant computer systems ::

_____ decision-making is a group decision-making process in which group members develop, and agree to support a decision in the best interest of the whole group or common goal. _____ may be defined professionally as an acceptable resolution, one that can be supported, even if not the "favourite" of each individual. It has its origin in the Latin word consensus, which is from consentio meaning literally feel together. It is used to describe both the decision and the process of reaching a decision. _____ decision-making is thus concerned with the process of deliberating and finalizing a decision, and the social, economic, legal, environmental and political effects of applying this process.

Exam Probability: **Medium**

31. *Answer choices:*

(see index for correct answer)

- a. Gbcast
- b. Superstabilization
- c. SpaceWire
- d. Toric code

Guidance: level 1

:: Help desk ::

Data center management is the collection of tasks performed by those responsible for managing ongoing operation of a data center This includes Business service management and planning for the future.

Exam Probability: **Medium**

32. *Answer choices:*

(see index for correct answer)

- a. Virtual help desk
- b. Technical support
- c. OTRS
- d. HEAT

Guidance: level 1

:: Metal heat treatments ::

_____ is a group of industrial and metalworking processes used to alter the physical, and sometimes chemical, properties of a material. The most common application is metallurgical. Heat treatments are also used in the manufacture of many other materials, such as glass. Heat treatment involves the use of heating or chilling, normally to extreme temperatures, to achieve a desired result such as hardening or softening of a material. Heat treatment techniques include annealing, case hardening, precipitation strengthening, tempering, carburizing, normalizing and quenching. It is noteworthy that while the term heat treatment applies only to processes where the heating and cooling are done for the specific purpose of altering properties intentionally, heating and cooling often occur incidentally during other manufacturing processes such as hot forming or welding.

Exam Probability: **High**

33. *Answer choices:*

(see index for correct answer)

- a. Quenching
- b. Hardening
- c. Ferritic nitrocarburizing
- d. Heat treating

Guidance: level 1

:: Production and manufacturing ::

_____ is a set of techniques and tools for process improvement. Though as a shortened form it may be found written as 6S, it should not be confused with the methodology known as 6S.

Exam Probability: **Medium**

34. *Answer choices:*

(see index for correct answer)

- a. Total productive maintenance
- b. Product lifecycle management
- c. Six Sigma
- d. PA512

Guidance: level 1

:: ::

An _____ is, most an organized examination or formal evaluation exercise. In engineering activities _____ involves the measurements, tests, and gauges applied to certain characteristics in regard to an object or activity. The results are usually compared to specified requirements and standards for determining whether the item or activity is in line with these targets, often with a Standard _____ Procedure in place to ensure consistent checking. _____ s are usually non-destructive.

Exam Probability: **High**

35. *Answer choices:*

(see index for correct answer)

- a. cultural
- b. Inspection
- c. Sarbanes-Oxley act of 2002
- d. imperative

Guidance: level 1

:: ::

Catalysis is the process of increasing the rate of a chemical reaction by adding a substance known as a _____ , which is not consumed in the catalyzed reaction and can continue to act repeatedly. Because of this, only very small amounts of _____ are required to alter the reaction rate in principle.

Exam Probability: **Low**

36. *Answer choices:*

(see index for correct answer)

- a. functional perspective
- b. cultural
- c. Character
- d. Catalyst

Guidance: level 1

:: E-commerce ::

_____ is the business-to-business or business-to-consumer or business-to-government purchase and sale of supplies, work, and services through the Internet as well as other information and networking systems, such as electronic data interchange and enterprise resource planning.

Exam Probability: **Low**

37. *Answer choices:*

(see index for correct answer)

- a. Quisk
- b. E-procurement
- c. Network Security Services
- d. MusicPass

Guidance: level 1

:: Manufacturing ::

A _____ is an object used to extend the ability of an individual to modify features of the surrounding environment. Although many animals use simple _____ s, only human beings, whose use of stone _____ s dates back hundreds of millennia, use _____ s to make other _____ s. The set of _____ s needed to perform different tasks that are part of the same activity is called gear or equipment.

Exam Probability: **High**

38. *Answer choices:*

(see index for correct answer)

- a. Tool
- b. Factory tour
- c. Agri-Fab, Inc.
- d. Lean production

Guidance: level 1

:: Lean manufacturing ::

_____ is a scheduling system for lean manufacturing and just-in-time manufacturing. Taiichi Ohno, an industrial engineer at Toyota, developed _____ to improve manufacturing efficiency. _____ is one method to achieve JIT. The system takes its name from the cards that track production within a factory. For many in the automotive sector, _____ is known as the "Toyota nameplate system" and as such the term is not used by some other automakers.

Exam Probability: **Medium**

39. *Answer choices:*

(see index for correct answer)

- a. Overall equipment effectiveness
- b. Kanban
- c. Agent-assisted automation
- d. Lean Six Sigma

Guidance: level 1

:: Project management ::

_____ is a work methodology emphasizing the parallelisation of tasks, which is sometimes called simultaneous engineering or integrated product development using an integrated product team approach. It refers to an approach used in product development in which functions of design engineering, manufacturing engineering, and other functions are integrated to reduce the time required to bring a new product to market.

Exam Probability: **High**

40. *Answer choices:*
(see index for correct answer)

- a. Advanced Integrated Practice
- b. Risk register
- c. Project plan
- d. Concurrent engineering

Guidance: level 1

:: ::

_____ refers to the confirmation of certain characteristics of an object, person, or organization. This confirmation is often, but not always, provided by some form of external review, education, assessment, or audit. Accreditation is a specific organization's process of _____ . According to the National Council on Measurement in Education, a _____ test is a credentialing test used to determine whether individuals are knowledgeable enough in a given occupational area to be labeled "competent to practice" in that area.

Exam Probability: **Medium**

41. *Answer choices:*
(see index for correct answer)

- a. open system
- b. Certification
- c. personal values
- d. similarity-attraction theory

Guidance: level 1

:: Product management ::

_____ s, also known as Shewhart charts or process-behavior charts, are a statistical process control tool used to determine if a manufacturing or business process is in a state of control.

Exam Probability: **Medium**

42. *Answer choices:*
(see index for correct answer)

- a. Trademark look
- b. Mature technology
- c. Whole product
- d. Service life

Guidance: level 1

:: Industrial processes ::

_____ is a technique involving the condensation of vapors and the return of this condensate to the system from which it originated. It is used in industrial and laboratory distillations. It is also used in chemistry to supply energy to reactions over a long period of time.

Exam Probability: **Low**

43. *Answer choices:*
(see index for correct answer)

- a. Die cutting
- b. Textile bleaching
- c. Photonic curing
- d. Reflux

Guidance: level 1

:: Management ::

In organizational studies, _____ is the efficient and effective development of an organization's resources when they are needed. Such resources may include financial resources, inventory, human skills, production resources, or information technology and natural resources.

Exam Probability: **Low**

44. *Answer choices:*

(see index for correct answer)

- a. Bed management
- b. Evidence-based management
- c. Dominant design
- d. Resource management

Guidance: level 1

:: Help desk ::

A high-explosive anti-tank warhead is a type of shaped charge explosive that uses the Munroe effect to penetrate thick tank armor. The warhead functions by having the explosive charge collapse a metal liner inside the warhead into a high-velocity superplastic jet. This superplastic jet is capable of penetrating armor steel to a depth of seven or more times the diameter of the charge but is usually used to immobilize or destroy tanks. Due to the way they work, they do not have to be fired as fast as an armor piercing shell, allowing less recoil. Contrary to a widespread misconception, the jet does not melt its way through armor, as its effect is purely kinetic in nature. The _____ warhead has become less effective against tanks and other armored vehicles due to the use of composite armor, explosive-reactive armor, and active protection systems which destroy the _____ warhead before it hits the tank. Even though _____ rounds are less effective against the heavy armor found on 2010s main battle tanks, _____ warheads remain a threat against less-armored parts of a main battle tank and against lighter armored vehicles or unarmored vehicles and helicopters.

Exam Probability: **Medium**

45. *Answer choices:*

(see index for correct answer)

- a. AetherPal
- b. KnowledgeBase Manager Pro
- c. GLPI
- d. Computer-aided maintenance

Guidance: level 1

:: Quality management ::

_____ ensures that an organization, product or service is consistent. It has four main components: quality planning, quality assurance, quality control and quality improvement. _____ is focused not only on product and service quality, but also on the means to achieve it. _____ , therefore, uses quality assurance and control of processes as well as products to achieve more consistent quality. What a customer wants and is willing to pay for it determines quality. It is written or unwritten commitment to a known or unknown consumer in the market . Thus, quality can be defined as fitness for intended use or, in other words, how well the product performs its intended function

Exam Probability: **Low**

46. *Answer choices:*

(see index for correct answer)

- a. Quality management
- b. ISO 9000
- c. Institute of Standards and Industrial Research of Iran
- d. Allied Quality Assurance Publications

Guidance: level 1

:: Natural materials ::

_____ is a finely-grained natural rock or soil material that combines one or more _____ minerals with possible traces of quartz , metal oxides and organic matter. Geologic _____ deposits are mostly composed of phyllosilicate minerals containing variable amounts of water trapped in the mineral structure. _____ s are plastic due to particle size and geometry as well as water content, and become hard, brittle and non–plastic upon drying or firing. Depending on the soil's content in which it is found, _____ can appear in various colours from white to dull grey or brown to deep orange-red.

Exam Probability: **Low**

47. *Answer choices:*

(see index for correct answer)

- a. Rubble
- b. Trass
- c. Clay
- d. Levant bole

Guidance: level 1

:: Supply chain management terms ::

In business and finance, _____ is a system of organizations, people, activities, information, and resources involved in moving a product or service from supplier to customer. _____ activities involve the transformation of natural resources, raw materials, and components into a finished product that is delivered to the end customer. In sophisticated _____ systems, used products may re-enter the _____ at any point where residual value is recyclable. _____ s link value chains.

Exam Probability: **Low**

48. *Answer choices:*

(see index for correct answer)

- a. Supply-chain management
- b. Consumables
- c. Overstock
- d. Supply chain

Guidance: level 1

:: Data management ::

_____ refers to a data-driven improvement cycle used for improving, optimizing and stabilizing business processes and designs. The _____ improvement cycle is the core tool used to drive Six Sigma projects. However, _____ is not exclusive to Six Sigma and can be used as the framework for other improvement applications.

Exam Probability: **High**

49. *Answer choices:*

(see index for correct answer)

- a. Data profiling
- b. QuickPar
- c. CommVault Systems
- d. Modular serializability

Guidance: level 1

:: Casting (manufacturing) ::

A _____ is a regularity in the world, man-made design, or abstract ideas. As such, the elements of a _____ repeat in a predictable manner. A geometric _____ is a kind of _____ formed of geometric shapes and typically repeated like a wallpaper design.

Exam Probability: **Low**

50. *Answer choices:*

(see index for correct answer)

- a. Permeability
- b. Pattern
- c. Tundish
- d. Entrainment defect

Guidance: level 1

:: Management ::

_____ is a method of quality control which employs statistical methods to monitor and control a process. This helps to ensure that the process operates efficiently, producing more specification-conforming products with less waste . SPC can be applied to any process where the "conforming product" output can be measured. Key tools used in SPC include run charts, control charts, a focus on continuous improvement, and the design of experiments. An example of a process where SPC is applied is manufacturing lines.

Exam Probability: **Medium**

51. *Answer choices:*

(see index for correct answer)

- a. Statistical process control
- b. Decentralized decision-making
- c. Scenario planning
- d. Adhocracy

Guidance: level 1

:: ::

In production, research, retail, and accounting, a _____ is the value of money that has been used up to produce something or deliver a service, and hence is not available for use anymore. In business, the _____ may be one of acquisition, in which case the amount of money expended to acquire it is counted as _____ . In this case, money is the input that is gone in order to acquire the thing. This acquisition _____ may be the sum of the _____ of production as incurred by the original producer, and further _____ s of transaction as incurred by the acquirer over and above the price paid to the producer. Usually, the price also includes a mark-up for profit over the _____ of production.

Exam Probability: **Low**

52. *Answer choices:*
(see index for correct answer)

- a. imperative
- b. empathy
- c. cultural
- d. Cost

Guidance: level 1

:: Management ::

_____ is the identification, evaluation, and prioritization of risks followed by coordinated and economical application of resources to minimize, monitor, and control the probability or impact of unfortunate events or to maximize the realization of opportunities.

Exam Probability: **Medium**

53. *Answer choices:*
(see index for correct answer)

- a. Event management
- b. SimulTrain
- c. Voice of the customer
- d. Communications management

Guidance: level 1

:: Metalworking ::

A _____ is a round object with various uses. It is used in _____ games, where the play of the game follows the state of the _____ as it is hit, kicked or thrown by players. _____ s can also be used for simpler activities, such as catch or juggling. _____ s made from hard-wearing materials are used in engineering applications to provide very low friction bearings, known as _____ bearings. Black-powder weapons use stone and metal _____ s as projectiles.

Exam Probability: **Medium**

54. *Answer choices:*

(see index for correct answer)

- a. Lock-N-Stitch
- b. Slotted angle
- c. Autofrettage
- d. Ball

Guidance: level 1

:: Materials science ::

An _____ is a polymer with viscoelasticity and very weak intermolecular forces, and generally low Young's modulus and high failure strain compared with other materials. The term, a portmanteau of elastic polymer, is often used interchangeably with rubber, although the latter is preferred when referring to vulcanisates. Each of the monomers which link to form the polymer is usually a compound of several elements among carbon, hydrogen, oxygen and silicon. _____ s are amorphous polymers maintained above their glass transition temperature, so that considerable molecular reconformation, without breaking of covalent bonds, is feasible. At ambient temperatures, such rubbers are thus relatively soft and deformable. Their primary uses are for seals, adhesives and molded flexible parts. Application areas for different types of rubber are manifold and cover segments as diverse as tires, soles for shoes, and damping and insulating elements. The importance of these rubbers can be judged from the fact that global revenues are forecast to rise to US$56 billion in 2020.

Exam Probability: **High**

55. *Answer choices:*

(see index for correct answer)

- a. Negative thermal expansion
- b. Microstructure
- c. Elastomer
- d. Damping capacity

Guidance: level 1

:: Computer memory companies ::

_____ Corporation is a Japanese multinational conglomerate headquartered in Tokyo, Japan. Its diversified products and services include information technology and communications equipment and systems, electronic components and materials, power systems, industrial and social infrastructure systems, consumer electronics, household appliances, medical equipment, office equipment, as well as lighting and logistics.

Exam Probability: **Low**

56. *Answer choices:*
(see index for correct answer)

- a. Alliance Semiconductor
- b. Dane-Elec
- c. ASint Technology
- d. Strontium Technology

Guidance: level 1

:: Business ::

The seller, or the provider of the goods or services, completes a sale in response to an acquisition, appropriation, requisition or a direct interaction with the buyer at the point of sale. There is a passing of title of the item, and the settlement of a price, in which agreement is reached on a price for which transfer of ownership of the item will occur. The seller, not the purchaser typically executes the sale and it may be completed prior to the obligation of payment. In the case of indirect interaction, a person who sells goods or service on behalf of the owner is known as a _____ man or _____ woman or _____ person, but this often refers to someone selling goods in a store/shop, in which case other terms are also common, including _____ clerk, shop assistant, and retail clerk.

Exam Probability: **High**

57. *Answer choices:*

(see index for correct answer)

- a. GoCardless
- b. Sales
- c. Distribution
- d. Business directory

Guidance: level 1

:: ::

_____ is a kind of action that occur as two or more objects have an effect upon one another. The idea of a two-way effect is essential in the concept of _____, as opposed to a one-way causal effect. A closely related term is interconnectivity, which deals with the _____ s of _____ s within systems: combinations of many simple _____ s can lead to surprising emergent phenomena. _____ has different tailored meanings in various sciences. Changes can also involve _____ .

Exam Probability: **Low**

58. *Answer choices:*

(see index for correct answer)

- a. process perspective
- b. levels of analysis
- c. open system
- d. Interaction

Guidance: level 1

:: Outsourcing ::

_____ is an institutional procurement process that continuously improves and re-evaluates the purchasing activities of a company. In the services industry, _____ refers to a service solution, sometimes called a strategic partnership, which is specifically customized to meet the client's individual needs. In a production environment, it is often considered one component of supply chain management. Modern supply chain management professionals have placed emphasis on defining the distinct differences between _____ and procurement. Procurement operations support tactical day-to-day transactions such as issuing Purchase Orders to suppliers, whereas _____ represents to strategic planning, supplier development, contract negotiation, supply chain infrastructure, and outsourcing models.

Exam Probability: **Low**

59. *Answer choices:*
(see index for correct answer)

- a. Strategic sourcing
- b. Request for proposal
- c. Pillsbury Winthrop Shaw Pittman
- d. Virtual CFO

Guidance: level 1

Commerce

Commerce relates to "the exchange of goods and services, especially on a large scale." It includes legal, economic, political, social, cultural and technological systems that operate in any country or internationally.

:: Securities (finance) ::

A _____ is a container that is traditionally constructed from stiff fibers, and can be made from a range of materials, including wood splints, runners, and cane. While most _____ s are made from plant materials, other materials such as horsehair, baleen, or metal wire can be used. _____ s are generally woven by hand. Some _____ s are fitted with a lid, while others are left open on top.

Exam Probability: **Low**

1. *Answer choices:*

(see index for correct answer)

- a. Basket
- b. Securities and Exchange Board of India Act, 1992
- c. Book entry
- d. Look-through approach

Guidance: level 1

:: Dot-com bubble ::

_____ is an internet portal launched in 1995 that provides a variety of content including news and weather, a metasearch engine, a web-based email, instant messaging, stock quotes, and a customizable user homepage. It is currently operated by IAC Applications of IAC, and _____ Networks. In the U.S., the main _____ site has long been a personal start page called My _____. _____ also operates an e-mail service, although it is no longer open for new customers.

Exam Probability: **Low**

2. *Answer choices:*

(see index for correct answer)

- a. Irrational exuberance
- b. Excite
- c. @Home Network
- d. Xoom

Guidance: level 1

:: ::

_____ is both a research area and a practical skill encompassing the ability of an individual or organization to "lead" or guide other individuals, teams, or entire organizations. Specialist literature debates various viewpoints, contrasting Eastern and Western approaches to _____, and also United States versus European approaches. U.S. academic environments define _____ as "a process of social influence in which a person can enlist the aid and support of others in the accomplishment of a common task".

Exam Probability: **Low**

3. *Answer choices:*

(see index for correct answer)

- a. functional perspective
- b. co-culture
- c. Leadership
- d. personal values

Guidance: level 1

:: Data interchange standards ::

_____ is the concept of businesses electronically communicating information that was traditionally communicated on paper, such as purchase orders and invoices. Technical standards for EDI exist to facilitate parties transacting such instruments without having to make special arrangements.

Exam Probability: **High**

4. *Answer choices:*

(see index for correct answer)

- a. Domain Application Protocol
- b. Interaction protocol
- c. ASC X12
- d. Common Alerting Protocol

Guidance: level 1

:: Marketing ::

The _____ is a foundation model for businesses. The _____ has been defined as the "set of marketing tools that the firm uses to pursue its marketing objectives in the target market". Thus the _____ refers to four broad levels of marketing decision, namely: product, price, place, and promotion. Marketing practice has been occurring for millennia, but marketing theory emerged in the early twentieth century. The contemporary _____ , or the 4 Ps, which has become the dominant framework for marketing management decisions, was first published in 1960. In services marketing, an extended _____ is used, typically comprising 7 Ps, made up of the original 4 Ps extended by process, people, and physical evidence. Occasionally service marketers will refer to 8 Ps, comprising these 7 Ps plus performance.

Exam Probability: **Medium**

5. *Answer choices:*

(see index for correct answer)

- a. Configurator
- b. Purchase funnel
- c. Product naming convention
- d. Marketing mix

Guidance: level 1

:: Customs duties ::

A _____ is a tax on imports or exports between sovereign states. It is a form of regulation of foreign trade and a policy that taxes foreign products to encourage or safeguard domestic industry. _____ s are the simplest and oldest instrument of trade policy. Traditionally, states have used them as a source of income. Now, they are among the most widely used instruments of protection, along with import and export quotas.

Exam Probability: **Medium**

6. *Answer choices:*

(see index for correct answer)

- a. Russian Customs Tariff
- b. Tariff
- c. Customs area
- d. Wines in bond

Guidance: level 1

:: Payment systems ::

_____ s are part of a payment system issued by financial institutions, such as a bank, to a customer that enables its owner to access the funds in the customer's designated bank accounts, or through a credit account and make payments by electronic funds transfer and access automated teller machines . Such cards are known by a variety of names including bank cards, ATM cards, MAC , client cards, key cards or cash cards.

Exam Probability: **High**

7. *Answer choices:*

(see index for correct answer)

- a. Manual fare collection
- b. Certified check
- c. Cheque truncation system
- d. Payment card

Guidance: level 1

:: Economic globalization ::

_____ is an agreement in which one company hires another company to be responsible for a planned or existing activity that is or could be done internally, and sometimes involves transferring employees and assets from one firm to another.

Exam Probability: **Low**

8. *Answer choices:*

(see index for correct answer)

- a. Outsourcing
- b. reshoring

Guidance: level 1

:: E-commerce ::

_____ is the business-to-business or business-to-consumer or business-to-government purchase and sale of supplies, work, and services through the Internet as well as other information and networking systems, such as electronic data interchange and enterprise resource planning.

Exam Probability: **High**

9. *Answer choices:*

(see index for correct answer)

- a. E-procurement
- b. ROPO
- c. Click farm
- d. Social shopping

Guidance: level 1

:: Management ::

Logistics is generally the detailed organization and implementation of a complex operation. In a general business sense, logistics is the management of the flow of things between the point of origin and the point of consumption in order to meet requirements of customers or corporations. The resources managed in logistics may include tangible goods such as materials, equipment, and supplies, as well as food and other consumable items. The logistics of physical items usually involves the integration of information flow, materials handling, production, packaging, inventory, transportation, warehousing, and often security.

Exam Probability: **High**

10. *Answer choices:*

(see index for correct answer)

- a. Design leadership
- b. Allegiance
- c. Social risk management
- d. Logistics Management

Guidance: level 1

:: Generally Accepted Accounting Principles ::

In accounting, _____ is the income that a business have from its normal business activities, usually from the sale of goods and services to customers. _____ is also referred to as sales or turnover. Some companies receive _____ from interest, royalties, or other fees. _____ may refer to business income in general, or it may refer to the amount, in a monetary unit, earned during a period of time, as in "Last year, Company X had _____ of $42 million". Profits or net income generally imply total _____ minus total expenses in a given period. In accounting, in the balance statement it is a subsection of the Equity section and _____ increases equity, it is often referred to as the "top line" due to its position on the income statement at the very top. This is to be contrasted with the "bottom line" which denotes net income.

Exam Probability: **Medium**

11. *Answer choices:*

(see index for correct answer)

- a. Write-off
- b. Profit
- c. Revenue
- d. Income statement

Guidance: level 1

:: Management accounting ::

_____ , or dollar contribution per unit, is the selling price per unit minus the variable cost per unit. "Contribution" represents the portion of sales revenue that is not consumed by variable costs and so contributes to the coverage of fixed costs. This concept is one of the key building blocks of break-even analysis.

Exam Probability: **High**

12. *Answer choices:*
(see index for correct answer)

- a. Institute of Certified Management Accountants
- b. Direct material price variance
- c. Indirect costs
- d. Contribution margin

Guidance: level 1

:: Management ::

_____ is the identification, evaluation, and prioritization of risks followed by coordinated and economical application of resources to minimize, monitor, and control the probability or impact of unfortunate events or to maximize the realization of opportunities.

Exam Probability: **Medium**

13. *Answer choices:*
(see index for correct answer)

- a. Risk management
- b. Organizational hologram
- c. Information excellence
- d. Supplier relationship management

Guidance: level 1

:: Project management ::

In political science, an _____ is a means by which a petition signed by a certain minimum number of registered voters can force a government to choose to either enact a law or hold a public vote in parliament in what is called indirect _____, or under direct _____, the proposition is immediately put to a plebiscite or referendum, in what is called a Popular initiated Referendum or citizen-initiated referendum).

Exam Probability: **Medium**

14. *Answer choices:*
(see index for correct answer)

- a. Aggregate project plan
- b. Project management triangle
- c. Bill of quantities
- d. Initiative

Guidance: level 1

:: E-commerce ::

E-commerce is the activity of buying or selling of products on online services or over the Internet. _____ draws on technologies such as mobile commerce, electronic funds transfer, supply chain management, Internet marketing, online transaction processing, electronic data interchange, inventory management systems, and automated data collection systems.

Exam Probability: **High**

15. *Answer choices:*
(see index for correct answer)

- a. Electronic commerce
- b. Variable pricing
- c. Online marketplace
- d. Mobimoneybox

Guidance: level 1

:: ::

Competition arises whenever at least two parties strive for a goal which cannot be shared: where one's gain is the other's loss.

Exam Probability: **High**

16. *Answer choices:*

(see index for correct answer)

- a. hierarchical
- b. open system
- c. Competitor
- d. levels of analysis

Guidance: level 1

:: Marketing ::

_____ —an information- and communication-based electronic exchange environment—is a relatively new concept in marketing. Since physical boundaries no longer interfere with buy/sell decisions, the world has grown into several industry specific _____ s which are integration of marketplaces through sophisticated computer and telecommunication technologies. The term _____ was introduced by Jeffrey Rayport and John Sviokla in 1994 in their article "Managing in the _____ " that appeared in Harvard Business Review. In the article the authors distinguished between electronic and conventional markets. In a _____ , information and/or physical goods are exchanged, and transactions take place through computers and networks. These networks consist of blogs, forum threads, and micro-blogging services like Twitter. Businesses and their customers are enabled to create conversations and two-way communications about products and services. These conversations may also happen outside the sphere of control of a given business, when a marketing campaign or customer-service issue captures the attention of web-savvy consumers.

Exam Probability: **High**

17. *Answer choices:*

(see index for correct answer)

- a. Marketspace
- b. Book of business
- c. Cannibalization
- d. Customer acquisition management

Guidance: level 1

:: ::

_____ refers to the overall process of attracting, shortlisting, selecting and appointing suitable candidates for jobs within an organization. _____ can also refer to processes involved in choosing individuals for unpaid roles. Managers, human resource generalists and _____ specialists may be tasked with carrying out _____, but in some cases public-sector employment agencies, commercial _____ agencies, or specialist search consultancies are used to undertake parts of the process. Internet-based technologies which support all aspects of _____ have become widespread.

Exam Probability: **Medium**

18. *Answer choices:*

(see index for correct answer)

- a. co-culture
- b. hierarchical perspective
- c. empathy
- d. functional perspective

Guidance: level 1

:: Commercial item transport and distribution ::

A _____ in common law countries is a person or company that transports goods or people for any person or company and that is responsible for any possible loss of the goods during transport. A _____ offers its services to the general public under license or authority provided by a regulatory body. The regulatory body has usually been granted "ministerial authority" by the legislation that created it. The regulatory body may create, interpret, and enforce its regulations upon the _____ with independence and finality, as long as it acts within the bounds of the enabling legislation.

Exam Probability: **Medium**

19. *Answer choices:*

(see index for correct answer)

- a. Common carrier
- b. Freight audit
- c. Hold
- d. Food distribution

Guidance: level 1

:: Workplace ::

_____ is asystematic determination of a subject's merit, worth and significance, using criteria governed by a set of standards. It can assist an organization, program, design, project or any other intervention or initiative to assess any aim, realisable concept/proposal, or any alternative, to help in decision-making; or to ascertain the degree of achievement or value in regard to the aim and objectives and results of any such action that has been completed. The primary purpose of _____, in addition to gaining insight into prior or existing initiatives, is to enable reflection and assist in the identification of future change.

Exam Probability: **Medium**

20. *Answer choices:*
(see index for correct answer)

- a. Micromanagement
- b. Workplace listening
- c. Queen bee syndrome
- d. Evaluation

Guidance: level 1

:: ::

The _____ is a political and economic union of 28 member states that are located primarily in Europe. It has an area of 4,475,757 km2 and an estimated population of about 513 million. The EU has developed an internal single market through a standardised system of laws that apply in all member states in those matters, and only those matters, where members have agreed to act as one. EU policies aim to ensure the free movement of people, goods, services and capital within the internal market, enact legislation in justice and home affairs and maintain common policies on trade, agriculture, fisheries and regional development. For travel within the Schengen Area, passport controls have been abolished. A monetary union was established in 1999 and came into full force in 2002 and is composed of 19 EU member states which use the euro currency.

Exam Probability: **Medium**

21. *Answer choices:*

(see index for correct answer)

- a. functional perspective
- b. personal values
- c. process perspective
- d. empathy

Guidance: level 1

:: E-commerce ::

IBM _____ also known as WCS is a software platform framework for e-commerce, including marketing, sales, customer and order processing functionality in a tailorable, integrated package. It is a single, unified platform which offers the ability to do business directly with consumers, with businesses, indirectly through channel partners, or all of these simultaneously. _____ is a customizable, scalable and high availability solution built on the Java - Java EE platform using open standards, such as XML, and Web services.

Exam Probability: **High**

22. *Answer choices:*

(see index for correct answer)

- a. United Nations Convention on the Use of Electronic Communications in International Contracts
- b. WebSphere Commerce
- c. TRADACOMS
- d. Eagle Cash

Guidance: level 1

:: Minimum wage ::

A _____ is the lowest remuneration that employers can legally pay their workers—the price floor below which workers may not sell their labor. Most countries had introduced _____ legislation by the end of the 20th century.

Exam Probability: **Medium**

23. *Answer choices:*

(see index for correct answer)

- a. Working poor
- b. Minimum Wage Fairness Act
- c. Minimum wage in Taiwan
- d. Guaranteed minimum income

Guidance: level 1

:: E-commerce ::

_____, cybersecurity or information technology security is the protection of computer systems from theft or damage to their hardware, software or electronic data, as well as from disruption or misdirection of the services they provide.

Exam Probability: **Medium**

24. *Answer choices:*
(see index for correct answer)

- a. Smscoin
- b. Allstar
- c. Auction software
- d. Andy Dunn

Guidance: level 1

:: ::

_____ is the practical authority granted to a legal body to administer justice within a defined field of responsibility, e.g., Michigan tax law. In federations like the United States, areas of _____ apply to local, state, and federal levels; e.g. the court has _____ to apply federal law.

Exam Probability: **Low**

25. *Answer choices:*
(see index for correct answer)

- a. deep-level diversity
- b. Character
- c. open system
- d. Jurisdiction

Guidance: level 1

:: Consumer theory ::

A _____ is a technical term in psychology, economics and philosophy usually used in relation to choosing between alternatives. For example, someone prefers A over B if they would rather choose A than B.

Exam Probability: **High**

26. *Answer choices:*

(see index for correct answer)

- a. Preference
- b. Autonomous consumption
- c. Marginal rate of substitution
- d. Price elasticity of demand

Guidance: level 1

:: Business law ::

The _____ , first published in 1952, is one of a number of Uniform Acts that have been established as law with the goal of harmonizing the laws of sales and other commercial transactions across the United States of America through UCC adoption by all 50 states, the District of Columbia, and the Territories of the United States.

Exam Probability: **Medium**

27. *Answer choices:*

(see index for correct answer)

- a. Uniform Commercial Code
- b. Statutory liability
- c. Legal tender
- d. Ladenschlussgesetz

Guidance: level 1

:: ::

A _____ manages, commands, directs, or regulates the behavior of other devices or systems using control loops. It can range from a single home heating controller using a thermostat controlling a domestic boiler to large Industrial _____ s which are used for controlling processes or machines.

Exam Probability: **High**

28. *Answer choices:*

(see index for correct answer)

- a. surface-level diversity
- b. Control system
- c. similarity-attraction theory
- d. Sarbanes-Oxley act of 2002

Guidance: level 1

:: Commodities ::

In economics, a _____ is an economic good or service that has full or substantial fungibility: that is, the market treats instances of the good as equivalent or nearly so with no regard to who produced them. Most commodities are raw materials, basic resources, agricultural, or mining products, such as iron ore, sugar, or grains like rice and wheat. Commodities can also be mass-produced unspecialized products such as chemicals and computer memory.

Exam Probability: **High**

29. *Answer choices:*

(see index for correct answer)

- a. Commodity
- b. Commodity money
- c. Sample grade
- d. Commoditization

Guidance: level 1

:: Quality management ::

_____ ensures that an organization, product or service is consistent. It has four main components: quality planning, quality assurance, quality control and quality improvement. _____ is focused not only on product and service quality, but also on the means to achieve it. _____ , therefore, uses quality assurance and control of processes as well as products to achieve more consistent quality. What a customer wants and is willing to pay for it determines quality. It is written or unwritten commitment to a known or unknown consumer in the market . Thus, quality can be defined as fitness for intended use or, in other words, how well the product performs its intended function

Exam Probability: **High**

30. *Answer choices:*

(see index for correct answer)

- a. Common Assessment Framework
- b. Quality policy
- c. Bureau Veritas
- d. Quality management

Guidance: level 1

:: Stock market ::

The _____ of a corporation is all of the shares into which ownership of the corporation is divided. In American English, the shares are commonly known as "_____ s". A single share of the _____ represents fractional ownership of the corporation in proportion to the total number of shares. This typically entitles the _____ holder to that fraction of the company's earnings, proceeds from liquidation of assets , or voting power, often dividing these up in proportion to the amount of money each _____ holder has invested. Not all _____ is necessarily equal, as certain classes of _____ may be issued for example without voting rights, with enhanced voting rights, or with a certain priority to receive profits or liquidation proceeds before or after other classes of shareholders.

Exam Probability: **High**

31. *Answer choices:*

(see index for correct answer)

- a. Stock
- b. Secondary shares

- c. Stock exchange
- d. Follow-on offering

Guidance: level 1

:: ::

Employment is a relationship between two parties, usually based on a contract where work is paid for, where one party, which may be a corporation, for profit, not-for-profit organization, co-operative or other entity is the employer and the other is the employee. Employees work in return for payment, which may be in the form of an hourly wage, by piecework or an annual salary, depending on the type of work an employee does or which sector she or he is working in. Employees in some fields or sectors may receive gratuities, bonus payment or stock options. In some types of employment, employees may receive benefits in addition to payment. Benefits can include health insurance, housing, disability insurance or use of a gym. Employment is typically governed by employment laws, regulations or legal contracts.

Exam Probability: **Low**

32. *Answer choices:*
(see index for correct answer)

- a. surface-level diversity
- b. similarity-attraction theory
- c. Personnel
- d. hierarchical

Guidance: level 1

:: ::

A _____ or _____ s is a type of footwear and not a specific type of shoe. Most _____ s mainly cover the foot and the ankle, while some also cover some part of the lower calf. Some _____ s extend up the leg, sometimes as far as the knee or even the hip. Most _____ s have a heel that is clearly distinguishable from the rest of the sole, even if the two are made of one piece. Traditionally made of leather or rubber, modern _____ s are made from a variety of materials. _____ s are worn both for their functionality protecting the foot and leg from water, extreme cold, mud or hazards or providing additional ankle support for strenuous activities with added traction requirements , or may have hobnails on their undersides to protect against wear and to get better grip; and for reasons of style and fashion.

Exam Probability: **High**

33. *Answer choices:*

(see index for correct answer)

- a. interpersonal communication
- b. co-culture
- c. Boot
- d. empathy

Guidance: level 1

:: ::

Business Model Canvas is a strategic management and lean startup template for developing new or documenting existing business models. It is a visual chart with elements describing a firm's or product's value proposition, infrastructure, customers, and finances. It assists firms in aligning their activities by illustrating potential trade-offs.

Exam Probability: **High**

34. *Answer choices:*

(see index for correct answer)

- a. Cost structure
- b. imperative
- c. information systems assessment
- d. process perspective

Guidance: level 1

:: ::

_____ is the exchange of capital, goods, and services across international borders or territories.

Exam Probability: **Low**

35. *Answer choices:*

(see index for correct answer)

- a. International trade
- b. interpersonal communication
- c. imperative
- d. hierarchical perspective

Guidance: level 1

:: ::

_____ is a concept of English common law and is a necessity for simple contracts but not for special contracts. The concept has been adopted by other common law jurisdictions, including the US.

Exam Probability: **High**

36. *Answer choices:*

(see index for correct answer)

- a. co-culture
- b. Sarbanes-Oxley act of 2002
- c. empathy
- d. hierarchical perspective

Guidance: level 1

:: Industry ::

_____ describes various measures of the efficiency of production. Often, a _____ measure is expressed as the ratio of an aggregate output to a single input or an aggregate input used in a production process, i.e. output per unit of input. Most common example is the labour _____ measure, e.g., such as GDP per worker. There are many different definitions of _____ and the choice among them depends on the purpose of the _____ measurement and/or data availability. The key source of difference between various _____ measures is also usually related to how the outputs and the inputs are aggregated into scalars to obtain such a ratio-type measure of _____ .

Exam Probability: **High**

37. *Answer choices:*

(see index for correct answer)

- a. Unexpected events
- b. Permissible exposure limit
- c. AS-Interface
- d. Productivity

Guidance: level 1

:: Investment ::

In finance, the benefit from an _____ is called a return. The return may consist of a gain realised from the sale of property or an _____ , unrealised capital appreciation, or _____ income such as dividends, interest, rental income etc., or a combination of capital gain and income. The return may also include currency gains or losses due to changes in foreign currency exchange rates.

Exam Probability: **Medium**

38. *Answer choices:*

(see index for correct answer)

- a. IFund
- b. Investment certificate
- c. Investment theory
- d. Investment function

Guidance: level 1

:: ::

_____ is the administration of an organization, whether it is a business, a not-for-profit organization, or government body. _____ includes the activities of setting the strategy of an organization and coordinating the efforts of its employees to accomplish its objectives through the application of available resources, such as financial, natural, technological, and human resources. The term " _____ " may also refer to those people who manage an organization.

Exam Probability: **High**

39. *Answer choices:*
(see index for correct answer)

- a. personal values
- b. hierarchical
- c. co-culture
- d. Sarbanes-Oxley act of 2002

Guidance: level 1

:: Materials ::

A _____ , also known as a feedstock, unprocessed material, or primary commodity, is a basic material that is used to produce goods, finished products, energy, or intermediate materials which are feedstock for future finished products. As feedstock, the term connotes these materials are bottleneck assets and are highly important with regard to producing other products. An example of this is crude oil, which is a _____ and a feedstock used in the production of industrial chemicals, fuels, plastics, and pharmaceutical goods; lumber is a _____ used to produce a variety of products including all types of furniture. The term " _____ " denotes materials in minimally processed or unprocessed in states; e.g., raw latex, crude oil, cotton, coal, raw biomass, iron ore, air, logs, or water i.e. "...any product of agriculture, forestry, fishing and any other mineral that is in its natural form or which has undergone the transformation required to prepare it for internationally marketing in substantial volumes."

Exam Probability: **Low**

40. *Answer choices:*

(see index for correct answer)

- a. Nordic Institute of Dental Materials
- b. Composition leather
- c. Raw material
- d. Rock

Guidance: level 1

:: Decision theory ::

A _____ is a deliberate system of principles to guide decisions and achieve rational outcomes. A _____ is a statement of intent, and is implemented as a procedure or protocol. Policies are generally adopted by a governance body within an organization. Policies can assist in both subjective and objective decision making. Policies to assist in subjective decision making usually assist senior management with decisions that must be based on the relative merits of a number of factors, and as a result are often hard to test objectively, e.g. work-life balance _____ . In contrast policies to assist in objective decision making are usually operational in nature and can be objectively tested, e.g. password _____ .

Exam Probability: **Medium**

41. *Answer choices:*
(see index for correct answer)

- a. ELECTRE
- b. Dominance-based rough set approach
- c. Causal decision theory
- d. Option grid

Guidance: level 1

:: International trade ::

In finance, an _____ is the rate at which one currency will be exchanged for another. It is also regarded as the value of one country's currency in relation to another currency. For example, an interbank _____ of 114 Japanese yen to the United States dollar means that ¥114 will be exchanged for each US$1 or that US$1 will be exchanged for each ¥114. In this case it is said that the price of a dollar in relation to yen is ¥114, or equivalently that the price of a yen in relation to dollars is $1/114.

Exam Probability: **High**

42. *Answer choices:*

(see index for correct answer)

- a. New International Economic Order
- b. Internationalization
- c. Camino de los chilenos
- d. Exchange rate

Guidance: level 1

:: E-commerce ::

Customer to customer markets provide an innovative way to allow customers to interact with each other. Traditional markets require business to customer relationships, in which a customer goes to the business in order to purchase a product or service. In customer to customer markets, the business facilitates an environment where customers can sell goods or services to each other. Other types of markets include business to business and business to customer.

Exam Probability: **Medium**

43. *Answer choices:*

(see index for correct answer)

- a. Mobile banking
- b. Digital certificate
- c. Helpling
- d. Demandware

Guidance: level 1

:: Marketing ::

_____ is a concept introduced in a book of the same name in 1999 by marketing expert Seth Godin. _____ is a non-traditional marketing technique that advertises goods and services when advance consent is given.

Exam Probability: **High**

44. *Answer choices:*

(see index for correct answer)

- a. Cola Wars
- b. Masstige

- c. Contribution margin-based pricing
- d. Pricing objectives

Guidance: level 1

:: ::

_____ is the collaborative effort of a team to achieve a common goal or to complete a task in the most effective and efficient way. This concept is seen within the greater framework of a team, which is a group of interdependent individuals who work together towards a common goal. Basic requirements for effective _____ are an adequate team size, available resources for the team to make use of, and clearly defined roles within the team in order for everyone to have a clear purpose. _____ is present in any context where a group of people are working together to achieve a common goal. These contexts include an industrial organization, athletics, a school, and the healthcare system. In each of these settings, the level of _____ and interdependence can vary from low, to intermediate, to high, depending on the amount of communication, interaction, and collaboration present between team members.

Exam Probability: **Low**

45. *Answer choices:*

(see index for correct answer)

- a. process perspective
- b. Teamwork
- c. similarity-attraction theory
- d. personal values

Guidance: level 1

:: Computer access control ::

_____ is the act of confirming the truth of an attribute of a single piece of data claimed true by an entity. In contrast with identification, which refers to the act of stating or otherwise indicating a claim purportedly attesting to a person or thing's identity, _____ is the process of actually confirming that identity. It might involve confirming the identity of a person by validating their identity documents, verifying the authenticity of a website with a digital certificate, determining the age of an artifact by carbon dating, or ensuring that a product is what its packaging and labeling claim to be. In other words, _____ often involves verifying the validity of at least one form of identification.

Exam Probability: **Medium**

46. *Answer choices:*
(see index for correct answer)

- a. Authentication
- b. NemID
- c. Mobilegov
- d. Mutual authentication

Guidance: level 1

:: Price fixing convictions ::

_____ is the flag carrier airline of the United Kingdom, headquartered at Waterside, Harmondsworth. It is the second largest airline in the United Kingdom, based on fleet size and passengers carried, behind easyJet. The airline is based in Waterside near its main hub at London Heathrow Airport. In January 2011 BA merged with Iberia, creating the International Airlines Group, a holding company registered in Madrid, Spain. IAG is the world's third-largest airline group in terms of annual revenue and the second-largest in Europe. It is listed on the London Stock Exchange and in the FTSE 100 Index. _____ is the first passenger airline to have generated more than $1 billion on a single air route in a year.

Exam Probability: **High**

47. *Answer choices:*
(see index for correct answer)

- a. AGC Glass Europe
- b. Hoffmann-La Roche

- c. British Airways
- d. Siemens

Guidance: level 1

:: ::

_____ is a type of government support for the citizens of that society. _____ may be provided to people of any income level, as with social security, but it is usually intended to ensure that the poor can meet their basic human needs such as food and shelter. _____ attempts to provide poor people with a minimal level of well-being, usually either a free- or a subsidized-supply of certain goods and social services, such as healthcare, education, and vocational training.

Exam Probability: **Low**

48. *Answer choices:*
(see index for correct answer)

- a. surface-level diversity
- b. Sarbanes-Oxley act of 2002
- c. levels of analysis
- d. similarity-attraction theory

Guidance: level 1

:: ::

Regulatory economics is the economics of regulation. It is the application of law by government or independent administrative agencies for various purposes, including remedying market failure, protecting the environment, centrally-planning an economy, enriching well-connected firms, or benefiting politicians.

Exam Probability: **Low**

49. *Answer choices:*
(see index for correct answer)

- a. interpersonal communication
- b. hierarchical
- c. Economic regulation
- d. deep-level diversity

Guidance: level 1

:: E-commerce ::

A _____ is a hosted service offering that acts as an intermediary between business partners sharing standards based or proprietary data via shared business processes. The offered service is referred to as "_____ services".

Exam Probability: **Medium**

50. *Answer choices:*
(see index for correct answer)

- a. Wanelo
- b. EPAS
- c. Donna Hoffman
- d. Value-added network

Guidance: level 1

:: ::

_____ Corporation is an American multinational technology company with headquarters in Redmond, Washington. It develops, manufactures, licenses, supports and sells computer software, consumer electronics, personal computers, and related services. Its best known software products are the _____ Windows line of operating systems, the _____ Office suite, and the Internet Explorer and Edge Web browsers. Its flagship hardware products are the Xbox video game consoles and the _____ Surface lineup of touchscreen personal computers. As of 2016, it is the world's largest software maker by revenue, and one of the world's most valuable companies. The word "_____" is a portmanteau of "microcomputer" and "software". _____ is ranked No. 30 in the 2018 Fortune 500 rankings of the largest United States corporations by total revenue.

Exam Probability: **Low**

51. *Answer choices:*
(see index for correct answer)

- a. empathy
- b. levels of analysis

- c. Microsoft
- d. cultural

Guidance: level 1

:: Business models ::

A _____, _____ company or daughter company is a company that is owned or controlled by another company, which is called the parent company, parent, or holding company. The _____ can be a company, corporation, or limited liability company. In some cases it is a government or state-owned enterprise. In some cases, particularly in the music and book publishing industries, subsidiaries are referred to as imprints.

Exam Probability: **High**

52. *Answer choices:*
(see index for correct answer)

- a. Very small business
- b. Subsidiary
- c. Utility computing
- d. Cooperative

Guidance: level 1

:: Regulators ::

A _____ is a public authority or government agency responsible for exercising autonomous authority over some area of human activity in a regulatory or supervisory capacity. An independent _____ is a _____ that is independent from other branches or arms of the government.

Exam Probability: **Medium**

53. *Answer choices:*
(see index for correct answer)

- a. Energy Resources Conservation Board
- b. Regulatory agency
- c. Alberta Energy Regulator
- d. Croatian Regulatory Authority for Network Industries

Guidance: level 1

:: ::

_____ is an American restaurant chain and international franchise which was founded in 1958 by Dan and Frank Carney. The company is known for its Italian-American cuisine menu, including pizza and pasta, as well as side dishes and desserts. _____ has 18,431 restaurants worldwide as of December 31, 2018, making it the world's largest pizza chain in terms of locations. It is a subsidiary of Yum! Brands, Inc., one of the world's largest restaurant companies.

Exam Probability: **High**

54. *Answer choices:*

(see index for correct answer)

- a. corporate values
- b. similarity-attraction theory
- c. open system
- d. Pizza Hut

Guidance: level 1

:: ::

The _____ is a U.S. business-focused, English-language international daily newspaper based in New York City. The Journal, along with its Asian and European editions, is published six days a week by Dow Jones & Company, a division of News Corp. The newspaper is published in the broadsheet format and online. The Journal has been printed continuously since its inception on July 8, 1889, by Charles Dow, Edward Jones, and Charles Bergstresser.

Exam Probability: **Low**

55. *Answer choices:*

(see index for correct answer)

- a. information systems assessment
- b. co-culture
- c. hierarchical perspective
- d. Wall Street Journal

Guidance: level 1

:: Management accounting ::

In economics, _____ s, indirect costs or overheads are business expenses that are not dependent on the level of goods or services produced by the business. They tend to be time-related, such as interest or rents being paid per month, and are often referred to as overhead costs. This is in contrast to variable costs, which are volume-related and unknown at the beginning of the accounting year. For a simple example, such as a bakery, the monthly rent for the baking facilities, and the monthly payments for the security system and basic phone line are _____ s, as they do not change according to how much bread the bakery produces and sells. On the other hand, the wage costs of the bakery are variable, as the bakery will have to hire more workers if the production of bread increases. Economists reckon _____ as a entry barrier for new entrepreneurs.

Exam Probability: **Medium**

56. *Answer choices:*

(see index for correct answer)

- a. Notional profit
- b. Environmental full-cost accounting
- c. Target income sales
- d. Fixed cost

Guidance: level 1

:: ::

Business is the activity of making one's living or making money by producing or buying and selling products . Simply put, it is "any activity or enterprise entered into for profit. It does not mean it is a company, a corporation, partnership, or have any such formal organization, but it can range from a street peddler to General Motors."

Exam Probability: **Medium**

57. *Answer choices:*

(see index for correct answer)

- a. process perspective
- b. Firm
- c. Sarbanes-Oxley act of 2002
- d. hierarchical perspective

Guidance: level 1

:: ::

_____ is the collection of techniques, skills, methods, and processes used in the production of goods or services or in the accomplishment of objectives, such as scientific investigation. _____ can be the knowledge of techniques, processes, and the like, or it can be embedded in machines to allow for operation without detailed knowledge of their workings. Systems applying _____ by taking an input, changing it according to the system's use, and then producing an outcome are referred to as _____ systems or technological systems.

Exam Probability: **High**

58. *Answer choices:*

(see index for correct answer)

- a. corporate values
- b. Technology
- c. interpersonal communication
- d. hierarchical perspective

Guidance: level 1

:: Business ethics ::

_____ is a type of harassment technique that relates to a sexual nature and the unwelcome or inappropriate promise of rewards in exchange for sexual favors. _____ includes a range of actions from mild transgressions to sexual abuse or assault. Harassment can occur in many different social settings such as the workplace, the home, school, churches, etc. Harassers or victims may be of any gender.

Exam Probability: **Low**

59. *Answer choices:*

(see index for correct answer)

- a. Jewish business ethics
- b. Ethical corporate social responsibility
- c. Sexual harassment
- d. Eating your own dog food

Guidance: level 1

Business ethics

Business ethics (also known as corporate ethics) is a form of applied ethics or professional ethics, that examines ethical principles and moral or ethical problems that can arise in a business environment. It applies to all aspects of business conduct and is relevant to the conduct of individuals and entire organizations. These ethics originate from individuals, organizational statements or from the legal system. These norms, values, ethical, and unethical practices are what is used to guide business. They help those businesses maintain a better connection with their stakeholders.

:: ::

MCI, Inc. was an American telecommunication corporation, currently a subsidiary of Verizon Communications, with its main office in Ashburn, Virginia. The corporation was formed originally as a result of the merger of _____ and MCI Communications corporations, and used the name MCI _____, succeeded by _____, before changing its name to the present version on April 12, 2003, as part of the corporation's ending of its bankruptcy status. The company traded on NASDAQ as WCOM and MCIP. The corporation was purchased by Verizon Communications with the deal finalizing on January 6, 2006, and is now identified as that company's Verizon Enterprise Solutions division with the local residential divisions being integrated slowly into local Verizon subsidiaries.

Exam Probability: **Low**

1. *Answer choices:*

(see index for correct answer)

- a. similarity-attraction theory
- b. surface-level diversity
- c. process perspective
- d. co-culture

Guidance: level 1

:: Statutory law ::

_____ or statute law is written law set down by a body of legislature or by a singular legislator. This is as opposed to oral or customary law; or regulatory law promulgated by the executive or common law of the judiciary. Statutes may originate with national, state legislatures or local municipalities.

Exam Probability: **Medium**

2. *Answer choices:*
(see index for correct answer)

- a. Statutory law
- b. Statute of repose
- c. ratification
- d. statute law

Guidance: level 1

:: Offshoring ::

A _____ is the temporary suspension or permanent termination of employment of an employee or, more commonly, a group of employees for business reasons, such as personnel management or downsizing an organization. Originally, _____ referred exclusively to a temporary interruption in work, or employment but this has evolved to a permanent elimination of a position in both British and US English, requiring the addition of "temporary" to specify the original meaning of the word. A _____ is not to be confused with wrongful termination. Laid off workers or displaced workers are workers who have lost or left their jobs because their employer has closed or moved, there was insufficient work for them to do, or their position or shift was abolished. Downsizing in a company is defined to involve the reduction of employees in a workforce. Downsizing in companies became a popular practice in the 1980s and early 1990s as it was seen as a way to deliver better shareholder value as it helps to reduce the costs of employers. Indeed, recent research on downsizing in the U.S., UK, and Japan suggests that downsizing is being regarded by management as one of the preferred routes to help declining organizations, cutting unnecessary costs, and improve organizational performance. Usually a _____ occurs as a cost cutting measure.

Exam Probability: **Low**

3. *Answer choices:*
(see index for correct answer)

- a. Programmers Guild
- b. Advanced Contact Solutions
- c. Global labor arbitrage
- d. Layoff

Guidance: level 1

:: United States federal defense and national security legislation ::

The USA _____ is an Act of the U.S. Congress that was signed into law by President George W. Bush on October 26, 2001. The title of the Act is a contrived three letter initialism preceding a seven letter acronym, which in combination stand for Uniting and Strengthening America by Providing Appropriate Tools Required to Intercept and Obstruct Terrorism Act of 2001. The acronym was created by a 23 year old Congressional staffer, Chris Kyle.

Exam Probability: **Low**

4. *Answer choices:*
(see index for correct answer)

- a. USA PATRIOT Act
- b. Patriot Act

Guidance: level 1

:: Trade unions ::

A _____ was a group formed of private citizens to administer law and order where they considered governmental structures to be inadequate. The term is commonly associated with the frontier areas of the American West in the mid-19th century, where groups attacked cattle rustlers and gangs, and people at gold mining claims. As non-state organizations no functioning checks existed to protect against excessive force or safeguard due process from the committees. In the years prior to the Civil War, some committees worked to free slaves and transport them to freedom.

Exam Probability: **Medium**

5. *Answer choices:*

(see index for correct answer)

- a. National trade union center
- b. Churn and burn
- c. Opposition to trade unions
- d. Company union

Guidance: level 1

:: United States law ::

The ABA _____, created by the American Bar Association, are a set of rules that prescribe baseline standards of legal ethics and professional responsibility for lawyers in the United States. They were promulgated by the ABA House of Delegates upon the recommendation of the Kutak Commission in 1983. The rules are merely recommendations, or models, and are not themselves binding. However, having a common set of Model Rules facilitates a common discourse on legal ethics, and simplifies professional responsibility training as well as the day-to-day application of such rules. As of 2015, 49 states and four territories have adopted the rules in whole or in part, of which the most recent to do so was the Commonwealth of the Northern Mariana Islands in March 2015. California is the only state that has not adopted the ABA Model Rules, while Puerto Rico is the only U.S. jurisdiction outside of confederation has not adopted them but instead has its own Código de Ética Profesional.

Exam Probability: **Low**

6. *Answer choices:*

(see index for correct answer)

- a. judgment notwithstanding the verdict
- b. Model Rules of Professional Conduct

Guidance: level 1

:: Parental leave ::

_____ , or family leave, is an employee benefit available in almost all countries. The term " _____ " may include maternity, paternity, and adoption leave; or may be used distinctively from "maternity leave" and "paternity leave" to describe separate family leave available to either parent to care for small children. In some countries and jurisdictions, "family leave" also includes leave provided to care for ill family members. Often, the minimum benefits and eligibility requirements are stipulated by law.

Exam Probability: **High**

7. *Answer choices:*

(see index for correct answer)

- a. Cleveland Board of Education v. LaFleur
- b. Pregnant Workers Directive
- c. Parental leave
- d. Pregnancy discrimination

Guidance: level 1

:: Labor rights ::

The _____ is the concept that people have a human _____ , or engage in productive employment, and may not be prevented from doing so. The _____ is enshrined in the Universal Declaration of Human Rights and recognized in international human rights law through its inclusion in the International Covenant on Economic, Social and Cultural Rights, where the _____ emphasizes economic, social and cultural development.

Exam Probability: **High**

8. *Answer choices:*

(see index for correct answer)

- a. Right to work
- b. The Hyatt 100
- c. Grievance
- d. Labor rights

Guidance: level 1

:: Renewable energy ::

_____ is the conversion of energy from sunlight into electricity, either directly using photovoltaics, indirectly using concentrated _____, or a combination. Concentrated _____ systems use lenses or mirrors and tracking systems to focus a large area of sunlight into a small beam. Photovoltaic cells convert light into an electric current using the photovoltaic effect.

Exam Probability: **Medium**

9. *Answer choices:*

(see index for correct answer)

- a. Seasonal thermal energy storage
- b. Energy transfer
- c. Cogeneration
- d. Waste heat recovery unit

Guidance: level 1

:: ::

_____ Corporation was an American energy, commodities, and services company based in Houston, Texas. It was founded in 1985 as a merger between Houston Natural Gas and InterNorth, both relatively small regional companies. Before its bankruptcy on December 3, 2001, _____ employed approximately 29,000 staff and was a major electricity, natural gas, communications and pulp and paper company, with claimed revenues of nearly $101 billion during 2000. Fortune named _____ "America's Most Innovative Company" for six consecutive years.

Exam Probability: **Low**

10. *Answer choices:*

(see index for correct answer)

- a. surface-level diversity
- b. interpersonal communication
- c. Enron
- d. functional perspective

Guidance: level 1

:: United Kingdom labour law ::

The _____ was a series of programs, public work projects, financial reforms, and regulations enacted by President Franklin D. Roosevelt in the United States between 1933 and 1936. It responded to needs for relief, reform, and recovery from the Great Depression. Major federal programs included the Civilian Conservation Corps, the Civil Works Administration, the Farm Security Administration, the National Industrial Recovery Act of 1933 and the Social Security Administration. They provided support for farmers, the unemployed, youth and the elderly. The _____ included new constraints and safeguards on the banking industry and efforts to re-inflate the economy after prices had fallen sharply. _____ programs included both laws passed by Congress as well as presidential executive orders during the first term of the presidency of Franklin D. Roosevelt.

Exam Probability: **High**

11. *Answer choices:*

(see index for correct answer)

- a. Report of the committee of inquiry on industrial democracy
- b. Employment Act 2008
- c. Coal Industry Commission Act 1919
- d. New Deal

Guidance: level 1

:: ::

The _____ to Fight AIDS, Tuberculosis and Malaria is an international financing organization that aims to "attract, leverage and invest additional resources to end the epidemics of HIV/AIDS, tuberculosis and malaria to support attainment of the Sustainable Development Goals established by the United Nations." A public-private partnership, the organization maintains its secretariat in Geneva, Switzerland. The organization began operations in January 2002. Microsoft founder Bill Gates was one of the first private foundations among many bilateral donors to provide seed money for the partnership.

Exam Probability: **Low**

12. *Answer choices:*

(see index for correct answer)

- a. co-culture
- b. open system
- c. hierarchical perspective
- d. functional perspective

Guidance: level 1

:: Business ethics ::

_____ is an area of applied ethics which deals with the moral principles behind the operation and regulation of marketing. Some areas of _____ overlap with media ethics.

Exam Probability: **High**

13. *Answer choices:*

(see index for correct answer)

- a. The Crooked E: The Unshredded Truth About Enron
- b. Pension spiking
- c. Enron Code of Ethics
- d. Equator Principles

Guidance: level 1

:: Electronic feedback ::

_____ occurs when outputs of a system are routed back as inputs as part of a chain of cause-and-effect that forms a circuit or loop. The system can then be said to feed back into itself. The notion of cause-and-effect has to be handled carefully when applied to _____ systems.

Exam Probability: **High**

14. *Answer choices:*

(see index for correct answer)

- a. Feedback
- b. feedback loop

Guidance: level 1

:: Environmental economics ::

_____ is an institutional arrangement designed to help producers in developing countries achieve better trading conditions. Members of the _____ movement advocate the payment of higher prices to exporters, as well as improved social and environmental standards. The movement focuses in particular on commodities, or products which are typically exported from developing countries to developed countries, but also consumed in domestic markets most notably handicrafts, coffee, cocoa, wine, sugar, fresh fruit, chocolate, flowers and gold. The movement seeks to promote greater equity in international trading partnerships through dialogue, transparency, and respect. It promotes sustainable development by offering better trading conditions to, and securing the rights of, marginalized producers and workers in developing countries. _____ is grounded in three core beliefs; first, producers have the power to express unity with consumers. Secondly, the world trade practices that currently exist promote the unequal distribution of wealth between nations. Lastly, buying products from producers in developing countries at a fair price is a more efficient way of promoting sustainable development than traditional charity and aid.

Exam Probability: **High**

15. *Answer choices:*

(see index for correct answer)

- a. Gashole
- b. The Green Collar Economy
- c. Environmental and Resource Economics
- d. Fair trade

Guidance: level 1

:: United States federal labor legislation ::

The _____ of 1988 is a United States federal law that generally prevents employers from using polygraph tests, either for pre-employment screening or during the course of employment, with certain exemptions.

Exam Probability: **Medium**

16. *Answer choices:*

(see index for correct answer)

- a. Employee Polygraph Protection Act
- b. Alien Contract Labor Law

- c. Workforce Investment Act of 1998
- d. Uniformed Services Employment and Reemployment Rights Act

Guidance: level 1

:: ::

_____ refers to a business initiative to increase the access between a company and their current and potential customers through the use of the Internet. The Internet allows the company to market themselves and attract new customers to their website where they can provide product information and better customer service. Customers can place orders electronically, therefore reducing expensive long distant phone calls and postage costs of placing orders, while saving time on behalf of the customer and company.

Exam Probability: **Medium**

17. *Answer choices:*

(see index for correct answer)

- a. surface-level diversity
- b. Global reach
- c. functional perspective
- d. Sarbanes-Oxley act of 2002

Guidance: level 1

:: ::

The _____ is an American stock exchange located at 11 Wall Street, Lower Manhattan, New York City, New York. It is by far the world's largest stock exchange by market capitalization of its listed companies at US$30.1 trillion as of February 2018. The average daily trading value was approximately US$169 billion in 2013. The NYSE trading floor is located at 11 Wall Street and is composed of 21 rooms used for the facilitation of trading. A fifth trading room, located at 30 Broad Street, was closed in February 2007. The main building and the 11 Wall Street building were designated National Historic Landmarks in 1978.

Exam Probability: **Low**

18. *Answer choices:*

(see index for correct answer)

- a. New York Stock Exchange
- b. hierarchical perspective
- c. functional perspective
- d. Sarbanes-Oxley act of 2002

Guidance: level 1

:: Criminal law ::

_____ is the body of law that relates to crime. It proscribes conduct perceived as threatening, harmful, or otherwise endangering to the property, health, safety, and moral welfare of people inclusive of one's self. Most _____ is established by statute, which is to say that the laws are enacted by a legislature. _____ includes the punishment and rehabilitation of people who violate such laws. _____ varies according to jurisdiction, and differs from civil law, where emphasis is more on dispute resolution and victim compensation, rather than on punishment or rehabilitation. Criminal procedure is a formalized official activity that authenticates the fact of commission of a crime and authorizes punitive or rehabilitative treatment of the offender.

Exam Probability: **Low**

19. *Answer choices:*
(see index for correct answer)

- a. complicit
- b. mitigating factor
- c. Self-incrimination
- d. Mala in se

Guidance: level 1

:: Data management ::

_____ is a form of intellectual property that grants the creator of an original creative work an exclusive legal right to determine whether and under what conditions this original work may be copied and used by others, usually for a limited term of years. The exclusive rights are not absolute but limited by limitations and exceptions to _____ law, including fair use. A major limitation on _____ on ideas is that _____ protects only the original expression of ideas, and not the underlying ideas themselves.

Exam Probability: **Medium**

20. *Answer choices:*

(see index for correct answer)

- a. Distributed concurrency control
- b. Data verification
- c. Data storage device
- d. Operational database

Guidance: level 1

:: ::

In ecology, a _____ is the type of natural environment in which a particular species of organism lives. It is characterized by both physical and biological features. A species' _____ is those places where it can find food, shelter, protection and mates for reproduction.

Exam Probability: **Medium**

21. *Answer choices:*

(see index for correct answer)

- a. co-culture
- b. Habitat
- c. open system
- d. hierarchical perspective

Guidance: level 1

:: Private equity ::

In finance, a high-yield bond is a bond that is rated below investment grade. These bonds have a higher risk of default or other adverse credit events, but typically pay higher yields than better quality bonds in order to make them attractive to investors.

Exam Probability: **High**

22. *Answer choices:*

(see index for correct answer)

- a. Private equity in the 1990s
- b. Junk bond
- c. LBO valuation model
- d. Earnout

Guidance: level 1

:: Management ::

The term _____ refers to measures designed to increase the degree of autonomy and self-determination in people and in communities in order to enable them to represent their interests in a responsible and self-determined way, acting on their own authority. It is the process of becoming stronger and more confident, especially in controlling one's life and claiming one's rights.

_____ as action refers both to the process of self-_____ and to professional support of people, which enables them to overcome their sense of powerlessness and lack of influence, and to recognize and use their resources. To do work with power.

Exam Probability: **Low**

23. *Answer choices:*
(see index for correct answer)

- a. Business-oriented architecture
- b. Empowerment
- c. Complementary assets
- d. Porter five forces analysis

Guidance: level 1

:: Anti-capitalism ::

_____ is a range of economic and social systems characterised by social ownership of the means of production and workers' self-management, as well as the political theories and movements associated with them. Social ownership can be public, collective or cooperative ownership, or citizen ownership of equity. There are many varieties of _____ and there is no single definition encapsulating all of them, with social ownership being the common element shared by its various forms.

Exam Probability: **Medium**

24. *Answer choices:*
(see index for correct answer)

- a. Deep Green Resistance
- b. Anti-capitalist

- c. Anarchist communism
- d. Socialism

Guidance: level 1

:: Management ::

A _____ describes the rationale of how an organization creates, delivers, and captures value, in economic, social, cultural or other contexts. The process of _____ construction and modification is also called _____ innovation and forms a part of business strategy.

Exam Probability: **Medium**

25. *Answer choices:*

(see index for correct answer)

- a. Reval
- b. Business model
- c. Fredmund Malik
- d. Action item

Guidance: level 1

:: Cognitive biases ::

In personality psychology, _____ is the degree to which people believe that they have control over the outcome of events in their lives, as opposed to external forces beyond their control. Understanding of the concept was developed by Julian B. Rotter in 1954, and has since become an aspect of personality studies. A person's "locus" is conceptualized as internal or external.

Exam Probability: **Low**

26. *Answer choices:*

(see index for correct answer)

- a. Serial position effect
- b. Physical attractiveness stereotype
- c. Positive illusions
- d. Locus of control

Guidance: level 1

:: ::

_____ is a cognitive process that elicits emotion and rational associations based on an individual's moral philosophy or value system. _____ stands in contrast to elicited emotion or thought due to associations based on immediate sensory perceptions and reflexive responses, as in sympathetic central nervous system responses. In common terms, _____ is often described as leading to feelings of remorse when a person commits an act that conflicts with their moral values. An individual's moral values and their dissonance with familial, social, cultural and historical interpretations of moral philosophy are considered in the examination of cultural relativity in both the practice and study of psychology. The extent to which _____ informs moral judgment before an action and whether such moral judgments are or should be based on reason has occasioned debate through much of modern history between theories of modern western philosophy in juxtaposition to the theories of romanticism and other reactionary movements after the end of the Middle Ages.

Exam Probability: **High**

27. *Answer choices:*
(see index for correct answer)

- a. Sarbanes-Oxley act of 2002
- b. process perspective
- c. Conscience
- d. interpersonal communication

Guidance: level 1

:: Minimum wage ::

A _____ is the lowest remuneration that employers can legally pay their workers—the price floor below which workers may not sell their labor. Most countries had introduced _____ legislation by the end of the 20th century.

Exam Probability: **Medium**

28. *Answer choices:*
(see index for correct answer)

- a. Minimum wage

- b. Minimum wage in the United States
- c. Guaranteed minimum income
- d. National Anti-Sweating League

Guidance: level 1

:: ::

The _____ was a severe worldwide economic depression that took place mostly during the 1930s, beginning in the United States. The timing of the _____ varied across nations; in most countries it started in 1929 and lasted until the late-1930s. It was the longest, deepest, and most widespread depression of the 20th century. In the 21st century, the _____ is commonly used as an example of how intensely the world's economy can decline.

Exam Probability: **Medium**

29. *Answer choices:*
(see index for correct answer)

- a. personal values
- b. Great Depression
- c. open system
- d. Character

Guidance: level 1

:: Production and manufacturing ::

_____ is a set of techniques and tools for process improvement. Though as a shortened form it may be found written as 6S, it should not be confused with the methodology known as 6S.

Exam Probability: **Low**

30. *Answer choices:*
(see index for correct answer)

- a. Digital materialization
- b. production control
- c. Earned value
- d. Fieldbus Foundation

Guidance: level 1

:: Socialism ::

_____ is a label used to define the first currents of modern socialist thought as exemplified by the work of Henri de Saint-Simon, Charles Fourier, Étienne Cabet and Robert Owen.

Exam Probability: **Medium**

31. *Answer choices:*

(see index for correct answer)

- a. The Triple Revolution
- b. Harvest Hills Cooperative Community
- c. Gucci socialist
- d. Class conflict

Guidance: level 1

:: ::

_____ is the study and management of exchange relationships. _____ is the business process of creating relationships with and satisfying customers. With its focus on the customer, _____ is one of the premier components of business management.

Exam Probability: **Medium**

32. *Answer choices:*

(see index for correct answer)

- a. corporate values
- b. deep-level diversity
- c. co-culture
- d. Marketing

Guidance: level 1

:: Culture ::

_____ is a society which is characterized by individualism, which is the prioritization or emphasis, of the individual over the entire group. _____ s are oriented around the self, being independent instead of identifying with a group mentality. They see each other as only loosely linked, and value personal goals over group interests. _____ s tend to have a more diverse population and are characterized with emphasis on personal achievements, and a rational assessment of both the beneficial and detrimental aspects of relationships with others. _____ s have such unique aspects of communication as being a low power-distance culture and having a low-context communication style. The United States, Australia, Great Britain, Canada, the Netherlands, and New Zealand have been identified as highly _____ s.

Exam Probability: **Medium**

33. *Answer choices:*

(see index for correct answer)

- a. Individualistic culture
- b. Low-context culture
- c. cultural framework
- d. Intracultural

Guidance: level 1

:: ::

An _____ is the release of a liquid petroleum hydrocarbon into the environment, especially the marine ecosystem, due to human activity, and is a form of pollution. The term is usually given to marine _____ s, where oil is released into the ocean or coastal waters, but spills may also occur on land. _____ s may be due to releases of crude oil from tankers, offshore platforms, drilling rigs and wells, as well as spills of refined petroleum products and their by-products, heavier fuels used by large ships such as bunker fuel, or the spill of any oily refuse or waste oil.

Exam Probability: **High**

34. *Answer choices:*

(see index for correct answer)

- a. corporate values
- b. functional perspective
- c. Oil spill

- d. imperative

Guidance: level 1

:: Renewable energy ::

A _____ is a fuel that is produced through contemporary biological processes, such as agriculture and anaerobic digestion, rather than a fuel produced by geological processes such as those involved in the formation of fossil fuels, such as coal and petroleum, from prehistoric biological matter. If the source biomatter can regrow quickly, the resulting fuel is said to be a form of renewable energy.

Exam Probability: **High**

35. *Answer choices:*

(see index for correct answer)

- a. Biofuel
- b. Carbon neutrality
- c. Algaculture
- d. National Solar Conference and World Renewable Energy Forum 2012

Guidance: level 1

:: Advertising techniques ::

The _____ is a story from the Trojan War about the subterfuge that the Greeks used to enter the independent city of Troy and win the war. In the canonical version, after a fruitless 10-year siege, the Greeks constructed a huge wooden horse, and hid a select force of men inside including Odysseus. The Greeks pretended to sail away, and the Trojans pulled the horse into their city as a victory trophy. That night the Greek force crept out of the horse and opened the gates for the rest of the Greek army, which had sailed back under cover of night. The Greeks entered and destroyed the city of Troy, ending the war.

Exam Probability: **Medium**

36. *Answer choices:*

(see index for correct answer)

- a. Trojan horse

- b. Surrogate advertising
- c. Display window
- d. Inconsistent comparison

Guidance: level 1

:: Timber industry ::

The _____ is an international non-profit, multi-stakeholder organization established in 1993 to promote responsible management of the world's forests. The FSC does this by setting standards on forest products, along with certifying and labeling them as eco-friendly.

Exam Probability: **Low**

37. *Answer choices:*
(see index for correct answer)

- a. Lumber
- b. Resistograph
- c. Greenheart Group
- d. Ottawa River timber trade

Guidance: level 1

:: Public relations terminology ::

_____ , also called "green sheen", is a form of spin in which green PR or green marketing is deceptively used to promote the perception that an organization's products, aims or policies are environmentally friendly. Evidence that an organization is _____ often comes from pointing out the spending differences: when significantly more money or time has been spent advertising being "green" , than is actually spent on environmentally sound practices. _____ efforts can range from changing the name or label of a product to evoke the natural environment on a product that contains harmful chemicals to multimillion-dollar marketing campaigns portraying highly polluting energy companies as eco-friendly.Publicized accusations of _____ have contributed to the term's increasing use.

Exam Probability: **Low**

38. *Answer choices:*
(see index for correct answer)

- a. Greenwashing
- b. Corporate pathos
- c. No comment
- d. Photo op

Guidance: level 1

:: Supply chain management terms ::

In business and finance, _____ is a system of organizations, people, activities, information, and resources involved in moving a product or service from supplier to customer. _____ activities involve the transformation of natural resources, raw materials, and components into a finished product that is delivered to the end customer. In sophisticated _____ systems, used products may re-enter the _____ at any point where residual value is recyclable. _____ s link value chains.

Exam Probability: **Low**

39. *Answer choices:*
(see index for correct answer)

- a. Cool Chain Quality Indicator
- b. Supply Chain
- c. Widget
- d. Capital spare

Guidance: level 1

:: Auditing ::

_____ is a general term that can reflect various types of evaluations intended to identify environmental compliance and management system implementation gaps, along with related corrective actions. In this way they perform an analogous function to financial audits. There are generally two different types of _____ s: compliance audits and management systems audits. Compliance audits tend to be the primary type in the US or within US-based multinationals.

Exam Probability: **High**

40. *Answer choices:*
(see index for correct answer)

- a. Audit trail
- b. Verified Audit Circulation
- c. Environmental audit
- d. BPA Worldwide

Guidance: level 1

:: Utilitarianism ::

_____ is a family of consequentialist ethical theories that promotes actions that maximize happiness and well-being for the majority of a population. Although different varieties of _____ admit different characterizations, the basic idea behind all of them is to in some sense maximize utility, which is often defined in terms of well-being or related concepts. For instance, Jeremy Bentham, the founder of _____ , described utility as

Exam Probability: **High**

41. *Answer choices:*
(see index for correct answer)

- a. Rule utilitarianism
- b. Hedonism
- c. Consequentialism
- d. Preference utilitarianism

Guidance: level 1

:: ::

A _____ service is an online platform which people use to build social networks or social relationship with other people who share similar personal or career interests, activities, backgrounds or real-life connections.

Exam Probability: **Low**

42. *Answer choices:*
(see index for correct answer)

- a. process perspective
- b. Social networking
- c. cultural
- d. imperative

:: Workplace ::

In business management, _____ is a management style whereby a manager closely observes and/or controls the work of his/her subordinates or employees.

Exam Probability: **Low**

43. *Answer choices:*
(see index for correct answer)

- a. Workplace revenge
- b. Work motivation
- c. Workplace romance
- d. Workplace listening

Guidance: level 1

:: ::

A _____ is a form of business network, for example, a local organization of businesses whose goal is to further the interests of businesses. Business owners in towns and cities form these local societies to advocate on behalf of the business community. Local businesses are members, and they elect a board of directors or executive council to set policy for the chamber. The board or council then hires a President, CEO or Executive Director, plus staffing appropriate to size, to run the organization.

Exam Probability: **Low**

44. *Answer choices:*
(see index for correct answer)

- a. functional perspective
- b. Chamber of Commerce
- c. cultural
- d. open system

Guidance: level 1

:: Industrial ecology ::

_____ is a strategy for reducing the amount of waste created and released into the environment, particularly by industrial facilities, agriculture, or consumers. Many large corporations view P2 as a method of improving the efficiency and profitability of production processes by technology advancements. Legislative bodies have enacted P2 measures, such as the _____ Act of 1990 and the Clean Air Act Amendments of 1990 by the United States Congress.

Exam Probability: **High**

45. *Answer choices:*
(see index for correct answer)

- a. Pollution Prevention
- b. Integrated chain management
- c. Thermoeconomics
- d. Design for the Environment

Guidance: level 1

:: Majority–minority relations ::

_____ , also known as reservation in India and Nepal, positive discrimination / action in the United Kingdom, and employment equity in Canada and South Africa, is the policy of promoting the education and employment of members of groups that are known to have previously suffered from discrimination. Historically and internationally, support for _____ has sought to achieve goals such as bridging inequalities in employment and pay, increasing access to education, promoting diversity, and redressing apparent past wrongs, harms, or hindrances.

Exam Probability: **Low**

46. *Answer choices:*
(see index for correct answer)

- a. cultural Relativism
- b. positive discrimination
- c. Affirmative action

Guidance: level 1

:: False advertising law ::

The Lanham Act is the primary federal trademark statute of law in the United States. The Act prohibits a number of activities, including trademark infringement, trademark dilution, and false advertising.

Exam Probability: **Low**

47. *Answer choices:*

(see index for correct answer)

- a. Lanham Act
- b. POM Wonderful LLC v. Coca-Cola Co.

Guidance: level 1

:: White-collar criminals ::

_____ refers to financially motivated, nonviolent crime committed by businesses and government professionals. It was first defined by the sociologist Edwin Sutherland in 1939 as "a crime committed by a person of respectability and high social status in the course of their occupation". Typical _____ s could include wage theft, fraud, bribery, Ponzi schemes, insider trading, labor racketeering, embezzlement, cybercrime, copyright infringement, money laundering, identity theft, and forgery. Lawyers can specialize in _____ .

Exam Probability: **Medium**

48. *Answer choices:*

(see index for correct answer)

- a. Du Jun
- b. White-collar crime

Guidance: level 1

:: Business ethics ::

A _____ is a person who exposes any kind of information or activity that is deemed illegal, unethical, or not correct within an organization that is either private or public. The information of alleged wrongdoing can be classified in many ways: violation of company policy/rules, law, regulation, or threat to public interest/national security, as well as fraud, and corruption. Those who become _____ s can choose to bring information or allegations to surface either internally or externally. Internally, a _____ can bring his/her accusations to the attention of other people within the accused organization such as an immediate supervisor. Externally, a _____ can bring allegations to light by contacting a third party outside of an accused organization such as the media, government, law enforcement, or those who are concerned. _____ s, however, take the risk of facing stiff reprisal and retaliation from those who are accused or alleged of wrongdoing.

Exam Probability: **High**

49. *Answer choices:*

(see index for correct answer)

- a. TG Soft
- b. Conscious business
- c. Corporate behaviour
- d. Whistleblower

Guidance: level 1

:: Office work ::

_____ is the process and behavior in human interactions involving power and authority. It is also a tool to assess the operational capacity and to balance diverse views of interested parties. It is also known as office politics and organizational politics. It is the use of power and social networking within an organization to achieve changes that benefit the organization or individuals within it. Influence by individuals may serve personal interests without regard to their effect on the organization itself. Some of the personal advantages may include access to tangible assets, or intangible benefits such as status or pseudo-authority that influences the behavior of others. On the other hand, organizational politics can increase efficiency, form interpersonal relationships, expedite change, and profit the organization and its members simultaneously. Both individuals and groups may engage in office politics which can be highly destructive, as people focus on personal gains at the expense of the organization. "Self-serving political actions can negatively influence our social groupings, cooperation, information sharing, and many other organizational functions." Thus, it is vital to pay attention to organizational politics and create the right political landscape. "Politics is the lubricant that oils your organization's internal gears."
Office politics has also been described as "simply how power gets worked out on a practical, day-to-day basis."

Exam Probability: **Medium**

50. *Answer choices:*
(see index for correct answer)

- a. Pink-collar worker
- b. Copier service
- c. Workplace politics
- d. Paperless office

Guidance: level 1

_____ is a bundle of characteristics, including ways of thinking, feeling, and acting, which humans are said to have naturally. The term is often regarded as capturing what it is to be human, or the essence of humanity. The term is controversial because it is disputed whether or not such an essence exists. Arguments about _____ have been a mainstay of philosophy for centuries and the concept continues to provoke lively philosophical debate. The concept also continues to play a role in science, with neuroscientists, psychologists and social scientists sometimes claiming that their results have yielded insight into _____. _____ is traditionally contrasted with characteristics that vary among humans, such as characteristics associated with specific cultures. Debates about _____ are related to, although not the same as, debates about the comparative importance of genes and environment in development.

Exam Probability: **High**

51. *Answer choices:*

(see index for correct answer)

- a. personal values
- b. cultural
- c. hierarchical
- d. Human nature

Guidance: level 1

:: Labour relations ::

_____ is a field of study that can have different meanings depending on the context in which it is used. In an international context, it is a subfield of labor history that studies the human relations with regard to work – in its broadest sense – and how this connects to questions of social inequality. It explicitly encompasses unregulated, historical, and non-Western forms of labor. Here, _____ define "for or with whom one works and under what rules. These rules determine the type of work, type and amount of remuneration, working hours, degrees of physical and psychological strain, as well as the degree of freedom and autonomy associated with the work."

Exam Probability: **Medium**

52. *Answer choices:*

(see index for correct answer)

- a. Labor relations
- b. Global Unions
- c. Minnesota Nurses Association
- d. Delta Board Council

Guidance: level 1

:: ::

_____ is the practice of deliberately managing the spread of information between an individual or an organization and the public. _____ may include an organization or individual gaining exposure to their audiences using topics of public interest and news items that do not require direct payment. This differentiates it from advertising as a form of marketing communications. _____ is the idea of creating coverage for clients for free, rather than marketing or advertising. But now, advertising is also a part of greater PR Activities. An example of good _____ would be generating an article featuring a client, rather than paying for the client to be advertised next to the article. The aim of _____ is to inform the public, prospective customers, investors, partners, employees, and other stakeholders and ultimately persuade them to maintain a positive or favorable view about the organization, its leadership, products, or political decisions. _____ professionals typically work for PR and marketing firms, businesses and companies, government, and public officials as PIOs and nongovernmental organizations, and nonprofit organizations. Jobs central to _____ include account coordinator, account executive, account supervisor, and media relations manager.

Exam Probability: **Medium**

53. *Answer choices:*
(see index for correct answer)

- a. functional perspective
- b. Public relations
- c. empathy
- d. personal values

Guidance: level 1

:: ::

The _____ is an 1848 political pamphlet by the German philosophers Karl Marx and Friedrich Engels. Commissioned by the Communist League and originally published in London just as the Revolutions of 1848 began to erupt, the Manifesto was later recognised as one of the world's most influential political documents. It presents an analytical approach to the class struggle and the conflicts of capitalism and the capitalist mode of production, rather than a prediction of communism's potential future forms.

Exam Probability: **Low**

54. *Answer choices:*

(see index for correct answer)

- a. hierarchical perspective
- b. personal values
- c. open system
- d. Sarbanes-Oxley act of 2002

Guidance: level 1

:: Industry ::

_____ is the manner in which a given entity has decided to address issues of energy development including energy production, distribution and consumption. The attributes of _____ may include legislation, international treaties, incentives to investment, guidelines for energy conservation, taxation and other public policy techniques. Energy is a core component of modern economies. A functioning economy requires not only labor and capital but also energy, for manufacturing processes, transportation, communication, agriculture, and more.

Exam Probability: **Medium**

55. *Answer choices:*

(see index for correct answer)

- a. Energy policy
- b. Consciousness Industry
- c. PROFINET
- d. Standard Industrial Classification

Guidance: level 1

:: Marketing ::

_____ is the marketing of products that are presumed to be environmentally safe. It incorporates a broad range of activities, including product modification, changes to the production process, sustainable packaging, as well as modifying advertising. Yet defining _____ is not a simple task where several meanings intersect and contradict each other; an example of this will be the existence of varying social, environmental and retail definitions attached to this term. Other similar terms used are environmental marketing and ecological marketing.

Exam Probability: **High**

56. *Answer choices:*

(see index for correct answer)

- a. Object Value
- b. Market sector
- c. Green marketing
- d. Customer acquisition cost

Guidance: level 1

:: ::

A _____ is an organization, usually a group of people or a company, authorized to act as a single entity and recognized as such in law. Early incorporated entities were established by charter . Most jurisdictions now allow the creation of new _____ s through registration.

Exam Probability: **Medium**

57. *Answer choices:*

(see index for correct answer)

- a. co-culture
- b. Corporation
- c. levels of analysis
- d. imperative

Guidance: level 1

:: Financial markets ::

The _____ is a United States federal government organization, established by Title I of the Dodd–Frank Wall Street Reform and Consumer Protection Act, which was signed into law by President Barack Obama on July 21, 2010. The Office of Financial Research is intended to provide support to the council.

Exam Probability: **High**

58. *Answer choices:*

(see index for correct answer)

- a. Financial Stability Oversight Council
- b. Reset
- c. Real-time economy
- d. Composite

Guidance: level 1

:: Television terminology ::

A _____ organization, also known as a non-business entity, not-for-profit organization, or _____ institution, is dedicated to furthering a particular social cause or advocating for a shared point of view. In economic terms, it is an organization that uses its surplus of the revenues to further achieve its ultimate objective, rather than distributing its income to the organization's shareholders, leaders, or members. _____ s are tax exempt or charitable, meaning they do not pay income tax on the money that they receive for their organization. They can operate in religious, scientific, research, or educational settings.

Exam Probability: **Low**

59. *Answer choices:*

(see index for correct answer)

- a. Satellite television
- b. distance learning
- c. Nonprofit
- d. not-for-profit

Guidance: level 1

Accounting

Accounting or accountancy is the measurement, processing, and communication of financial information about economic entities such as businesses and corporations. The modern field was established by the Italian mathematician Luca Pacioli in 1494. Accounting, which has been called the "language of business", measures the results of an organization's economic activities and conveys this information to a variety of users, including investors, creditors, management, and regulators.

:: Accounting source documents ::

_____ is a letter sent by a customer to a supplier to inform the supplier that their invoice has been paid. If the customer is paying by cheque, the _____ often accompanies the cheque. The advice may consist of a literal letter or of a voucher attached to the side or top of the cheque.

Exam Probability: **High**

1. *Answer choices:*
(see index for correct answer)

- a. Credit memorandum
- b. Remittance advice
- c. Banknote
- d. Invoice

Guidance: level 1

:: Accounting terminology ::

In accounting/accountancy, _____ are journal entries usually made at the end of an accounting period to allocate income and expenditure to the period in which they actually occurred. The revenue recognition principle is the basis of making _____ that pertain to unearned and accrued revenues under accrual-basis accounting. They are sometimes called Balance Day adjustments because they are made on balance day.

Exam Probability: **High**

2. *Answer choices:*

(see index for correct answer)

- a. Impairment cost
- b. Accrued liabilities
- c. double-entry bookkeeping
- d. Checkoff

Guidance: level 1

:: Finance ::

_____, in finance and accounting, means stated value or face value. From this come the expressions at par, over par and under par.

Exam Probability: **High**

3. *Answer choices:*

(see index for correct answer)

- a. Par value
- b. XBRLS
- c. Senior stretch loan
- d. Social enterprise lending

Guidance: level 1

:: Business models ::

A _____, _____ company or daughter company is a company that is owned or controlled by another company, which is called the parent company, parent, or holding company. The _____ can be a company, corporation, or limited liability company. In some cases it is a government or state-owned enterprise. In some cases, particularly in the music and book publishing industries, subsidiaries are referred to as imprints.

Exam Probability: **High**

4. *Answer choices:*

(see index for correct answer)

- a. Independent business
- b. Subsidiary
- c. The India Way
- d. Business-agile enterprise

Guidance: level 1

:: Economic globalization ::

_____ is an agreement in which one company hires another company to be responsible for a planned or existing activity that is or could be done internally, and sometimes involves transferring employees and assets from one firm to another.

Exam Probability: **Low**

5. *Answer choices:*

(see index for correct answer)

- a. global financial
- b. Outsourcing

Guidance: level 1

:: Accounting terminology ::

_____ are liabilities that reflect expenses that have not yet been paid or logged under accounts payable during an accounting period; in other words, a company's obligation to pay for goods and services that have been provided for which invoices have not yet been received. Examples would include accrued wages payable, accrued sales tax payable, and accrued rent payable.

Exam Probability: **Medium**

6. *Answer choices:*
(see index for correct answer)

- a. profit and loss statement
- b. Internal auditing
- c. Accrued liabilities
- d. Record to report

Guidance: level 1

:: Cash flow ::

_____ s are narrowly interconnected with the concepts of value, interest rate and liquidity. A _____ that shall happen on a future day tN can be transformed into a _____ of the same value in t0.

Exam Probability: **Low**

7. *Answer choices:*
(see index for correct answer)

- a. Cash flow loan
- b. Cash flow
- c. Cash carrier
- d. Propequity

Guidance: level 1

:: Management accounting ::

In _____ or managerial accounting, managers use the provisions of accounting information in order to better inform themselves before they decide matters within their organizations, which aids their management and performance of control functions.

Exam Probability: **Medium**

8. *Answer choices:*

(see index for correct answer)

- a. Pre-determined overhead rate
- b. Total benefits of ownership
- c. Management accounting
- d. Relevant cost

Guidance: level 1

:: Accounting in the United States ::

_____ refers to a Memorandum of Understanding signed in September 2002 between the Financial Accounting Standards Board , the US standard setter, and the International Accounting Standards Board . The agreement is so called as it was reached in Norwalk.

Exam Probability: **Medium**

9. *Answer choices:*

(see index for correct answer)

- a. Governmental Accounting Standards Board
- b. Association of Government Accountants
- c. Positive assurance
- d. Norwalk Agreement

Guidance: level 1

:: Management accounting ::

A _____ is a part of a business which is expected to make an identifiable contribution to the organization's profits.

Exam Probability: **Medium**

10. *Answer choices:*

(see index for correct answer)

- a. Target income sales
- b. Dual overhead rate
- c. Profit center
- d. Extended cost

Guidance: level 1

:: Accounting terminology ::

_____ is an independent, objective assurance and consulting activity designed to add value to and improve an organization's operations. It helps an organization accomplish its objectives by bringing a systematic, disciplined approach to evaluate and improve the effectiveness of risk management, control and governance processes. _____ achieves this by providing insight and recommendations based on analyses and assessments of data and business processes. With commitment to integrity and accountability, _____ provides value to governing bodies and senior management as an objective source of independent advice. Professionals called internal auditors are employed by organizations to perform the _____ activity.

Exam Probability: **High**

11. *Answer choices:*
(see index for correct answer)

- a. double-entry bookkeeping
- b. Fair value accounting
- c. Internal auditing
- d. Impairment cost

Guidance: level 1

:: Taxation ::

_____ refers to instances where a taxpayer can delay paying taxes to some future period. In theory, the net taxes paid should be the same. Taxes can sometimes be deferred indefinitely, or may be taxed at a lower rate in the future, particularly for deferral of income taxes.

Exam Probability: **Low**

12. *Answer choices:*
(see index for correct answer)

- a. Steuerberater
- b. Tax Analysts
- c. Paulette
- d. Tax policy

Guidance: level 1

:: Expense ::

An _____ , operating expenditure, operational expense, operational expenditure or opex is an ongoing cost for running a product, business, or system. Its counterpart, a capital expenditure , is the cost of developing or providing non-consumable parts for the product or system. For example, the purchase of a photocopier involves capex, and the annual paper, toner, power and maintenance costs represents opex. For larger systems like businesses, opex may also include the cost of workers and facility expenses such as rent and utilities.

Exam Probability: **Low**

13. *Answer choices:*

(see index for correct answer)

- a. Corporate travel
- b. Business overhead expense disability insurance
- c. Tax expense
- d. Accretion expense

Guidance: level 1

:: Banking ::

A _____ is a financial institution that accepts deposits from the public and creates credit. Lending activities can be performed either directly or indirectly through capital markets. Due to their importance in the financial stability of a country, _____ s are highly regulated in most countries. Most nations have institutionalized a system known as fractional reserve _____ ing under which _____ s hold liquid assets equal to only a portion of their current liabilities. In addition to other regulations intended to ensure liquidity, _____ s are generally subject to minimum capital requirements based on an international set of capital standards, known as the Basel Accords.

Exam Probability: **High**

14. *Answer choices:*

(see index for correct answer)

- a. Bank
- b. Anonymous Internet banking

- c. Soft probe
- d. Master transaction agreement

Guidance: level 1

:: Financial ratios ::

The _____ is a financial ratio indicating the relative proportion of equity used to finance a company's assets. The two components are often taken from the firm's balance sheet or statement of financial position, but the ratio may also be calculated using market values for both, if the company's equities are publicly traded.

Exam Probability: **Medium**

15. *Answer choices:*
(see index for correct answer)

- a. Debt-to-income ratio
- b. Equity ratio
- c. Retention rate
- d. Return on net assets

Guidance: level 1

:: Financial ratios ::

_____ is a measure of how revenue growth translates into growth in operating income. It is a measure of leverage, and of how risky, or volatile, a company's operating income is.

Exam Probability: **Low**

16. *Answer choices:*
(see index for correct answer)

- a. Operating leverage
- b. Quick ratio
- c. Omega ratio
- d. PEG ratio

Guidance: level 1

:: ::

An _____ , for United States federal income tax, is a closely held corporation that makes a valid election to be taxed under Subchapter S of Chapter 1 of the Internal Revenue Code. In general, _____ s do not pay any income taxes. Instead, the corporation's income or losses are divided among and passed through to its shareholders. The shareholders must then report the income or loss on their own individual income tax returns.

Exam Probability: **Low**

17. *Answer choices:*

(see index for correct answer)

- a. hierarchical
- b. S corporation
- c. similarity-attraction theory
- d. functional perspective

Guidance: level 1

:: International taxation ::

_____ is the levying of tax by two or more jurisdictions on the same declared income, asset, or financial transaction. Double liability is mitigated in a number of ways, for example.

Exam Probability: **High**

18. *Answer choices:*

(see index for correct answer)

- a. European Union withholding tax
- b. Currency transaction tax
- c. Foreign personal holding company
- d. Robin Hood tax

Guidance: level 1

:: Inventory ::

It requires a detailed physical count, so that the company knows exactly how many of each goods brought on specific dates remained at year end inventory. When this information is found, the amount of goods are multiplied by their purchase cost at their purchase date, to get a number for the ending inventory cost.

Exam Probability: **Low**

19. *Answer choices:*

(see index for correct answer)

- a. Buffer stock
- b. Stock-taking
- c. Spare part
- d. Stock demands

Guidance: level 1

:: Generally Accepted Accounting Principles ::

A _____ or reacquired stock is stock which is bought back by the issuing company, reducing the amount of outstanding stock on the open market .

Exam Probability: **High**

20. *Answer choices:*

(see index for correct answer)

- a. Cost principle
- b. Paid in capital
- c. Matching principle
- d. Operating income

Guidance: level 1

:: Accounting systems ::

In accounting, a business or an organization and its owners are treated as two separately identifiable parties. This is called the _____ . The business stands apart from other organizations as a separate economic unit. It is necessary to record the business's transactions separately, to distinguish them from the owners' personal transactions. This helps to give a correct determination of the true financial condition of the business. This concept can be extended to accounting separately for the various divisions of a business in order to ascertain the financial results for each division. Under the business _____ , a business holds separate entity and distinct from its owners. "The entity view holds the business 'enterprise to be an institution in its own right separate and distinct from the parties who furnish the funds"

Exam Probability: **Medium**

21. *Answer choices:*
(see index for correct answer)

- a. Installment sales method
- b. Public expenditure tracking system
- c. Entity concept
- d. Accounting practice

Guidance: level 1

:: Types of business entity ::

A _____ is a partnership in which some or all partners have limited liabilities. It therefore can exhibit elements of partnerships and corporations. In a LLP, each partner is not responsible or liable for another partner's misconduct or negligence. This is an important difference from the traditional partnership under the UK Partnership Act 1890, in which each partner has joint and several liability. In a LLP, some or all partners have a form of limited liability similar to that of the shareholders of a corporation. Unlike corporate shareholders, the partners have the right to manage the business directly. In contrast, corporate shareholders must elect a board of directors under the laws of various state charters. The board organizes itself and hires corporate officers who then have as "corporate" individuals the legal responsibility to manage the corporation in the corporation's best interest. A LLP also contains a different level of tax liability from that of a corporation.

Exam Probability: **High**

22. *Answer choices:*

(see index for correct answer)

- a. Delaware General Corporation Law
- b. Multi-divisional form
- c. European economic interest grouping
- d. Shelf corporation

Guidance: level 1

:: Tax credits ::

A _____ is a tax incentive which allows certain taxpayers to subtract the amount of the credit they have accrued from the total they owe the state. It may also be a credit granted in recognition of taxes already paid or, as in the United Kingdom, a form of state support.

Exam Probability: **High**

23. *Answer choices:*

(see index for correct answer)

- a. Foreign tax credit
- b. Child tax credit
- c. New Markets Tax Credit Program
- d. Tax credit

Guidance: level 1

:: Accounting terminology ::

Double-entry bookkeeping, in accounting, is a system of bookkeeping so named because every entry to an account requires a corresponding and opposite entry to a different account. The double entry has two equal and corresponding sides known as debit and credit. The left-hand side is debit and right-hand side is credit. For instance, recording a sale of $100 might require two entries: a debit of $100 to an account named "Stock" and a credit of $100 to an account named "Revenue."

Exam Probability: **Low**

24. *Answer choices:*

(see index for correct answer)

- a. outstanding balance
- b. Record to report
- c. Double-entry accounting
- d. Capital appreciation

Guidance: level 1

:: Stock market ::

A _____, securities exchange or bourse, is a facility where stock brokers and traders can buy and sell securities, such as shares of stock and bonds and other financial instruments. _____ s may also provide for facilities the issue and redemption of such securities and instruments and capital events including the payment of income and dividends. Securities traded on a _____ include stock issued by listed companies, unit trusts, derivatives, pooled investment products and bonds. _____ s often function as "continuous auction" markets with buyers and sellers consummating transactions via open outcry at a central location such as the floor of the exchange or by using an electronic trading platform.

Exam Probability: **High**

25. *Answer choices:*
(see index for correct answer)

- a. Common stock
- b. Stock Exchange
- c. Penny stock
- d. Reverse stock split

Guidance: level 1

:: Management accounting ::

_____ accounting is a traditional cost accounting method introduced in the 1920s, as an alternative for the traditional cost accounting method based on historical costs.

Exam Probability: **Medium**

26. *Answer choices:*
(see index for correct answer)

- a. Process costing

- b. Fixed assets management
- c. Standard cost
- d. Direct material total variance

Guidance: level 1

:: Management ::

_____ is the identification, evaluation, and prioritization of risks followed by coordinated and economical application of resources to minimize, monitor, and control the probability or impact of unfortunate events or to maximize the realization of opportunities.

Exam Probability: **Low**

27. *Answer choices:*

(see index for correct answer)

- a. Risk management
- b. Fredmund Malik
- c. Reval
- d. Hierarchical organization

Guidance: level 1

:: Real estate valuation ::

_____ or OMV is the price at which an asset would trade in a competitive auction setting. _____ is often used interchangeably with open _____, fair value or fair _____, although these terms have distinct definitions in different standards, and may or may not differ in some circumstances.

Exam Probability: **Medium**

28. *Answer choices:*

(see index for correct answer)

- a. Extraordinary assumptions and hypothetical conditions
- b. Market value
- c. Highest and best use
- d. Sales comparison approach

Guidance: level 1

:: Accounting terminology ::

Accounts are typically defined by an identifier and a caption or header and are coded by account type. In computerized accounting systems with computable quantity accounting, the accounts can have a quantity measure definition.

Exam Probability: **High**

29. *Answer choices:*

(see index for correct answer)

- a. Accounts payable
- b. Chart of accounts
- c. Capital appreciation
- d. Total absorption costing

Guidance: level 1

:: Management accounting ::

_____ is the process of recording, classifying, analyzing, summarizing, and allocating costs associated with a process,after that developing various courses of action to control the costs. Its goal is to advise the management on how to optimize business practices and processes based on cost efficiency and capability. _____ provides the detailed cost information that management needs to control current operations and plan for the future.

Exam Probability: **Medium**

30. *Answer choices:*

(see index for correct answer)

- a. Cost accounting
- b. Total benefits of ownership
- c. Investment center
- d. Chartered Institute of Management Accountants

Guidance: level 1

:: ::

The U.S. _____ is an independent agency of the United States federal government. The SEC holds primary responsibility for enforcing the federal securities laws, proposing securities rules, and regulating the securities industry, the nation's stock and options exchanges, and other activities and organizations, including the electronic securities markets in the United States.

Exam Probability: **Medium**

31. *Answer choices:*

(see index for correct answer)

- a. corporate values
- b. Securities and Exchange Commission
- c. Character
- d. levels of analysis

Guidance: level 1

:: Income taxes ::

An _____ is a tax imposed on individuals or entities that varies with respective income or profits. _____ generally is computed as the product of a tax rate times taxable income. Taxation rates may vary by type or characteristics of the taxpayer.

Exam Probability: **Low**

32. *Answer choices:*

(see index for correct answer)

- a. Income splitting
- b. Income tax
- c. Negative income tax
- d. Income tax in Singapore

Guidance: level 1

:: Taxation ::

In a tax system, the _____ is the ratio at which a business or person is taxed. There are several methods used to present a _____ : statutory, average, marginal, and effective. These rates can also be presented using different definitions applied to a tax base: inclusive and exclusive.

Exam Probability: **High**

33. *Answer choices:*

(see index for correct answer)

- a. Tax rate
- b. Tax lien
- c. Fair market value
- d. Taxpayer receipt

Guidance: level 1

:: Accounting terminology ::

_____ is an accounting system for recording resources whose use has been limited by the donor, grant authority, governing agency, or other individuals or organisations or by law. It emphasizes accountability rather than profitability, and is used by Nonprofit organizations and by governments. In this method, a fund consists of a self-balancing set of accounts and each are reported as either unrestricted, temporarily restricted or permanently restricted based on the provider-imposed restrictions.

Exam Probability: **Low**

34. *Answer choices:*

(see index for correct answer)

- a. Capital expenditure
- b. Fund accounting
- c. Absorption costing
- d. Statement of financial position

Guidance: level 1

:: Fundamental analysis ::

_____ is the monetary value of earnings per outstanding share of common stock for a company.

Exam Probability: **Low**

35. *Answer choices:*

(see index for correct answer)

- a. Growth stock
- b. Earnings per share
- c. Terminal value
- d. economic Value Added

Guidance: level 1

:: Accounting ::

_____ is the recording of financial transactions, and is part of the process of accounting in business. Transactions include purchases, sales, receipts, and payments by an individual person or an organization/corporation. There are several standard methods of _____ , including the single-entry and double-entry _____ systems. While these may be viewed as "real" _____ , any process for recording financial transactions is a _____ process.

Exam Probability: **Low**

36. *Answer choices:*

(see index for correct answer)

- a. Pipeline planning
- b. Clearing account
- c. LEA Global
- d. Accountant General

Guidance: level 1

:: Actuarial science ::

The _____ is the greater benefit of receiving money now rather than an identical sum later. It is founded on time preference.

Exam Probability: **Medium**

37. *Answer choices:*

(see index for correct answer)

- a. Catastrophe modeling
- b. Extreme value theory
- c. Risk
- d. Time value of money

Guidance: level 1

:: Financial ratios ::

_____ is a financial ratio that indicates the percentage of a company's assets that are provided via debt. It is the ratio of total debt and total assets.

Exam Probability: **Medium**

38. *Answer choices:*

(see index for correct answer)

- a. Debt-to-income ratio
- b. Loss ratio
- c. Statutory liquidity ratio
- d. Debt ratio

Guidance: level 1

:: Business law ::

The expression " _____ " is somewhat confusing as it has a different meaning based on the context that is under consideration. From a product characteristic stand point, this type of a lease, as distinguished from a finance lease, is one where the lessor takes residual risk. As such, the lease is non full payout. From an accounting stand point, this type of lease results in off balance sheet financing.

Exam Probability: **Medium**

39. *Answer choices:*

(see index for correct answer)

- a. Business method patent
- b. Operating lease

- c. Ease of doing business index
- d. Contract failure

Guidance: level 1

:: International Financial Reporting Standards ::

_____, usually called IFRS, are standards issued by the IFRS Foundation and the International Accounting Standards Board to provide a common global language for business affairs so that company accounts are understandable and comparable across international boundaries. They are a consequence of growing international shareholding and trade and are particularly important for companies that have dealings in several countries. They are progressively replacing the many different national accounting standards. They are the rules to be followed by accountants to maintain books of accounts which are comparable, understandable, reliable and relevant as per the users internal or external. IFRS, with the exception of IAS 29 Financial Reporting in Hyperinflationary Economies and IFRIC 7 Applying the Restatement Approach under IAS 29, are authorized in terms of the historical cost paradigm. IAS 29 and IFRIC 7 are authorized in terms of the units of constant purchasing power paradigm.IAS 2 is related to inventories in this standard we talk about the stock its production process etcIFRS began as an attempt to harmonize accounting across the European Union but the value of harmonization quickly made the concept attractive around the world. However, it has been debated whether or not de facto harmonization has occurred. Standards that were issued by IASC are still within use today and go by the name International Accounting Standards , while standards issued by IASB are called IFRS. IAS were issued between 1973 and 2001 by the Board of the International Accounting Standards Committee . On 1 April 2001, the new International Accounting Standards Board took over from the IASC the responsibility for setting International Accounting Standards. During its first meeting the new Board adopted existing IAS and Standing Interpretations Committee standards . The IASB has continued to develop standards calling the new standards " _____ ".

Exam Probability: **Low**

40. *Answer choices:*

(see index for correct answer)

- a. IAS 7
- b. IAS 39
- c. IFRS 5
- d. IAS 2

Guidance: level 1

:: Auditing ::

A _____ , also called "Internal _____ ", is a term of financial audit, internal audit and Enterprise Risk Management. It means the overall attitude, awareness and actions of directors and management regarding the internal control system and its importance to the entity. They express it in management style, corporate culture, values, philosophy and operating style, the organisational structure, and human resources policies and procedures.

Exam Probability: **Low**

41. *Answer choices:*

(see index for correct answer)

- a. Mazars
- b. Walk-through test
- c. Control environment
- d. Assurance services

Guidance: level 1

:: Accounting ::

_____ are key sources of information and evidence used to prepare, verify and/or audit the financial statements. They also include documentation to prove asset ownership for creation of liabilities and proof of monetary and non monetary transactions.

Exam Probability: **Medium**

42. *Answer choices:*

(see index for correct answer)

- a. Accounting period
- b. Clearing account
- c. Morison International
- d. Accounting research

Guidance: level 1

:: Management accounting ::

_____ is an accountancy practice, the aim of which is to provide an offset to the mark-to-market movement of the derivative in the profit and loss account. There are two types of hedge recognized. For a fair value hedge the offset is achieved either by marking-to-market an asset or a liability which offsets the P&L movement of the derivative. For a cash flow hedge some of the derivative volatility into a separate component of the entity's equity called the cash flow hedge reserve. Where a hedge relationship is effective, most of the mark-to-market derivative volatility will be offset in the profit and loss account. _____ entails much compliance - involving documenting the hedge relationship and both prospectively and retrospectively proving that the hedge relationship is effective.

Exam Probability: **High**

43. *Answer choices:*
(see index for correct answer)

- a. Hedge accounting
- b. Relevant cost
- c. Institute of Cost and Management Accountants of Bangladesh
- d. Responsibility center

Guidance: level 1

:: Ethically disputed business practices ::

_____, in accounting, is the act of intentionally influencing the process of financial reporting to obtain some private gain. _____ involves the alteration of financial reports to mislead stakeholders about the organization's underlying performance, or to "influence contractual outcomes that depend on reported accounting numbers."

Exam Probability: **Medium**

44. *Answer choices:*
(see index for correct answer)

- a. Earnings management
- b. Nokku kooli
- c. Tobashi scheme
- d. Bioprospecting

Guidance: level 1

:: Generally Accepted Accounting Principles ::

In accrual accounting, the revenue recognition principle states that expenses should be recorded during the period in which they are incurred, regardless of when the transfer of cash occurs. Conversely, cash basis accounting calls for the recognition of an expense when the cash is paid, regardless of when the expense was actually incurred.

Exam Probability: **Medium**

45. *Answer choices:*

(see index for correct answer)

- a. Long-term liabilities
- b. Provision
- c. Access to finance
- d. Cash method of accounting

Guidance: level 1

:: Inventory ::

Costs are associated with particular goods using one of the several formulas, including specific identification, first-in first-out , or average cost. Costs include all costs of purchase, costs of conversion and other costs that are incurred in bringing the inventories to their present location and condition. Costs of goods made by the businesses include material, labor, and allocated overhead. The costs of those goods which are not yet sold are deferred as costs of inventory until the inventory is sold or written down in value.

Exam Probability: **Low**

46. *Answer choices:*

(see index for correct answer)

- a. Inventory control problem
- b. Safety stock
- c. Cost of goods sold
- d. Decomposition

Guidance: level 1

:: Management accounting ::

In finance, the _____ or net present worth applies to a series of cash flows occurring at different times. The present value of a cash flow depends on the interval of time between now and the cash flow. It also depends on the discount rate. NPV accounts for the time value of money. It provides a method for evaluating and comparing capital projects or financial products with cash flows spread over time, as in loans, investments, payouts from insurance contracts plus many other applications.

Exam Probability: **Low**

47. *Answer choices:*

(see index for correct answer)

- a. Variance
- b. Net present value
- c. Variable Costing
- d. Constraints accounting

Guidance: level 1

:: Corporate crime ::

_____ LLP, based in Chicago, was an American holding company. Formerly one of the "Big Five" accounting firms, the firm had provided auditing, tax, and consulting services to large corporations. By 2001, it had become one of the world's largest multinational companies.

Exam Probability: **High**

48. *Answer choices:*

(see index for correct answer)

- a. Langbar International
- b. Tip and Trade
- c. Ovson Egg
- d. Medco Health Solutions

Guidance: level 1

:: Generally Accepted Accounting Principles ::

The term _____ is most often used to describe a practice or document that is provided as a courtesy or satisfies minimum requirements, conforms to a norm or doctrine, tends to be performed perfunctorily or is considered a formality.

Exam Probability: **Low**

49. *Answer choices:*

(see index for correct answer)

- a. Cash method of accounting
- b. Pro forma
- c. Insurance asset management
- d. Closing entries

Guidance: level 1

:: Budgets ::

_____ is a method of budgeting in which all expenses must be justified and approved for each new period. Developed by Peter Pyhrr in the 1970s, _____ starts from a "zero base" at the beginning of every budget period, analyzing needs and costs of every function within an organization and allocating funds accordingly, regardless of how much money has previously been budgeted to any given line item.

Exam Probability: **Low**

50. *Answer choices:*

(see index for correct answer)

- a. Budget
- b. Link budget
- c. Personal budget
- d. Zero-based budgeting

Guidance: level 1

:: Accounting systems ::

In accounting, the controlling account is an account in the general ledger for which a corresponding subsidiary ledger has been created. The subsidiary ledger allows for tracking transactions within the controlling account in more detail. Individual transactions are posted both to the controlling account and the corresponding subsidiary ledger, and the totals for both are compared when preparing a trial balance to ensure accuracy.

Exam Probability: **Medium**

51. *Answer choices:*

(see index for correct answer)

- a. Control account
- b. Purchase ledger
- c. Controlling account
- d. Standard accounting practice

Guidance: level 1

:: ::

_____ is a process whereby a person assumes the parenting of another, usually a child, from that person's biological or legal parent or parents. Legal _____ s permanently transfers all rights and responsibilities, along with filiation, from the biological parent or parents.

Exam Probability: **High**

52. *Answer choices:*

(see index for correct answer)

- a. deep-level diversity
- b. similarity-attraction theory
- c. interpersonal communication
- d. Adoption

Guidance: level 1

:: Accounting in the United States ::

The _____ is the source of generally accepted accounting principles used by state and local governments in the United States. As with most of the entities involved in creating GAAP in the United States, it is a private, non-governmental organization.

Exam Probability: **Medium**

53. *Answer choices:*

(see index for correct answer)

- a. Beta Alpha Psi
- b. Revolving fund
- c. Other comprehensive basis of accounting
- d. The Wheat Committee

Guidance: level 1

:: Business economics ::

_____ is one of the constituents of a leasing calculus or operation. It describes the future value of a good in terms of absolute value in monetary terms and it is sometimes abbreviated into a percentage of the initial price when the item was new.

Exam Probability: **High**

54. *Answer choices:*

(see index for correct answer)

- a. Residual value
- b. Seasonal industry
- c. Gross operating surplus
- d. Inclusive business finance

Guidance: level 1

:: United States Generally Accepted Accounting Principles ::

A _____ is a set of U.S. government financial statements comprising the financial report of a state, municipal or other governmental entity that complies with the accounting requirements promulgated by the Governmental Accounting Standards Board. GASB provides standards for the content of a CAFR in its annually updated publication Codification of Governmental Accounting and Financial Reporting Standards. The U.S. Federal Government adheres to standards determined by the Federal Accounting Standards Advisory Board.

Exam Probability: **Low**

55. *Answer choices:*

(see index for correct answer)

- a. Comprehensive income
- b. Available for sale
- c. Comprehensive annual financial report
- d. FIN 46

Guidance: level 1

:: United States Generally Accepted Accounting Principles ::

In the United States, a _____ is one of the five governmental fund types established by GAAP. It is classified as a restricted true endowment fund for governments and non-profit organizations. Put simply, a _____ may be used to generate and disburse money to those entitled to receive payments by qualification or agreement, as in the case of Alaska citizens or residents that satisfy the rules for payment from their _____ from State oil revenues. It was first introduced through GASB Statement 34. The name of the fund comes from the purpose of the fund: a sum of equity used to permanently generate payments to maintain some financial obligation. Also, a fund can only be classified as a _____ if the money is used to report the status of a restricted financial resource. The resource is restricted in the sense that only earnings from the resource are used and not the principal. For example, a fund can be classified as a _____ if it is being used to pay for accounting services for a perpetual endowment of a government-run cemetery or financial endowments towards a government-run library.

Exam Probability: **Medium**

56. *Answer choices:*

(see index for correct answer)

- a. Impaired asset
- b. Permanent fund
- c. Accounting for leases in the United States
- d. FIN 46

Guidance: level 1

:: ::

The _____ of 1934 is a law governing the secondary trading of securities in the United States of America. A landmark of wide-ranging legislation, the Act of '34 and related statutes form the basis of regulation of the financial markets and their participants in the United States. The 1934 Act also established the Securities and Exchange Commission, the agency primarily responsible for enforcement of United States federal securities law.

Exam Probability: **Medium**

57. *Answer choices:*
(see index for correct answer)

- a. hierarchical perspective
- b. surface-level diversity
- c. Sarbanes-Oxley act of 2002
- d. Securities Exchange Act

Guidance: level 1

:: Auditing ::

An _____ is a security-relevant chronological record, set of records, and/or destination and source of records that provide documentary evidence of the sequence of activities that have affected at any time a specific operation, procedure, or event. Audit records typically result from activities such as financial transactions, scientific research and health care data transactions, or communications by individual people, systems, accounts, or other entities.

Exam Probability: **High**

58. *Answer choices:*
(see index for correct answer)

- a. Audit trail
- b. Mitigating control
- c. Legal auditing

- d. Recovery Auditing

Guidance: level 1

:: Manufacturing ::

_____ costs are all manufacturing costs that are related to the cost object but cannot be traced to that cost object in an economically feasible way.

Exam Probability: **Low**

59. *Answer choices:*
(see index for correct answer)

- a. Part number
- b. Sewing
- c. Gunsmith
- d. Process manufacturing

Guidance: level 1

INDEX: Correct Answers

Foundations of Business

1. : Bankruptcy

2. c: Sharing

3. b: Availability

4. : Health

5. c: Return on investment

6. c: Stock

7. b: Credit card

8. : Energies

9. d: Technology

10. a: Income statement

11. d: Officer

12. b: Exercise

13. d: Federal Trade Commission

14. c: Sales

15. : Total quality management

16. b: Strategic alliance

17. a: Economic Development

18. : Evaluation

19. d: Preferred stock

20. d: Performance

21. a: Labor relations

22. : Sony

23. b: Chart

24. a: Cooperative

25. a: Organizational structure

26. d: Incentive

27. b: Negotiation

28. b: Risk management

29. d: Limited liability

30. : Quality control

31. a: E-commerce

32. a: Good

33. d: Specification

34. c: Ownership

35. d: Accounting

36. a: Currency

37. : Industrial Revolution

38. d: Human resources

39. a: Management

40. c: Customs

41. d: Policy

42. c: Land

43. : Exchange rate

44. : Pattern

45. d: Solution

46. d: Advertising

47. b: Insurance

48. a: Brand

49. b: Commerce

50. a: Competitive advantage

51. a: Problem

52. a: Contract

53. d: Patent

54. a: Project

55. c: Innovation

56. d: Information

57. c: Investment

58. d: Internal Revenue Service

59. a: Competitor

Management

1. d: Procurement

2. a: Overtime

3. a: Statistical process control

4. b: Customer

5. : Management

6. d: Economies of scale

7. c: Joint venture

8. : Certification

9. a: Expert power

10. c: Forecasting

11. a: Offshoring

12. a: Delegation

13. a: Tariff

14. : Strategic management

15. a: Assessment center

16. b: Management system

17. a: Ownership

18. : Discipline

19. b: Sexual harassment

20. c: Best practice

21. : Centralization

22. a: World Trade Organization

23. a: Incentive

24. d: Risk management

25. : Transactional leadership

26. a: Job satisfaction

27. d: Bureaucracy

28. : Project manager

29. : Process control

30. d: Quality assurance

31. : Emotional intelligence

32. a: Collaboration

33. a: Performance appraisal

34. a: Explanation

35. : Income

36. d: Ambiguity

37. b: Trade

38. a: Social loafing

39. d: Authority

40. : Cost

41. b: Partnership

42. a: Halo effect

43. : Glass ceiling

44. b: Project management

45. c: Specification

46. a: Mediation

47. c: Logistics

48. b: Intranet

49. c: Product design

50. b: Empowerment

51. d: Balanced scorecard

52. a: Change management

53. : Schedule

54. d: Entrepreneurship

55. a: Cost leadership

56. d: European Union

57. : Franchising

58. c: Efficiency

59. c: Market share

Business law

1. d: Insider trading

2. a: Tort

3. b: Asset

4. c: Affirmative action

5. b: Deed

6. c: Issuer

7. d: Intellectual property

8. a: Secured transaction

9. b: Warehouse receipt

10. b: Clayton Act

11. b: Berne Convention

12. : Duty of care

13. a: Identity theft

14. b: S corporation

15. a: Mens rea

16. a: Labor relations

17. a: Negligence

18. a: Misrepresentation

19. d: Purchasing

20. c: Patent

21. : Precedent

22. : Bad faith

23. d: Offeror

24. : Revenue

25. b: Broker

26. c: Commerce Clause

27. b: Employment discrimination

28. : Statute of limitations

29. : Board of directors

30. d: Subsidiary

31. a: Warranty

32. a: Policy

33. c: Trustee

34. : Private law

35. b: Utilitarianism

36. a: Product liability

37. b: Consideration

38. d: Sexual harassment

39. c: Investment

40. a: National Labor Relations Board

41. d: Income

42. : Jurisdiction

43. b: Statute

44. a: Auction

45. a: Administrative law

46. c: Due diligence

47. : Forgery

48. b: Environmental Protection

49. a: Jury

50. d: Mirror image rule

51. c: Directed verdict

52. b: Beneficiary

53. c: Voidable

54. b: Punitive

55. c: Argument

56. a: Liquidated damages

57. a: Cyberspace

58. c: Anticipatory repudiation

59. b: Uniform Electronic Transactions Act

Finance

1. a: Fraud

2. : Market price

3. d: Capital structure

4. d: Economy

5. : Worksheet

6. b: Operating expense

7. a: Primary market

8. : Average Cost

9. d: Operating lease

10. b: Tax expense

11. a: Partnership

12. d: Bank reconciliation

13. d: Liquidation

14. a: Selling

15. d: Wall Street

16. c: Financial accounting

17. : Risk assessment

18. : Exchange rate

19. a: Ending inventory

20. d: Shareholder

21. b: Forward contract

22. a: General journal

23. c: Limited liability

24. : Rate risk

25. d: Earnings per share

26. a: Perpetual inventory

27. a: Deferral

28. : Board of directors

29. a: Dividend yield

30. b: Expected return

31. a: Accountant

32. b: Finished good

33. d: Pension

34. b: Debt ratio

35. d: Demand

36. b: Money market

37. b: Double taxation

38. b: Mortgage

39. : Payroll

40. : Call option

41. b: Operating Income

42. b: Public Company Accounting Oversight Board

43. b: Issuer

44. c: Presentation

45. a: Industry

46. b: Accounting

47. d: Debenture

48. a: Bond market

49. d: Quick ratio

50. a: Cost accounting

51. a: Internal rate of return

52. c: Financial instrument

53. c: Loan

54. a: Capital expenditure

55. c: Asset

56. : Certified Public Accountant

57. : Arbitrage

58. c: Activity-based costing

59. c: Pension fund

Human resource management

1. d: Substance abuse

2. a: Socialization

3. : Data collection

4. a: Committee

5. c: Sexual harassment

6. : Trainee

7. : Merit pay

8. c: Pension

9. d: Kelly Services

10. b: Severance package

11. : Performance appraisal

12. b: Rating scale

13. c: Collective bargaining

14. a: Absenteeism

15. a: Social loafing

16. c: Authoritarianism

17. : Information overload

18. a: Self-assessment

19. : Right-to-work law

20. c: Behavior modification

21. d: Hostile work environment

22. d: Glass ceiling

23. a: Disability insurance

24. c: Competitive advantage

25. a: Decentralization

26. d: Strategic planning

27. c: Survey research

28. a: Case interview

29. c: Intuition

30. c: Labor relations

31. c: Organizational justice

32. a: Balance sheet

33. : Job sharing

34. : Criterion validity

35. b: Hazard

36. c: Workforce planning

37. d: Succession planning

38. b: Vertical integration

39. b: Interactional justice

40. : Bargaining unit

41. c: National Institute for Occupational Safety and Health

42. d: Distance learning

43. a: Construct validity

44. d: Needs assessment

45. : Employment

46. : Strategic management

47. d: E-HRM

48. : Test validity

49. c: Officer

50. d: Locus of control

51. a: Performance improvement

52. c: Six Sigma

53. a: Sweatshop

54. a: Psychological contract

55. : Business model

56. : Employee Free Choice Act

57. d: Realistic job preview

58. d: Xerox Corporation

59. c: Unfair labor practice

Information systems

1. c: Top-level domain

2. d: Virtual reality

3. : User interface

4. c: Geographic information system

5. a: Web mining

6. : Facebook

7. : Worm

8. c: Random access

9. c: Authentication protocol

10. c: Supply chain management

11. a: Backup

12. a: Web content

13. c: Debit card

14. a: Consumer-to-consumer

15. a: Information management

16. b: Carnivore

17. d: Online advertising

18. : Telnet

19. b: Information ethics

20. d: Decision-making

21. d: Semantic Web

22. c: Knowledge management

23. d: Payment Card Industry Data Security Standard

24. c: Content management

25. d: Data integrity

26. b: Information flow

27. : Spamming

28. d: Operating system

29. c: Unstructured data

30. b: Google Calendar

31. d: Wiki

32. c: Collision

33. d: Strategic planning

34. a: Enterprise systems

35. : Information systems

36. c: Vulnerability

37. : Big data

38. : Flash memory

39. : Information literacy

40. b: Entity-relationship

41. a: Extensible Markup Language

42. d: One Laptop per Child

43. d: System

44. d: Query language

45. a: Database model

46. : Enterprise information system

47. : PageRank

48. : Blog

49. b: Pop-up ad

50. : Master data

51. d: Wide Area Network

52. b: Tacit knowledge

53. a: First mover advantage

54. : Yelp

55. a: Netflix

56. a: Gmail

57. : Search engine

58. b: Market share

59. c: Expert system

Marketing

1. d: Product development

2. a: Direct marketing

3. c: Marketing communications

4. : Intellectual property

5. b: Mass media

6. : Business-to-business

7. c: Manager

8. b: Customer satisfaction

9. b: Appeal

10. b: Manufacturing

11. d: Sponsorship

12. d: Research and development

13. c: Microsoft

14. c: Trade association

15. c: Google

16. b: Product manager

17. : Convenience

18. d: Competitive intelligence

19. d: Persuasion

20. a: Complaint

21. : Social network

22. a: Management

23. a: Presentation

24. d: Universal Product Code

25. a: Consumer Protection

26. c: Negotiation

27. c: Primary data

28. c: Information technology

29. c: Monopoly

30. b: Product differentiation

31. a: Industry

32. : Target market

33. a: Patent

34. : Investment

35. a: Competition

36. d: Merchant

37. c: Code

38. d: Penetration pricing

39. b: Subsidiary

40. b: Public

41. b: Merchandising

42. : Consultant

43. d: Direct selling

44. c: Project

45. b: Psychographic

46. : Stock

47. d: Commercialization

48. : Reinforcement

49. b: Ford

50. : Public relations

51. a: Economies of scale

52. d: Infomercial

53. c: Resource

54. c: Customer retention

55. : Need

56. d: Coupon

57. d: Wholesale

58. : Competitive advantage

59. c: Warranty

Manufacturing

1. a: Chemical industry

2. c: Average cost

3. b: Accreditation

4. b: Performance

5. b: Change management

6. b: Knowledge management

7. : Process flow diagram

8. b: Resource allocation

9. b: Stakeholder management

10. : Sharing

11. d: Bullwhip effect

12. c: American Society for Quality

13. b: Reorder point

14. a: Planning

15. d: Lean manufacturing

16. c: Service quality

17. c: Furnace

18. a: Supply chain risk management

19. d: Licensed production

20. : Property

21. c: Control limits

22. b: Perfect competition

23. a: Expediting

24. : Total quality management

25. a: Electronic data interchange

26. a: Natural resource

27. : Check sheet

28. : Chemical reaction

29. d: Steering committee

30. d: Project team

31. : Consensus

32. b: Technical support

33. d: Heat treating

34. c: Six Sigma

35. b: Inspection

36. d: Catalyst

37. b: E-procurement

38. a: Tool

39. b: Kanban

40. d: Concurrent engineering

41. b: Certification

42. : Control chart

43. d: Reflux

44. d: Resource management

45. : HEAT

46. a: Quality management

47. c: Clay

48. d: Supply chain

49. : DMAIC

50. b: Pattern

51. a: Statistical process control

52. d: Cost

53. : Risk management

54. d: Ball

55. c: Elastomer

56. : Toshiba

57. b: Sales

58. d: Interaction

59. a: Strategic sourcing

Commerce

1. a: Basket

2. b: Excite

3. c: Leadership

4. : Electronic data interchange

5. d: Marketing mix

6. b: Tariff

7. d: Payment card

8. a: Outsourcing

9. a: E-procurement

10. d: Logistics Management

11. c: Revenue

12. d: Contribution margin

13. a: Risk management

14. d: Initiative

15. a: Electronic commerce

16. c: Competitor

17. a: Marketspace

18. : Recruitment

19. a: Common carrier

20. d: Evaluation

21. : European Union

22. b: WebSphere Commerce

23. : Minimum wage

24. : Computer security

25. d: Jurisdiction

26. a: Preference

27. a: Uniform Commercial Code

28. b: Control system

29. a: Commodity

30. d: Quality management

31. a: Stock

32. c: Personnel

33. c: Boot

34. a: Cost structure

35. a: International trade

36. : Consideration

37. d: Productivity

38. : Investment

39. : Management

40. c: Raw material

41. : Policy

42. d: Exchange rate

43. : Consumer-to-consumer

44. : Permission marketing

45. b: Teamwork

46. a: Authentication

47. c: British Airways

48. : Welfare

49. c: Economic regulation

50. d: Value-added network

51. c: Microsoft

52. b: Subsidiary

53. b: Regulatory agency

54. d: Pizza Hut

55. d: Wall Street Journal

56. d: Fixed cost

57. b: Firm

58. b: Technology

59. c: Sexual harassment

Business ethics

1. : WorldCom

2. a: Statutory law

3. d: Layoff

4. b: Patriot Act

5. : Vigilance committee

6. b: Model Rules of Professional Conduct

7. c: Parental leave

8. a: Right to work

9. : Solar power

10. c: Enron

11. d: New Deal

12. : Global Fund

13. : Marketing ethics

14. a: Feedback

15. d: Fair trade

16. a: Employee Polygraph Protection Act

17. b: Global reach

18. a: New York Stock Exchange

19. : Criminal law

20. : Copyright

21. b: Habitat

22. b: Junk bond

23. b: Empowerment

24. d: Socialism

25. b: Business model

26. d: Locus of control

27. c: Conscience

28. a: Minimum wage

29. b: Great Depression

30. : Six Sigma

31. : Utopian socialism

32. d: Marketing

33. a: Individualistic culture

34. c: Oil spill

35. a: Biofuel

36. a: Trojan horse

37. : Forest Stewardship Council

38. a: Greenwashing

39. b: Supply Chain

40. c: Environmental audit

41. : Utilitarianism

42. b: Social networking

43. : Micromanagement

44. b: Chamber of Commerce

45. a: Pollution Prevention

46. c: Affirmative action

47. a: Lanham Act

48. b: White-collar crime

49. d: Whistleblower

50. c: Workplace politics

51. d: Human nature

52. a: Labor relations

53. b: Public relations

54. : Communist Manifesto

55. a: Energy policy

56. c: Green marketing

57. b: Corporation

58. a: Financial Stability Oversight Council

59. c: Nonprofit

Accounting

1. b: Remittance advice

2. : Adjusting entries

3. a: Par value

4. b: Subsidiary

5. b: Outsourcing

6. c: Accrued liabilities

7. b: Cash flow

8. c: Management accounting

9. d: Norwalk Agreement

10. c: Profit center

11. c: Internal auditing

12. : Tax deferral

13. : Operating expense

14. a: Bank

15. b: Equity ratio

16. a: Operating leverage

17. b: S corporation

18. : Double taxation

19. : Specific identification

20. : Treasury stock

21. c: Entity concept

22. : Limited liability partnership

23. d: Tax credit

24. c: Double-entry accounting

25. b: Stock Exchange

26. c: Standard cost

27. a: Risk management

28. b: Market value

29. b: Chart of accounts

30. a: Cost accounting

31. b: Securities and Exchange Commission

32. b: Income tax

33. a: Tax rate

34. b: Fund accounting

35. b: Earnings per share

36. : Bookkeeping

37. d: Time value of money

38. d: Debt ratio

39. b: Operating lease

40. : International Financial Reporting Standards

41. c: Control environment

42. : Accounting records

43. a: Hedge accounting

44. a: Earnings management

45. : Matching principle

46. c: Cost of goods sold

47. b: Net present value

48. : Arthur Andersen

49. b: Pro forma

50. d: Zero-based budgeting

51. a: Control account

52. d: Adoption

53. : Governmental Accounting Standards Board

54. a: Residual value

55. c: Comprehensive annual financial report

56. b: Permanent fund

57. d: Securities Exchange Act

58. a: Audit trail

59. : Manufacturing overhead

CPSIA information can be obtained
at www.ICGtesting.com
Printed in the USA
LVHW051624301019
635718LV00005B/724/P